Incarnation and Myth: *Th*

Incarnation and Myth:
The Debate Continued

Edited by
Michael Goulder

WILLIAM B. EERDMANS PUBLISHING COMPANY
GRAND RAPIDS, MICHIGAN

Editor's Foreword and arrangement © Michael Goulder 1979

First published 1979 by SCM Press, Ltd, London
First American edition published 1979 through special arrangement with SCM by Wm. B. Eerdmans Publishing Co., Grand Rapids, Michigan 49503.

Library of Congress Cataloging in Publication Data

Main entry under title:

Incarnation and myth.

Papers from a meeting held at the University of Birmingham, July 10-12, 1978, sponsored by the Cadbury Trust and the Dept. of Extramural Studies, University of Birmingham.
Includes indexes.
1. The myth of God Incarnate — Congresses.
2. Incarnation — Congresses. I. Goulder, M. D.
II. Cadbury Trust. III. Birmingham, Eng. University Dept. of Extra-Mural Studies.
BT220.I52   232'.1   79-16509
ISBN 0-8028-1199-X

Contents

Foreword
Michael Goulder

The Myth of God Incarnate was published in July, 1977, and it immediately set off the biggest theological controversy in Britain since *Honest to God* fifteen years earlier. It provoked hostile reviews in most of the religious and secular press; it was answered within six weeks by *The Truth of God Incarnate*, and later by *God Incarnate*; it sold thirty thousand copies in the first eight months, twenty-four thousand of them in Britain; and a call was made by the Church of England Evangelical Council (*Truth, error and discipline in the church*) for the five Anglican authors to resign their orders. Only in the course of time did more reasoned criticism come to the fore.

The puzzle is why the book should have caused so strong a reaction. There can be no doubt that its message had often been stated before, and sometimes better stated; and that some of the essays in the book were unreadable by many of those who bought it. The provocative title certainly was in part the reason for its 'success', for many people missed the *double entendre* intended; between myth as a story of profound meaning by which men guide their lives, and myth as a fairy-tale, not true. The distinction of some of the essayists was also a factor: for Professor Wiles was Regius Professor of Divinity at Oxford, and had been Chairman of the Church of England Doctrine Commission, Dr Nineham had been Regius Professor of Divinity at Cambridge and weighty in the church's councils, Canon Houlden had been Principal of Ripon College, Cuddesdon, a leading Anglican theological college, Professor Hick had been an outstanding defender of the faith in philosophical writings, and Mr Cupitt was a nationally known spokesman for the church on the television. Dr Young and I were less well-known: but the essayists were plainly respected English churchmen, not radical German theologians. It is hard to deny, however, that an important part of the scandal was due to the *prima facie* plausibility of the book's thesis. The possibility of doubting the truth of Christ's divinity was in the air, not only for fringe churchmen but for a number of regular worshippers. I am not the only contributor to whom it has been said, 'We've thought this for years'.

It seemed to Professor Hick and myself that the interest which the book had sparked off should not be allowed to spend itself in heated polemics, and that it would be a good idea to hold a colloquy, or conversation, between the seven essayists and a group of their leading critics. The possibility of financing such a colloquy arose from two facts. The Cadbury Trust had already shown itself generous in supporting previous conferences which Professor Hick had organized, and was willing to sponsor this enterprise also; and the Department of Extramural Studies in the University of Birmingham, whose Staff Tutor in Theology I am, exists to promote public discussion of just such issues. We were able therefore to hold a series of meetings in Birmingham from 10th to 12th July, 1978, seven of them being private sessions each lasting about two hours, and three of them being public debates of similar length in the evenings, each attended in the event by about a hundred people. I should like to record our appreciation here both for the financial backing we received from the Trust, and for the friendly co-operation we had from members of the Birmingham Extramural Department, and from Garth House, where the conversations were held.

The principal difficulty we faced was in the choice of 'critics', so I circularized the *Myth* essayists for their advice, and a list was produced. Naturally not everyone invited was able to attend, and we were especially disappointed not to have Professor John Macquarrie and Fr Herbert McCabe, both of whom had written interesting reviews. However, we were delighted that Professor Basil Mitchell of Oxford agreed to act as Chairman, knowing his reputation for fair-mindedness as well as his important work in the philosophy of religion; and the seven who finally accepted as participants either were distinguished, or were becoming distinguished, as theologians leaning towards orthodoxy. Three of them were from Cambridge: Mr Brian Hebblethwaite, the Dean of Queens' College and occasional antagonist to Mr Cupitt on television; Dr Nicholas Lash, a Roman Catholic and recently elected Norris-Hulse Professor of Divinity; and Professor Charles Moule, doyen New Testament scholar and author of the recently published *The Origin of Christology*. Professor Stephen Sykes of Durham had been joint editor of a volume of essays on our subject, *Christ, Faith and History*. Professor Graham Stanton, of the University of London King's College, was secretary of the international Society of New Testament Studies, and author of a study of the New Testament preaching of Jesus. Bishop Lesslie Newbigin, currently Moderator of the United Reformed Church, had been a distinguished missionary and author. Dr John Rodwell, of the University of Lancaster, was a younger theological thinker and a researcher in biological sciences. We felt very satisfied both that all the *Myth* essayists were able to come and that such an able and interesting group of opponents were there to discuss the issues with them. Everyone was invited to prepare a paper in advance, and copies were circulated to save time for discussion at the Colloquy itself.

Several possible perils could be foreseen. First the whole thing was set up in unhappy similarity to a Seven-a-Side Rugby Match, with Professor Mitchell to blow the whistle, and there might be strong feelings and a bad atmosphere. On the other hand universal good manners and a supply of the best University wine might result in a failure to come to grips with the hard issues. The fact that neither of these things occurred was due in a considerable degree to the Chairman's skill. The meetings were extremely friendly throughout, but strong things were said, and there was some cut and much thrust. A less successfully avoided threat was the possibility that the papers would not overlap enough to make a common conversation possible: for there were fourteen speakers for the ten sessions, and some of the pairings were inevitably marriages of less than obvious convenience. Nevertheless it was felt that the discussion had made a number of valuable points, and that it might be of interest to a larger circle of people if a publisher could be found. Hence the present volume.

Books of essays are often indigestible: the reader is asked to take in the thought of a dozen or more subtle minds each starting from a different point, and he finds so various a diet hard to assimilate. I have therefore been so bold as to do a certain amount of reorganizing; shuffling the order, dividing some papers in two, inviting Comments and Replies to Comments, adding a series of brief headings, and notes of my own. I hope that in this way the reader will find the complex and difficult subject predigested into some of its component topics, and thus easier to master. To this end I have been greatly helped by Professor Wiles' essay, 'A Survey of the Issues in the *Myth* debate'. This paper isolates two preliminary questions and five main issues which have been discussed in reviews and comments, and I have taken these seven heads as the outline of the book. The questions are:

1. Are the authors of *The Myth* still Christians?
2. How far has 'incarnation' changed its meaning in modern discussion, and are we speaking of a 'literal' incarnation?

3. Is the doctrine of the incarnation logically coherent?

4. Do all Christian doctrines stand and fall together?

5. Is the New Testament evidence of the incarnation clear or ambiguous?

6. Is a satisfactory compromise possible between the centrality of Christ and the claims of other faiths?

7. Granted the cultural conditioning of all Christians, including ourselves, can *we* believe in the incarnation?

The extent to which these topics were discussed at the Colloquy naturally varied, and the book reflects that imbalance. Where there is a single contribution to a question, I have simply printed it under the number and heading: for instance, only Mr Hebblethwaite has made a short comment on 1. In other cases there may be two independent contributions, as in 2, where half of Dr Lash's original paper 2A and a comment by Mr Hebblethwaite 2B discuss the issue without reference to each other. Where the colloquists are either answering one another, or are dealing with a limited sub-topic, I have indicated this by small Roman numbers: thus Professor Hick in 6(ii) is replying to Mr Hebblethwaite in 6(i), and there are four related comments on 4A, 'Incarnation and Atonement', numbered 4A(i), etc. I hope that this numbering system will be of help to the reader in relating the essays to each other. Sometimes essays have not belonged comfortably in any one of my Procrustean beds, and I have had to choose between chopping off their feet like the giant of old, and leaving them as they are with an apology and a cross-reference. In such cases I have let the reader know as best I can.

It might have seemed natural to follow a chronological order and to take the biblical questions first; but I have held them over for two reasons, one logical, the other practical. As Professor Mitchell writes, 'If it is true that the doctrine of the incarnation is incoherent, that settles it. If it is true that there is no continuous identity of doctrine, that settles it too. If, however, the doctrine is not found ready made in the New Testament, it is still possible to argue that it is implicit there, so that doesn't settle it ... The more general questions should come first.' The practical reason is that biblical discussion involves more technical argument, which may be formidable to the general reader.

Two final points should be made. The first is the regret of all of us that Dr Nineham has been unable to present a written contribution. His 'astonished' and interesting comments were a major feature of the Colloquy, and it was sad that his many commitments have compelled him to withdraw from a part in the publication.

Secondly I am most grateful to all the contributors who have made my task as editor a simple one; by their punctuality in sending their essays in face of other urgent work; by their willingness to revise and rewrite; and by their invariable good humour, even in the face of the theological divisions. We have faced a common theological task in elucidating the doctrine of the incarnation, and we have done what we could with it together, happily.

September, 1978   MICHAEL GOULDER

A Survey of Issues in the *Myth* Debate
Maurice Wiles

The Myth of God Incarnate is an untidy book. The response to it has been equally untidy. I like to think that this untidiness arises because the debate involves a live grappling with complex issues and is not simply due to muddle – though it would be an unusual theological debate if muddle didn't play a substantial part on both sides. What I want to do in this paper is to sort out some of the issues that have arisen and outline at least the basic shape of the more important arguments involved. I hope this may provide a context in which to place some of the particular issues that we shall discuss in this colloquy and may help to show what issues are in need of further work and clarification. I shall set out what I have to say under three headings.

1. *Is the issue raised by the book one that can properly be raised as a matter of theological interpretation within Christianity?*

In one sense it may not make a great deal of difference whether critics of the book and its arguments think that they are doing a bit of apologetics or that they are taking part in an inter-Christian theological debate – provided they are prepared (as most of them are) to give reasons for their objections. But there is a difference to the feel of the argument if someone thinks the position he is attacking is not merely theologically mistaken but outside the bounds of possible forms of Christian belief. There are at least four different grounds (not all mutually exclusive of one another) on which it has been claimed that the position (or, to give due weight to differences within the book itself, the cluster of positions) taken by the authors of the book is not merely mistaken but incompatible with genuinely Christian faith.

(*a*) *The conservative evangelical objection.* You can see the book as Michael Green does in the simile with which he opens *The Truth of God Incarnate*,[1] as expressing the final act of infidelity in a gradual dismemberment of 'traditional full-blooded Christianity, complete with an inspired Bible and an incarnate Christ'. But the objection, in the form that he develops it in the preface to that book, would involve an equally curt dismissal of most of the forms in which Christian belief has been expressed since the emergence of critical scholarship of the kind that has developed over the last 200 years.

(*b*) *The Barthian objection.* You can see it, as Alasdair Heron does in the *Scottish Journal of Theology*[2] as a tired and discredited resuscitation of nineteenth-century ideas doomed to failure because it does not accept the Barthian insistence that the incarnation is the basic given from which all Christian faith and all Christian theology derive.

(*c*) *The conservative Roman Catholic objection.* You can see it, as Herbert McCabe does in *New Blackfriars* (December 1977), as ruled out of court from the start because it conflicts with the church's formal self-definition at the Council of Chalcedon.[3]

(*d*) *The 'historical faith' objection.* This is the objection of many Anglicans, who are not in principle as hostile to the findings of critical scholarship as (*a*). While reluctant to give such absolutely determinative authority to a particular council as (*c*), they would still see Chalcedon as giving expression to a fundamental feature of the church's faith down the ages. Their position is well expressed in the words of Peter Cornwell in his parish letter of the University Church of St Mary's in Oxford (August 1977), where he gives it as his judgment 'that this book produces a form of Christianity so unlike what we have been led to believe Christianity to be that it is misleading to call it Christianity'.

I have set these four positions out briefly and starkly, because I don't intend to enter into detailed debate with them here. The first three positions lay claim to an absoluteness of judgment on specific theological issues of a kind that seems to me unwarranted. The counter-objections I would want to put would have to deal with the epistemological grounds for claiming such absoluteness of judgment. The fourth position is in my view more broadly and thus more soundly based. It can very properly be used as one argument within the debate, but I do not think it should be allowed to prejudge the issue at stake. In other words I do not think the conclusions of the book (in so far as it can be said to have conclusions) can properly be treated as in themselves placing it outside the sphere of Christian belief, without careful prior consideration of the context, the form and the substance of the arguments on which those conclusions are based.

Although I cannot deal with these positions at all fully, I have thought it important to draw attention to their existence, because of the way they may influence the judgments people make on more specific questions in the course of discussion. The issues that arise there are not straightforward; there are no knock-down arguments. Our assessment in each instance is a matter of judgment. How we judge the evidence in any particular case will quite rightly be influenced by our prior expectations as Christians about what is likely to be true in the light of the past history of Christian faith. I am prepared to accept that that prior expectation puts a burden of proof on the shoulders of those who question the viability of the traditional conception of incarnation. But to accept a burden of proof is a very different thing from accepting that the question ought not to be raised or that, if raised, it can only be answered one way by anyone laying claim to the name of Christian.

So far I have written as if the issue at stake was quite clear. I described it just now as the question of 'the viability of the traditional conception of incarnation'. And this leads me to my second heading:

2. *What is being questioned in questioning the traditional doctrine of the incarnation?*

A good deal of criticism has been directed at the use of the word 'myth' in the book. Some (but by no means all) of what has been said on that score I accept as justifiable. Certainly there is scope for further clarification. But we must not exaggerate how much can be achieved by closer definition of such terms as 'myth', 'model', 'image', 'symbol', 'analogy', etc. Provided the basically oblique and analogical character of religious language is recognized, further progress depends not simply on distinguishing the various forms of language at an abstract or theoretical level. That process needs to go hand in hand with consideration of the substantive issues themselves.

The discussion to which the book has given rise has highlighted for me the variety of senses in which the word 'incarnation' is used. It seems to me now that the word 'incarnation' is almost as slippery as the word 'myth', and that anyone who wants to use it in serious theological discussion must spell out the sense in which he is using it if serious confusion is to be avoided.[4]

Geoffrey Lampe's book, *God as Spirit*,[5] provides an illustration of the flexibility with which the term is used. In that book he develops a Spirit-Christology which explicitly disavows the conceptions alike of a personal pre-existent and post-existent Christ. Nevertheless, he regards his position as expounding the idea of Christ's incarnation. For him there is a 'continuous incarnation of God as Spirit in the spirits of men', and while the incarnate presence of God in Jesus is for him unique it is not unique *qua* being incarnation (p. 23). It is not simply a matter of the idea of a pre-existent Son not being integral to his understanding of incarnation; it is actually inconsistent with it. 'When Jesus is identified with the pre-existent Son', he writes, 'belief in a true incarnation of God in Jesus is weakened' (p. 142). At the other end of the scale (and there are several stopping-points in between) 'incarnation' is restricted to that which is claimed to be unique about Jesus. I take two succinct statements of it. 'This doctrine [of the incarnation] expresses, so far as human words permit, the central belief of Christians that God himself without ceasing to be God has come amongst us, not just in but *as* a particular man, at a particular time and place. The human life lived and the death died have been held quite literally to *be* the human life and death of God himself in one of the modes of his own eternal being'[6]. And in *New Blackfriars* (August 1977 p. 352) Herbert McCabe speaks of 'the Christian doctrine that Jesus was not a "spiritual visitant" but a man who was God'.

This seems to me to come much closer to 'the traditional conception of incarnation'. At the formal level it is identical. But as soon as we move beyond the purely formal level, the issue ceases to be quite so straightforward. I would venture to claim that for virtually all Christians before the twentieth century this affirmation that Jesus is both God and man has given rise to a number of special problems relating to the human life of Jesus – questions about his miraculous powers, the nature of his knowledge and, perhaps most acutely, his knowledge of and relationship to God. For many theologians today these problems are still real problems. Some deal with them very cavalierly, some with immense care and sophistication. But for the moment I want to stress what seems to me the very important distinction between those for whom they do arise as problems calling for special treatment and those for whom they do not. For Hebblethwaite and McCabe, if I understand them aright, no such problems arise. Hebblethwaite entirely disavows 'the "docetic" tendencies of early Christianity which found it hard to believe, for example, that Jesus shared the limitations of human psychology and knowledge'[7] and McCabe describes such questions as having no 'logical connection with the incarnation'[8]. For them the humanity of Jesus really is one with ours in all its limitations. But it remains equally and unequivocally true that he is God.

Something like this seems to me to be the form in which many of the most sensitive upholders of 'traditional incarnational doctrine' are defending that position today. Here there is need for a much more careful dialogue than has so far taken place. Many of the arguments that are directed against earlier forms of incarnational doctrine seem to such people to hold only against docetic distortions of the doctrine and so miss their mark. I think they use that riposte too sweepingly, but I agree that many of the arguments do not meet the position that they hold. Hence the need for further dialogue. But one thing that I would want to ask for as a starting-point for this comparatively new dialogue is the recognition that, despite the continuity at the formal level, their position is significantly different from what has been held in the past. This point is made very briefly in the original book both by me (pp. 5–6) and by Don Cupitt (pp. 134–7). If we are right in this, then the *onus probandi* of which I spoke is much more evenly shared between the two sides of the debate. And just as I accept that many of the arguments that are raised against incarnational doctrine may not be valid against their position, so I believe they will find that many of the arguments that gave rise to the earlier incarnational doctrine do not fit anything like as well as evidence for that form of the doctrine that they wish to maintain. Unless they are prepared to take the short cut of appealing to Chalcedon or to the past doctrinal tradition as decisive in themselves, they need to set out carefully the grounds for accepting their position in the form that they affirm it. I am not aware that that task has yet been done, and I do not think it will prove an easy one.

3. *What then are the crucial issues of debate?*

One of the main difficulties of the discussion, as with all theological discussion, is the number of closely interrelated issues involved. I list five that seem to me to be of major importance.

(i) *Logical coherence*

I take first the question: Is the doctrine of the incarnation logically coherent? If it could be shown that the doctrine was strictly non-sensical, the basic issue in the debate would have been settled at a stroke – and we could either pack up and go home or move on to the work of reconstruction. But I am innately suspicious of arguments in a discussion of this sort that claim to be as sweeping and as conclusive as this one would be. And I don't, in fact, think it can be shown clearly and decisively that the doctrine is nonsense. I do believe, however, that the challenge to logical coherence (however hoary) remains a serious one and ought to be taken seriously. I do not think the issue falls into the square-circle class (to use John Hick's example) because there the absoluteness of the contradition can be demonstrated in a decisive and formal way. It is much harder to plot the border-line between sense and nonsense in talking about the mystery of God. But, though more difficult to detect, it is still possible to talk nonsense about God. It is generally agreed that the omnipotence of God does not mean his ability to do things that are logically self-contradictory – like creating square-circles. It seems clear to me that in creating beings other than himself with a measure of genuine freedom and creativity, the omnipotent God restricts his omnipotence (in one sense of the word 'power') in a way that is mysterious but not self-contradictory; indeed that in another sense of the word 'power', such a creation is an expression of divine power. If one goes on to say that God actually becomes one of those creatures, while remaining God, this can be presented rhetorically as a further and supreme expression of that divine self-limitation which is also the power of divine love. But there does seem to be a difference in the logic when we move over to speaking of God *being* a part of his own creation or a part of that creation *being* God. *Prima facie* this does seem to me to involve a logical self-contradiction. Herbert McCabe in *New Blackfriars* (December 1977) has tried to per-suade me that it could not be a matter of logical contradiction. I am not altogether clear about the force of his argument. But I do find some of his statements about the meaning of the doctrine so odd, that I remain unconvinced about their logical coherence. 'Part of the doctrine of the incarnation is that the person of Jesus is *uncre-ated*' (p. 550). 'A human person just is a person with a human nature and it makes absolutely no difference to the logic of this whether the same person does or does not exist from eternity as divine' (p. 552). *If* that does make sense, it is the sort of sense that needs very compelling reasons to persuade me to accept it. More clarification on the purely logical issues seems to be needed here. Pending that, this serious doubt about the logical coherence of the doctrine remains for me a factor in the debate which moves the *onus probandi* in the direction of the defenders of the doctrine.

(ii) *Coherence with other Christian doctrines*

The doctrine of the incarnation is sometimes defended as necessary to the continued affirmation of other Christian doc-trines. Dr Macquarrie put the point forcibly when he wrote: 'Chris-tian doctrines are so closely interrelated that if you take away one, several others tend to collapse. After incarnation is thrown out, is the doctrine of the Trinity bound to go? What kind of doctrine of atonement remains possible? Would the Eucharist be reduced simply to a memorial service?'[9] It is clearly right to insist on the interrelatedness of doctrines; but it is misleading to speak of possible 'collapse', as if their interrelation was like that of a set of dominoes. Doctrines are always undergoing modification, and leading to modification in other doctrines by doing so. Dr Macquarrie's challenge is a proper one to make, and one that those of us who are unhappy with traditional incarnational doctrine ought to meet. But it takes time. In the case of the first two of Dr Macquarrie's questions, I would claim to have provided an outline sketch of the shape that an answer might take in my essay appended to the Church of England Doctrine report, *Christian Believing*,[10] and in Chapter IV of *The Remaking of Christian Doctrine*,[11] respectively. But much more certainly needs to be done. At this stage I can only express a confidence that it can be done; that when the view that Jesus is to be identified with God is replaced by one in which he symbolizes and expresses God's action towards the world, an appropriate reconstruction of Christian belief will prove possible. The working out of such a programme would, no doubt, serve incidentally to reveal whether the difference between the transcendentalist Cupitt and his more immanentist colleagues is as deep as some of our critics believe it to be. But the real difficulty will be how we are to assess whether such a reconstruction is appropriate or not. For if it is to be judged by the standard of past formulas or even by that of the expectations to which past formulas have given rise, it will inevitably be found wanting. The problem of criteria of assessment is particularly acute here. Even more than the production of such a doctrinal scheme, its assessment will require time. Like the particular issue with which we are concerned in this colloquy, it will require to be thought out, talked out, prayed out and lived out in the life of the church over a period of time before we will be in a position to make anything like a definitive judgment about it.

Brian Hebblethwaite makes a point similar to that made by Dr Macquarrie when he claims that the doctrine of the incarnation is essential to any belief in a God who encounters us in a genuinely personal way and who takes responsibility for the world's evil.[12] This point, too, I have tried to deal with in *The Remaking of Christian Doctrine*.[13] But Hebblethwaite's argument can be turned on its head, and I am genuinely uncertain which way up it functions better. For if it is logically conceivable (as Hebblethwaite's view of the incarnation insists that it is) for God to be actually identified with a human person without in any way taking away from the full and genuine humanity of that human person, it follows that God does not, in fact, draw near to us as individual men and women or share our suffering as directly as apparently he could. And that is not out of respect for our freedom nor because of our lack of response; for were one of those the reason it would mean either that Jesus was not genuinely free (in which case his humanity would be impaired) or that the incarnation depended upon his response (a view which the traditional understanding of incarnation has been unwilling to countenance). I raise the argument in the context of that put forward by Hebblethwaite, which I think to be an important and religiously attractive one, because my counter-argument does at the very least show that his argument can be looked at from a very different angle in a way that suggests it may not be as forceful as it appears at first sight.

John Baker[14] takes this point to its furthest limit when he claims that the argument of the book suggests the dispensability of God altogether. But his argument points only to the dispensability of an interventionist view of God, and that is surely a very different matter. That shorthand way of indicating how I would want to meet his challenge should not be taken to mean that there is no problem. Of course, there are serious difficulties in speaking of God's activity in history today, and there is some justice in the complaints of those who say that, having emphasized the difficulties in holding an incarnational belief today, we have in places spoken too easily of God's activity and of divine providence. One can't of course deal with every problem at the same time. I want simply to comment that the two problems, though related, are not identical, and that elsewhere some of us (and others who think along similar lines) have made some attempt to spell out how those other ideas might best be understood today. But there is much more work for theologians to do here – whatever their position about incarnation.

(iii) *The evidence of the New Testament and Christian origins*

It is generally agreed that the text of the New Testament points in a much less direct way to any doctrine of the incarnation (in the sense in which I am using that phrase) than it has been thought to do during most of Christian history. We cannot therefore expect the interpretation of the relevant New Testament evidence to be a clear or straightforward matter.

Perhaps the most important recent discussion of it, germane to the debate, is to be found in Professor Moule's *The Origin of Christology*,[15] which though not a response to the book itself is not unrelated to the ideas and discussions that lie behind it. In that book he points to two features of the New Testament as justifying the claim that even if our revised understanding of the text points less directly, it points no less surely in the direction of incarnational belief. The first is his claim that the acknowledged development within the New Testament itself is such that one should see 'all the various estimates of Jesus reflected in the New Testament as, in essence, only attempts to describe what was already there from the beginning' (pp. 3–4). Secondly he claims that the texts bear witness to a continuing experience of Jesus himself so that where Mr Houlden argues that 'the understanding of Jesus as the pre-existent agent in creation was rooted in an experience, as a result of him, of freshness in relation to *everything*', Professor Moule wants not only to say 'as a result of him' but also to claim that 'they experienced Jesus himself as in a dimension transcending the human and the temporal' (p. 138). Inevitably these are matters of judgment, where no clear-cut criteria are available. How does one decide whether a later belief is simply drawing out what was implicit from the start? (According to *The Listener* for 30 March, 1978, Cardinal Hume affirms that 'the position of the Pope is implicit in Scripture itself'. How should such a claim be assessed?) Since Mr Houlden and Professor Moule are both generalizing from the language of a number of different writers and translating their way of speaking into a very different idiom, how do we decide which is the fairer summary? In the last analysis a choice can, I suspect, only be made by way of accepting that account which seems to us preferable on much wider grounds than simply the direct evidence of the texts themselves.

John Baker, in his review in the *Journal of Theological Studies*, regards the book's major weakness as the failure of the authors (apart from Michael Goulder) to deal with the evidence of the resurrection. But can this really play the decisive role he expects from it? Only, it seems to me, if one thinks that something like Pannenberg's argument is valid as a form of strictly historical reasoning, or if one were to claim that inability to provide a convincing historical reconstruction of the events immediately following the crucifixion was itself confirmation of a traditionally 'realist' account of the resurrection. That is not to deny the importance of the kind of work he asks for, but only to express the conviction that, however carefully done, it will still be characterized by the same ambiguity that belongs to the rest of the New Testament evidence.

These are, of course, only a sample of the sort of evidence the more sensitive New Testament scholar is likely to adduce. I think we have to accept that that evidence is likely to remain pretty inconclusive. Furthermore it is not going to be of as major importance as it has been thought to be in the past. Even if it were less ambiguous than I believe it in fact to be, it would still be far from decisive on the issue at stake. As John Ashton puts it, in his review of *The Myth of God Incarnate* in *Scripture Bulletin* (Winter 1977), 'the question to be answered is surely not whether our ancestors believed in the divinity of Christ; but rather, can we, in this scientific age continue to do so.'

(iv) *The finality, uniqueness, universality or centrality of Jesus*

The sense of living in an evolutionary world, which we all share in a way which our forefathers did not and could not, makes the whole idea of the finality of Jesus more problematic than it used to be. We can react to this in two ways – either by saying that in the strong form in which it has been maintained in the past, the idea is no longer possible for us in view of our changed understanding of the world; or by saying that just because the idea is so problematic, we can only hold on to the kind of centrality for Jesus Christ for which our religious sense cries out if we maintain a strong form of incarnation doctrine. I think this is one of the most influential motives leading people to stress the vital need to maintain the doctrine of the incarnation: fear that without it the centre would not hold. I find it more difficult to know how it should be assessed as a ground for holding the doctrine.

In the heading to this section I have used a variety of cognate but not identical terms, all of which are frequently used with reference to Jesus. Our situation in relation to them seems to me to have changed as a result of our changing attitude to the significance of other religious traditions. Various attempts have been made to suggest how a strong incarnational doctrine can be compatible with a positive evaluation of other faiths – e.g., by stressing the concept of an inclusive rather than an exclusive uniqueness. These need careful exploration, but I have to say that I do not as yet know of any which seem to me to be true to incarnational doctrine as understood in the past, while at the same time allowing a genuine openness to the positive significance of other faiths.

My own view is that where the categorical and absolute character of the religious demand as it impinges on the Christian, is tied to the historical person of Jesus in a strictly metaphysical way (as in traditional incarnation doctrine), that does involve a pre-judgment of the potential significance of other religious faiths in the economy of God, of a kind that is very hard to justify from our standpoint within one particular stream of religious and cultural development. I do not think it is the categorical character of the religious demand that needs to be abandoned, but rather the linking of it in its absoluteness to the figure of Jesus by the kind of reasoning expressed in traditional incarnation doctrine. Thus it is precisely the kind of support which many people desiderate in relation to the religious centrality of Jesus that makes me uneasy. Much more needs to be done to spell out the kind of position I am suggesting here.[16] It does involve an element of risk, in the sense that it allows that faith may come to take significantly different forms in the future. But perhaps that is part of the risk of faith itself. I do not think it undermines the categorical element that properly belongs to religious faith, but may rather help to ensure that it is properly directed.

(v) *The significance of 'cultural conditioning'*

A number of critics have accused the authors of the book of being guilty of the 'genetic fallacy'. They have understood the argument to be of the form: we can show how the development of the doctrine of the incarnation was influenced by the philosophical, religious and cultural conditions of the day; thereby we have shown it to be false and not deserving contemporary credence. If that were the argument, it would certainly be a very bad one. It is not; though the claim is being made that the way in which the development of the doctrine was related to the particular ideas of its time is of significance in at least two ways.

In the first instance it is significant in relation to a very common form of argument. It is often claimed that incarnational doctrine goes so strongly against the grain of the religious and intellectual assumptions of the age, that nothing could have been strong enough to lead the church to develop it except the overwhelming force of the fact that that was what had happened. The historical evidence adduced shows, I believe, that the emergence of the doctrine, though still very striking, is not quite as extraordinary a phenomenon as that argument asserts. In my view there is force both in the argument and the counter-argument, and there is no clear way of settling where the balance of judgment should lie.

But it is significant also as a reminder of the point already made in the quotation from John Ashton. There is a general difference of outlook or world-view between the early centuries of our era and the present. That is not to claim that the attitudes of everyone living in the first century or in the twentieth are uniform, nor to claim that the differences between the two ages are absolute (as

Gerald Downing rightly insists in *The Modern Churchman*, Winter 1977). But that it is proper to speak of a 'culture gap' between them, however difficult it may be to spell it out with precision, I remain convinced despite Downing's strictures. The doctrine of the incarnation is in the first instance a doctrine of its own age, determined on the basis of the ideas and knowledge of the time. We ought not therefore to take it over without reassessment in the light of the ideas and knowledge of our own age – which is not to imply that our age's ideas and knowledge are any less culturally conditioned or that we do not need to be self-critical about them too.

NOTES

1. Michael Green (ed.), *The Truth of God Incarnate*, Hodder & Stoughton 1977.
2. Alasdair Heron in *Scottish Journal of Theology*, vol. 31, no. 1, 1978.
3. McCabe makes other criticisms of the book as well which merit serious attention. See the subsequent references in this paper and my fuller rejoinder to him in *New Blackfriars*, December 1977.
4. This feeling was strongly reinforced by the discussion of the colloquy itself. There was strong criticism of the legitimacy of speaking at all of a 'traditional doctrine of the incarnation' in view of the immense variety of ways in which 'incarnation' has been understood in the history of the church. In spite of that challenge it still seems to me legitimate to do so and I would stand by the definition I gave on p. 1 of *The Myth of God Incarnate*, (ed., John Hick, SCM Press 1977) 'that Jesus of Nazareth is unique in the precise sense that, while being fully man, it is true of him and of him alone, that he is also fully God, the second person of the co-equal Trinity'.
5. G. W. H. Lampe, *God as Spirit*, Oxford University Press 1977.
6. Brian Hebblethwaite, 'Incarnation – the Essence of Christianity' in *Theology*, March 1977, p. 85: italics original. Note also the use of the word 'literally' here. It helps to show how some of the authors of the book have spoken of a 'literal' understanding of incarnation, for which they have been criticized.
7. *The Truth of God Incarnate*, p. 102.
8. McCabe, *New Blackfriars*, December 1977, p. 354.
9. *The Truth of God Incarnate*, p. 144.
10. *Christian Believing*, SPCK 1976.
11. Maurice Wiles, *The Remaking of Christian Doctrine*, SCM Press 1974.
12. Hebblethwaite, *Theology*, March 1977, pp. 87–8.
13. *The Remaking of Christian Doctrine*, pp. 69–72, 117–20.
14. John A. Baker in *Journal of Theological Studies*, April 1978, p. 297.
15. C. F. D. Moule, *The Origin of Christology*, Cambridge University Press 1977.
16. I have attempted to do this in a paper entitled 'Christian Theology in an Age of Religious Studies' which appears in *Explorations in Theology 4*, SCM Press 1979.

1 · Are the Authors of *The Myth* still Christians?

The Myth and Christian Faith
Brian Hebblethwaite

It is surely both proper and inevitable that our discussions centred on questions of truth and meaning. The substantive debate was over what precisely is the content of Christian belief and how it can be and ought to be expressed in the language of today. Of course there is and always has been considerable difference of opinion on these matters not only amongst ordinary believers, but between different more or less institutional forms of Christian community, and between theologians within and across the borders of the denominations. But there must be some limit to the variety of doctrinal statement within the broad spectrum of the Christian churches if they are to retain any recognizable identity and if they are to be taken seriously as having something definite, let alone true, to say.

Now it might be argued that greater flexibility can be admitted amongst the faithful than amongst the clergy commissioned, among other things, to teach the faith. It might also be argued that greater exploratory freedom can be granted to the church's theologians than can ever be expected to find expression in official formulations of doctrine. These factors complicate the task of stating the limits of tolerable diversity in Christian self-understanding. But even if we may not readily be able to locate the boundary between what is recognizably Christian and what is not, some views surely stand way beyond any conceivable limit.

Admittedly the church has no business to repudiate anyone who feels something of the attraction of the figure of Jesus or the desire to associate himself with the Christian community in one of its many forms. But equally the church may reasonably hope that those attracted in this way will be drawn further into an appreciation of the content of the Christian faith as it has been handed down over the centuries. Its clergy are commissioned to teach that faith, and they have a special responsibility to that tradition, not just to the attractive power of Jesus and his church. For example it is hard to suppose that the so-called Christian atheism of the sixties was a tolerable variant of Christian doctrine. And indeed the authors of *The Myth* and their critics are agreed that faith in God is a necessary condition of genuinely Christian faith.

But do the doctrines of the incarnation and the Trinity belong, in the same way, to the essence of Christianity? I am persuaded that they do. It is these doctrines, expressed in all the creeds and confessions of the historic churches, that have given Christian belief its characteristic shape down the centuries. In subscribing to those doctrines, I am, first and foremost, stating my belief that they are true, that they are as near as one can get to the heart of God's revelation of himself in Jesus. In the second place I feel the moral and religious force of those doctrines in ways which I have tried to articulate in my contribution to this debate. But thirdly, I find myself considering these matters as a participant in what I think of as the body of Christ, the community of those who by adoption and grace are united with God through the risen Christ and drawn consciously within the sphere of the operations of the Spirit. It is a direct consequence of this that I cannot suppose the church's credal faith to have have been mistaken over so central a matter as the divinity of Christ, whatever the incidental errors and inadequacies there may have been in the church's understanding of its faith. In other words, I share the 'historical faith' objection (*d*) which Maurice Wiles outlines in his paper (above p. 2).

I am persuaded then not only that I must try to refute the views expressed in *The Myth*, but also that the church ought definitely to repudiate those views. Let me be quite explicit. I know that these views are being advanced now, as at earlier times, by Christians – Christians, in the sense of churchmen and followers of Christ, whom I still want to greet as fellow members in the body of Christ; but they are not, to my mind, Christian views, in the sense of views which the church could ever endorse as permissible variants within the broad spectrum of its official doctrine. I do not want to unchurch my colleagues and friends. I want this debate to continue within the body. But, I would urge, the fact that a number of Christian theologians no longer subscribe to the Christian doctrines of the incarnation and the Trinity should not deflect the church, through its bishops, its councils and its liturgies, from teaching and commending its trinitarian and incarnational faith.

2 · Are We Speaking of a 'Literal' Incarnation?

Maurice Wiles discussed a wider question: 'How far has "incarnation" changed its meaning in modern discussion, and are we speaking of a "literal" incarnation?' The former point is touched on in several later contributions, for example John Hick's 3B(ii), 'Is there a Doctrine of the Incarnation?', or Frances Young's conundrum 3B(v). I have included here two discussions of the latter point only, of which Brian Hebblethwaite's is addressed to it directly and Nicholas Lash's takes it in a broader context. This was originally the first half of his essay, the second appearing as 7B, 'Christology and the Future of Truth'. It will be noted that the two 'critics' reach apparently opposite conclusions. My own discussion of 'Paradox and Mystification' is also related to the linguistic issue, 3B(iii).

A   Interpretation and Imagination
Nicholas Lash

In December 1882, Cardinal Newman, reflecting on the 'apparent opposition' between the 'respective truths of science and religion', remarked: 'I consider ... that it is not reason that is against us, but imagination. The mind, after having, to the utter neglect of the Gospels, lived in science, experiences, on coming back to Scripture, an utter strangeness in what it reads.'[1]

This 'utter strangeness' of the biblical texts or, at least, of New Testament beliefs, hopes, thought-patterns and methods of argument as interpreted by a critical-historical study of Christian origins, is a recurrent theme in the work of Dr Dennis Nineham. And for Nineham, as for Newman, a failure or incapacity of the imagination is seen as central to the dilemma of the contemporary Christian. 'The characteristic religious difficulty today', he writes, 'is a metaphysical difficulty, at any rate in this sense: where men seem to need help above all is at the level of the *imagination*; they need some way of envisaging realities such as God, creation and providence imaginatively in a way which does no violence to the rest of what they know to be true.'[2]

That way of putting the matter ascribes too unquestioned an authority to 'the rest of what we know to be true'. The more or less uncritical 'taking on board' of cultural, class and group assumptions accounts for the great majority of the things that we suppose ourselves to 'know to be true'. Perhaps one of the 'great divides' in contemporary Christianity is between those who expect the gospel effectively to challenge conventional and accepted attitudes and beliefs, including religious beliefs, and those who, in practice, do not entertain any such expectation.

With this not unimportant qualification, let us accept, at least provisionally, the 'Newman–Nineham' statement of the problem. If we do so, we shall then need to ask: What conditions would have to be satisfied in order that the present incapacities of our Christian imagination could be overcome, and the scriptures (or the Fathers, the Schoolmen, the Reformers) lose their 'utter strangeness'?

It is important to notice that, even if we were to succeed in appropriately specifying these conditions, it would not necessarily follow that they could, in fact, be met. The accessibility of past to present has more the quality of a gift than of the content of a claim. One sure way of distorting, or destroying, communication between persons is to assert: 'Of course I can understand you: you are my wife (or mother, or brother)'. I see no reason to suppose that there may not be long periods in the life of a culture, as of an individual, in which 'nothing makes much sense', not even that which we continue to confess, in darkness, to be the written witness to the Word of God. (And, in such circumstances, confession will be closer cousin to prayer than to assertion.)

It is also important to notice that it is what Newman calls the '*utter*' strangeness of the text which constitutes, or appears to constitute, the problem, and not the text's strangeness *tout court*. If a text (any text, not only biblical texts) entirely loses its 'strangeness', its 'otherness', we can be certain of one of two things: either it has lost all interest and significance for us, or we have misinterpreted it. Why? Because a text that has entirely lost its strangeness, its otherness, is a text to which we have ceased to *listen*. 'Serious understanding', says George Steiner, 'depends on a linguistic and cultural experience of resistant difference.'[3]

Dennis Nineham suggests that, for the healing of our imagination, we may have to wait for a 'prophet'. Without disparaging prophecy,[4] I suspect that we have to look further afield: to profound transformations of language, relationship, behaviour and social institution; to something of a revolution in what Professor Raymond Williams has called our 'structures of feeling'.[5] In the meantime, however, there are perhaps at least some provisional steps that can be taken. In order to indicate what, where our theological discourse is concerned, some of these provisional steps might be, I propose to comment on the way in which several of the contributors to *The Myth of God Incarnate* handle the distinction between 'literal' and 'metaphorical' discourse. I shall suggest that, in handling this distinction as they do, they appear to be making assumptions concerning rationality, objectivity and interpretation which are highly questionable. I shall use the concept of 'imagination' in order to indicate an alternative hermeneutical strategy, from the standpoint of which not only does the relationship between historical interpretation and 'systematic' theology take a different form from that apparently envisaged by most of the contributors to *The Myth* but which, in so doing, invites us to reconsider the question: In asking whether or not, and in what sense,

Jesus could be said to be the incarnate Son of God, what sort of question are we asking? In a later contribution to this collection I shall offer an impressionistic sketch of one way in which what I take to be the central thrust of much 'classical' christological reflection could be expressed in a contemporary idiom.

Before propounding remedies for the healing of our imagination, we perhaps need to look more closely at the *concept* of 'imagination'. Running through several of the contributions to *The Myth of God Incarnate* there is an assumption that 'literal' discourse is 'objective', fact-asserting, whereas imaginative, metaphorical, symbolic or mythological discourse is 'subjective', expressive of attitudes. This assumption is most clearly evident in John Hick's essay,[6] but there are traces of it in the contributions by Frances Young (cf. pp. 34–35) and Leslie Houlden (cf. pp. 129–130). Its oddness becomes apparent when we reflect on the fact that ninety per cent of commonsense and scientific discourse is saturated with metaphorical usage. The assumption embodies, I suspect, a highly questionable account of the supposedly contrasting activities of 'reasoning' and 'imagining', according to which the former ascetically and disinterestedly strives for 'objectivity', whereas the latter is preoccupied, quite 'unscientifically' and somewhat self-indulgently, with how the individual or the group feels or perceives things to be.

And yet, the appropriate exercise of imagination is, as every novelist knows, as strenuous, costly and ascetic an enterprise as is any other intellectually and morally responsible use of the human mind. The poet is as impatient of imprecision, as constrained by that of which he seeks to speak, as is the historian or the physicist. In every field of discourse, practical or theoretical, literary or scientific, the quest for appropriate speech is a quest for precision that is fearful of illusion. To say exactly what one wants truthfully to say is as important for the poet as it is for the physicist, for the lover as it is for the astronomer, for the housewife shopping in Sainsbury's (who does not wish to pay the wrong price for the wrong commodity) as it is for the theologian.

Instead of contrasting 'reason' and 'imagination', I should prefer to suggest that *imagination is the intellect in quest of appropriate precision*. The function of 'appropriate', in that definition, is to serve as a reminder that types of human discourse are bewilderingly and irreducibly various, and that what is to count as 'precision', in any particular field of discourse, cannot be precisely stipulated in advance, but will emerge in the course of enquiry, discussion and critical reflection.

Nevertheless, I think we can say that the abandoment of the quest for appropriate precision, in our response to people and to texts, to practical challenges and to theoretical puzzles, betokens a form of intellectual sloth which may not inappropriately be described as a failure of the imagination. As Professor Hans-Georg Gadamer has said: 'It is imagination . . . that is the decisive function of the scholar.'[7] Newman's famous passage, in the thirteenth of his *University Sermons*, likening the 'genius' to a skilled mountain-climber, perhaps provides an illustration of the sort of thing that he has in mind.[8]

Where historical interpretation is concerned, there may well be beliefs, customs or modes of thought, characteristic of cultural contexts and belief-systems other than our own, which remain 'utterly strange', resisting all our attempts to understand. There is nothing dishonourable in the admission: 'I cannot understand this text.' But there is something smacking of arrogance in the widespread tendency to present alien beliefs or thought-patterns as manifestly ridiculous. In terms of my definition, this tendency exhibits an absence or failure of imagination.

Thus, several of the contributors to *The Myth* appear to assume that biblical, patristic, medieval and Reformation theologians were unaware of our (supposedly) 'sharp' distinction between 'literal' and 'metaphorical' usage and that, as a result, they talked a great deal of what *we* can see (even though they could not) to be arrant nonsense.

So, for example, John Hick asks, concerning the 'ancient language of divine sonship', whether the king was 'thought of as literally or as metaphorically the son of God' (p. 175). and comments: 'The question is probably too sharply posed; for the early cultures did not draw our modern distinction' (p. 175). He asserts that, if we distinguish between literal statements and 'metaphorical, poetic, symbolic and mythological statements, the Nicene formula was undoubtedly intended to be understood literally'.[9] Then comes the *coup de grâce*: 'That Jesus was God the Son incarnate is not literally true, since it has no literal meaning.'[10] Thus, according to Hick, the fathers of Nicea unwittingly taught meaningless nonsense. To be sure, they are generously acquitted of idiocy: they did the best they could, lacking the inestimable benefit of our sharp distinction.

Leaving on one side (because I shall return to it later) Professor Hick's curious assumption that the distinction between 'literal' and 'metaphorical' usage is straightforward and 'sharp', it does not seem to have occurred to him that it is possible to employ, in practice, distinctions of linguistic usage that are not reflexively appropriated in theoretical form. And yet this is what most of us do most of the time. Few people, lacking any reflexive awareness of rules for differentiating 'literal' from 'metaphorical' usage would, on being told that it was 'raining cat and dogs', telephone the RSPCA. In order to use language with richness, flexibility, nuance and precision, it is not necessary to be an expert logician. I suggest, in other words, that, in our attempts to understand what the New Testament writers, or the Fathers of the church, who sought to bend received linguistic resources to new purposes, were up to, it may be important to distinguish between sophisticated linguistic practice and more or less fully developed theoretical reflection on that practice.

I agree with Professor Hick that we cannot, today, avoid asking (for example), 'what kind of language-use one is engaging in when one says that "Jesus was God the Son incarnate" ' (p. 177). For some strange reason, however (and here the failure seems to be one of information rather than of imagination) Hick supposes that 'Such questions ... have only been posed directly in the recent past in which philosophical attention has been directed systematically upon the uses of language' (p. 177; cf. p. 181). One would hardly guess from that passage that medieval theology, from Anselm and Abelard to Aquinas and Nicholas of Cusa, was dominated by a preoccupation with just such issues in philosophical logic.

How are we to avoid that imaginative failure which presents alien modes of thought, not merely as unavailable for our use (which they may indeed frequently be) but as in principle unusable by any human being whose intellectual sophistication we could acknowledge to be equivalent or superior to our own?

In any conversation between two people, each statement can be construed as the answer to an actual or possible question. Misunderstanding is often cleared up when we discover that the question to which the other person was in fact 'replying' was not the question which we thought we had 'heard' behind his statement. Similarly, in our attempts to understand, not a living partner in dialogue, but an ancient text, it is always advisable to ask: To what *questions* are the metaphors, analogies, patterns of argument in the text the attempted outline or form of an answer?

For such a strategy to be fruitful, and for its results to appear interesting, the questions to which the text is a form of response must be questions which *we* could seriously entertain as significant.

Where the interpretation of the New Testament, or of any text which treats of central issues of Christian belief, are concerned, however, there would appear to be what Newman called an 'antecedent probability' that the questions *are* of abiding significance, for they are questions of death and life, of man's predicament and God's activity, of grace and freedom.

But there is a snag. In serious discussion with other people, we grow in understanding not only of the other, but also of ourselves. Good interpretation, they say, changes the interpreter. In the measure that we lack critical self-awareness, we are incapable of understanding other people. Or, to put it in terms of my model of question and answer: in order to 'hear' the question to which the language of the text is a form of response, the skills of the historian are not enough; we also need critically to reflect on our experience and our language, in quest of more precise formulation of the questions to which this language of ours is the more or less spontaneous responsive expression.

At the head of the second part of Gadamer's massive study of *Truth and Method* stands a quotation from Luther: 'Qui non intelligit res, non potest ex verbis sensum elicere.'[11] 'The person who doesn't understand the subject-matter cannot make sense of the language.' Where problems of christology are concerned, there is obviously a sense in which we cannot hope to understand the subject-matter, for it is the mystery of man reflected on in the light of the mystery of God. But at least we can proceed with caution and with a sense of that mystery of which the texts seek to speak. Beyond asserting, and presenting the assertions as transparently obvious and informative, that God is not 'literally' our Father (p. 34) or 'literally' a person (p. 34), that Jesus is not 'literally' divine (pp. 171, 188, 202) or 'literally' risen (p. 201), the authors of *The Myth* seem quite untroubled by questions concerning the legitimacy and the limits of human discourse concerning God. Indeed, it almost seems as if, for them, christological problems are not problems about the meaning of 'God' at all. Which is odd.

I am brought back, for the last time, to the thread which, perhaps more than any other, binds together the contributors to the book: namely, the assumption that there is a clear and straightforward distinction between 'literal' and 'metaphorical' uses of language, and that this distinction is applicable, with equal straightforwardness, to problems of christology.

The imagination, I have suggested, is the intellect in quest of appropriate precision. If it is true for us, as creatures of history, that some understanding of our past is a necessary condition of an

accurate grasp of our present predicament and of our respon-
sibilities for the future, it is also true that a measure of critical
self-understanding of our present predicament is a necessary condition of an accurate 'reading' of our past. We do not *first* understand the past and *then* proceed to seek to understand the present.
The relationship between these two dimensions of our quest for
meaning and truth is dialectical: they mutually inform, enable,
correct and enlighten each other.

Thus, for example, where theological enquiry is concerned, the
systematic theologian is not like the runner in the second leg of a
relay race, waiting impatiently to receive the baton from the historian (who in fact never reaches him, for the historian's task is
never finished). It is rather that the systematic theologian and the
exegete or church historian represent, at the level of academic
specialization, two dialectically related dimensions of all our
attempts, in the present, to relate responsibly both to our past and
to our future.

I have suggested that there are, in *The Myth of God Incarnate*,
signs of imaginative failure in the contributors' quest for understanding of the past. But I also wish to suggest that, in the crude-
ness and imprecision of their distinction between 'literal' and
'metaphorical' usage, there is a similar failure in their apprehen-
sion of the problems of the present. For that distinction, thus abstractly drawn, corresponds neither to the variety and complexity of
our experience (as constituted and expressed in language) nor to
the efforts made, by philosophers and literary critics, critically to
reflect upon our uses of language. To take just two examples of
shades whose hovering presence might have been expected to dis-
turb the tranquillity of the 'mythographers': Wittgenstein's work
has been around for some time, and it is nearly fifty years since
William Empson first published his study of *Seven Types of
Ambiguity*.[12]

Nothing that I have said in this paper is intended to give comfort
to those who suppose that, if someone says that Jesus is God the
Son incarnate, he is saying something 'obviously' intelligible,
significant or true. Quite the contrary. The authors of *The Myth*, in
employing what seem to me to be crude tools and an interpretative
strategy which is, in its positivism, strangely old-fashioned, are
nevertheless discussing issues of inescapable significance and centrality that may not simply be brushed aside. My complaint is that
the authors of *The Myth* are not sufficiently *puzzled* by classical
christological models. They are quite confident both that they
know exactly how those models were used in the past and that they

are no longer available today as expressions of what we believe concerning Jesus the Christ. I do not share their confidence on either score.

NOTES

1. Charles Stephen Dessain (ed.), *Letters and Diaries of John Henry Newman*, XXX, Clarendon Press 1976, pp. 159–160.

2. Dennis Nineham, *Explorations in Theology, 1*, SCM Press 1977, p. 4.

3. George Steiner, *After Babel*, Oxford University Press 1975, p. 379. Elsewhere he speaks of the 'elucidative strangeness' of the language of translation (p. 395). I am grateful to Dr Rowan Williams, who commented most helpfully on a draft of this paper, for drawing my attention to Steiner's treatment of hermeneutical problems.

4. Which I can hardly afford to do, since I have myself made a similar suggestion: cf; Nicholas Lash, 'The Church and Christ's Freedom', *Concilium*, III, 10, 1974, pp. 98–109.

5. Raymond Williams, *The Long Revolution*, Penguin Books 1965, pp. 63–64.

6. Cf. John Hick (ed.), *The Myth of God Incarnate*, SCM Press 1977, pp. 177–178. Until further notice, page references in the text are to this collection.

7. Hans-Georg Gadamer, *Philosophical Hermeneutics*, University of California Press 1977, p. 12.

8. Cf. John Henry Newman, *Fifteen Sermons Preached Before the University of Oxford*, Longmans 1871, pp. 256–257.

9. *The Myth*, p. 177. Bernard Lonergan is equally confident that, in the concept of 'substance', the fathers of Nicea 'found a word which they employed in a metaphorical sense' ('The Dehellenization of Dogma', *A Second Collection*, Darton Longman & Todd 1974, p. 23). Lonergan's treatment of the matter is perhaps overschematic, but his discussion of what it was that Nicea was and was not attempting to do is nevertheless illuminating. For a more nuanced account, cf. G. C. Stead, *Divine Substance*, Clarendon Press 1977.

10. *The Myth*, p. 178. Dr Nineham is similarly confident that, for centuries, 'the doctrine of the incarnation was taken as a statement of an *objective metaphysical fact*, that Jesus was *literally* divine' (p. 188), and he tells us that 'a situation of galloping cultural change ... has brought the doctrine of the *literal* divinity of Jesus into question' (p. 202, my stress in both passages).

11. Hans-Georg Gadamer, *Truth and Method*, Sheed & Ward 1975, p. 151.

12. Where the near impossible task and responsibility of christological discourse is concerned, it is perhaps Empson's 'seventh type' which would most repay careful study by the theologian.

B The Incarnation and Modern Theology
Brian Hebblethwaite

In each generation, theologians have to explore and re-state the doctrines of the church in the light of advancing knowledge, both of science and of history. Thus the doctrine of creation has been re-stated in the light of our vastly increased understanding of cosmology and evolution. But it remains the doctrine of creation. We affirm, with the tradition, that this whole evolving universe depends for its being and purpose on the creative will and act of God. The doctrine of the fall has also been re-stated, perhaps even more radically, in the light of this same knowledge and of the history of man. But it remains the doctrine of the fall. We affirm, with the tradition, that man, through the pressures both of heredity and environment and through the corruption of his will, falls very far short of the divine intention, and stands in need of redemption. The doctrine of the incarnation, too, has been re-stated in the light of greatly increased historical, cultural and psychological realism about what it is to be a man, and a man of first-century Palestine at that. But it remains the doctrine of the incarnation. We affirm, with the tradition, that, out of his great love, and in order to reconcile men to himself, God, without ceasing to be God, came amongst us as one of us, making himself vulnerable to suffering and evil.

In each case, such re-statement is a matter of advance rather than retreat. Theologically speaking, the doctrine of creation is more profoundly grasped when it is articulated in terms of metaphysical dependence; the doctrine of the fall is more profoundly grasped when it is articulated in terms of the radical gap between human achievement and the divine purpose; and the doctrine of the incarnation is more profoundly grasped when it is articulated in terms of kenosis – when the human vehicle or expression of God's presence and action in our midst is taken absolutely seriously in every facet of his human being.

There is surely a sense in which we may speak of a 'literal' incarnation. Literal uses of words are to be contrasted with metaphorical uses. One of the dictionary definitions of 'literal' says that it is applied 'to the relatively primary sense of a word'. Clearly many words used of God are used in secondary senses, metaphorically, that is – as when we call God 'the Rock of Ages'. With other words, the case is not so clear. Aquinas distinguished the analogical from the metaphorical on the grounds that some perfections, such as love, mind, will and (?) action are predicated of God as, in reality, their primary exemplar, on which their normal everyday exemplifications ultimately depend. This complicates the issue since there is still a sense (Aquinas calls it the 'modus significandi') in which the ordinary uses are primary and the theological uses secondary and extended. But in order of being (the 'res significata') the priority is reversed. This means that, by contrast with metaphorical talk, analogical talk ceases to be figurative and secondary. One might say that the analogical sense comes to constitute the primary 'literal' sense for fundamental theology. Fortunately these complications need not bother us here; for there is a third class of words used in religion and theology in neither metaphorical nor analogical senses. These are words like 'holy', 'sin', and indeed 'God', which are coined for religious purposes in the first place. Their religious or theological use is in every way primary. There can be no question but that they are used 'literally' in such contexts. 'Incarnation' falls into this category. The dictionary tells us that its earliest and still prevalent sense is that of the incarnation of God in Christ. It is general uses, meaning 'embodiment', as when we say that 'the Senior Tutor is the veritable incarnation of good sense', that are the secondary, metaphorical senses. We can indeed speak of a 'literal' incarnation.

Of course the fact that a word like 'incarnation' is used in its primary sense for a mysterious and baffling act of the transcendent God in making himself personally present and known in human form means that it is by no means a clear-cut, easily comprehensible and fully articulated concept. We do not grasp the essence of the incarnation any more than we grasp the essence of God. But the literal uses of all these special religious words inevitably include mystery. They are specifically designed to refer, literally, to that which necessarily eludes our full cognitive grasp.

I might add that I have no hesitation whatsoever in standing by what I wrote in my *Theology* article (March 1977): 'the human life lived and the death died have been held quite literally to be the human life and death of God himself in one of the modes of his own eternal being' – though I grant that that takes us back to the *analogy* of *being* ('analogy', as I said being included within the 'literal', by contrast with the 'metaphorical').

3 · Is the Doctrine of the Incarnation Logically Coherent?

A (i) Jesus and the Meaning of 'God'
Don Cupitt

Christians are often thought to be people who believe that Jesus is God. In fact, however, few theologians would accept that formula without qualification, for the apparently simple expression 'Jesus is God' is capable of many interpretations and conceals many difficulties. A short analysis of it may help to clarify our current controversies.

Each of the three words deserves some comment.

1. *Jesus*

It has been held that proper names have no semantic import. They do not describe individuals, but are merely devices for designating them. But if proper names have no content, what is at issue when we debate whether or not Jesus existed? What are the criteria for the correct use of the name?

There are two main theories about the use of proper names. According to *the descriptive theory of naming* the proper name Jesus comes associated with a set of descriptions that are currently believed to apply to him. Though in itself contentless, the name in use has a cloud of descriptive associations around it, and it is true to say that Jesus existed if there was indeed an individual to whom many of these descriptions applied. We say 'many' of the descriptions, and not 'all', because it is possible for one or two descriptions to fail without serious uncertainty being introduced.

The other theory of the use of proper names looks back to the setting-in-life in which their use first became established. According to the *causal theory of naming* present-day uses of the name Jesus stand in a continuous historical succession of uses of the name going back to times in the past when an individual was called Jesus to his face by his contemporaries. The reference of the name is given by that causal chain running back to an individual who regularly answered to the name. When someone names Jesus now he names the individual who went by that name in the time of Pontius Pilate. No doubt what people called out sounded more like 'Yeshu', but that is only a minor point.

Jesus lived a long time ago, and the set of empirical descriptions, titles and theological claims surrounding his name is controversial and has varied a good deal. It would seem that we need the requirements of *both* theories to be met if we are to be reasonably assured that when we speak of Jesus we all know and agree whom we are talking about. We need both historical continuity in the use of the name, and also sufficient stability in the descriptive associations surrounding the name. And there's the rub, for as all theologians know the picture of Jesus presented by historians, by the gospel writers, by the writers of the epistles, in the creeds, and in modern talk about him seem to differ appreciably, so that one can begin to feel very uncertain as to how far all these descriptions are compatible with each other and how many of them really are applicable to the Jesus who was called by that name to his face.

Here is matter for a great deal of controversy. I propose to short-circuit it by simply stipulating that when we use the name Jesus we designate first and foremost the individual who answered to that name in Galilee, and of whom a certain minimum description established by historians is for the most part true. We need to mention the description because the name was a common one; and my view supposes that if we could send a triumvirate of time-travellers on a commission of enquiry (I will nominate Dr Geza Vermes, Mr Michael Grant and Dr Dennis Nineham) they would know whom to look for and be able to recognize the right man when they found him.

However, it is possible that our commission of enquiry might be unable to agree in fixing upon a single individual to whom subsequent use of the name Jesus can be traced. The case might turn out to be like that of St John who is perhaps a composite figure created out of a number of descriptions (son of Zebedee, author of the Fourth Gospel, beloved disciple, author of the Apocalypse, the elder, exiled on Patmos, etc.). If our commission of enquiry also looked into the case of John they might report back that the dozen or so descriptions associated with the name of John really need to be distributed among several individuals; and Jesus might turn out to be like that. Again, it might turn out that there was someone who satisfied the requirement of the causal theory of names, but was so different from the figure described in the gospels that he failed to satisfy the requirement of the descriptive theory of names. And since the nature of history is such that my hypothetical experiment cannot be performed, I have to allow for such possibilities. They cannot be ruled out.

But we can only trust the evidence we have. If we were persuaded that there was no single historical individual who was approximately what historians suppose Jesus to have been, and back to whom all subsequent use of the name can be traced, then our whole view of Christianity would have to change radically. We would have to see Christianity as a mythical-dogmatic system of ideas within which the status of Jesus would be established axiomatically. It would not be a factual matter in any sense, but a matter of definition. The status of Jesus would be no more open to question than the powers of the Queen in a game of chess.

The contrast between the two accounts of the logic of Christian discourse is so great that one must simply choose between them according to the available evidence. To me it seems that the evidence still supports the historical rather than the axiomatic view of Jesus. So I hold that in Christian language the name Jesus should be used primarily as designating an historical individual. The statement 'Jesus is God' is not a definition but a synthetic assertion to whose truth or falsity historical evidence is relevant.

Everyone agrees that there was some elaboration after his death of the descriptions surrounding Jesus' name. I hold that these theological elaborations must not be developed so far as to make the reference of the name uncertain. What is said of Jesus must be something that can plausibly be said of the historical individual who answered to that name.

I repeat that it seems to me a matter of logic that the status of the name Jesus is determined either on the historical model or on the axiomatic model. Either the name designates the man from Nazareth, or it is a very different kind of term whose meaning is given by the way it is used in, for example, the *Quincunque Vult*. Between these two different views one must simply choose, and I choose the historical model and assume it henceforth.

2. *God*

It is convenient to turn next to the word 'God'. Philosophers have discussed whether the word God is a proper name or a predicable term, but the discussion has been rather trivial, taking little account of the history of religions. Ideas of God are found in almost all cultures and are of great antiquity and diversity. It may empirically be the case that most English use of the word God is influenced by its prehistory in the Latin, Greek, Aramaic and Hebrew languages, but nowadays we cannot assume that classical and Judeo-Christian culture have a prescriptive right to lay down the logic of the word. The most we can claim is that they are internally wide-ranging enough to cover most of the ground.

With this proviso, I suggest that the word God has five main kinds of use:

G1 A God may be defined relatively as anything which becomes the object of a religious attitude. In an extended sense it may be said that a man's god is his belly (Phil. 3.19), but more typically something is set up or established as the object of a cult. So it is said that the children of Israel went a-whoring after the Baalim and made Baal-berith their god (Judg. 8.33). The most universal metaphor, perhaps, is that of exaltation, for when something becomes my god it becomes the object of my highest concern.

G2 'God' may be used as a predicable, or more exactly a sortal term. In this use it is historically continuous with the use of Elohim and El in Hebrew. There are two main ideas here:

G2A As a sortal term, a God is a being which is a member of the class of divine beings. Gods may differ greatly in character and in their degree of authority and power, but they are thought of as belonging to a kind.

G2B The monotheistic use of 'God' presupposes an intense, exclusive concentration of divinity in a single focus. Thus God becomes a title, or descriptive expression with unique reference. In this use it is equivalent to such standard English expressions as the Deity, the Godhead, the Almighty, the Lord, the Supreme Being, the Most High, the Holy One and their equivalents in Hebrew and other languages.

Some people argue that the use of God as a predicable term has an ampler descriptive content than these phrases imply, and should include such expressions as *the Creator of the World*. I disagree, because it can be and has been disputed whether God is the Creator, in a sense in which it cannot be disputed that God is the Most High. Incidentally, I have put G2A and G2B together because the formulation of monotheism ('There is *only one* God') takes place against a polytheistic background.

G3 A step lower, there are some divinities who are inferior or subordinate divinities, divinities only by permission. They are felt to have some religious power, but not autonomously. In the Hebrew Bible members of Yahweh's court, angels and the gods of foreign nations are called gods in this sense. The various mediating principles and half-personified divine attributes described in the Bible also belong in this class.

G4 Divinity is communicable to men, and there are a number of senses in which human beings are called gods, both in the biblical tradition and outside it. His exalted office brings him close to heaven, so that a *king* may be thought of as 'God' in so far as he is endowed by virtue of his office with the fullness of divine power and authority. In the Hebrew Bible the clearest case is Psalm 45.6, but there are also many disputed instances, and other examples range from the Pharaohs to seventeenth-century European monarchs. A *judge* exercises a divine function, and in ancient Israel to go before a judge was to go before God (Ex. 21.6; 22.8, etc.). Power over life and death is divine, and as modern medicine develops *doctors* even today may be spoken of as becoming gods or wielding godlike powers.

In ancient times one who dealt with the deity became suffused with the divine holiness. Something of the divine glory shone in Moses' face and he had to be veiled (Ex. 34.29–35). Deification, or participation in God by grace, can be regarded as the general destiny of all God's people, as the discussion in John 10.33–36 shows. Jesus is seen as the pre-eminent example of this, the one who is most a son of God.

G5 But against these various extensions of divinity, to other gods, to inferior gods and to men there stands the final use of God as the proper name of an individual, addressed in the vocative: 'O God', 'Thou God'. Far in the past now lies the use of the proper name Yahweh for the God of Israel. But the logic of God's proper name is somewhat different from that of other proper names. God is not thought of as being assigned the Name, but as revealing it. And God reveals the Name, not to the world at large, but to one particular community. The Name, in short, stands for the religious system peculiar to one people by which that people identify their God and gain privileged access to their God. The Name may come to be regarded as a mystery too sacred to be uttered; or, as the faith becomes more universal in its outreach, it may be dropped. In Christianity there is no proper name for God, but the system of salvation through which God is identified, the Way, may be summed up in a phrase like 'the Father of Jesus Christ' or in the traditional threefold Name, 'the Father, the Son and the Holy Spirit'.

Such are the main uses of the word God, and very complex they are. Their variety can perhaps be explained in terms of two underlying themes:

First, there is God's relation to worship. A God may be thought of as something postulated by the practice of worship (G1), as that actual individual who alone deserves worship (G2B), or as one who is alone rightly worshipped by those privileged to receive the revelation of God's true Name (G5).

Secondly, there is the question of how far and in what ways godhood can be shared, whether equally (G2A), or in varying degress (G3), or by communication (G4).

3. *Is*

We now turn to consider the innocent-seeming little word 'is' in the statement 'Jesus is God'. I suggest that three ways of construing it are relevant to theology.

B1   The first is the 'is' of *identity*: the individual named Jesus is identical with the individual named God. The 'is' of identity requires that 'God' be understood either in sense (G5) or in sense (G2B). 'Jesus' and 'God' are two ways of designating one and the same individual. Sometimes Christian rhetoric seems to approximate to this view but strictly speaking no theologian would defend it, and it seems to be prohibited by the rule for the use of the name Jesus which I have already laid down. 'Jesus is identical with God the individual' is not reconcilable with well-established historical descriptions of Jesus such as that he was a Jew, that he believed in God and that he prayed to God.

B2   The second use of 'is' is for *predication*. To say Jesus is God is to say Jesus is divine, for he has the characteristics a thing must have in order to count as being divine. When people say this they presumably mean that Jesus is more than just posited as a god (G1), and more than just a man divinized by grace (G4). There was a good deal of experimentation in early times with ideas of Jesus as a subordinate divine or heavenly being (G3). Christianity arose in a strongly monotheistic setting, and it was scarely possible to think of him as one of the Gods (G2A). But to call him divine in the full Jewish monotheistic sense (G2B) was to go back to the 'is' of identity (B1). So whatever people wanted to say by way of predicating divinity of Jesus, there were acute difficulties. (G3) was the most popular solution, perhaps, Jesus being linked with some subordinate heavenly being such as God's Word or Wisdom.

B3   Finally, the third use of 'is' is for *acclamation*, and it corresponds to (G1). The acclamation 'Jesus is Lord!' may possibly be so understood. The younger Pliny thought of early Christian worship like this, for he thought that the believers sang hymns to Christ as if he were a god. People might feel impelled to cry out 'Long live the King!', 'Küng for Pope!' or 'Thatcher for Prime Minister!', disregarding any possible embarrassment to the present holders of those offices; and similarly the early Christians may have acclaimed Jesus as if he were a god to them, positing him as divine without thought of the theological problems this must one day raise. For example, in John 20.17 the risen Jesus speaks of God the Father as his God and ours; but a little later Thomas acclaims Jesus as 'my Lord and my God!' (verse 28) and we are not told how what Thomas says is compatible with what Jesus has said.

The B3 interpretation, 'Jesus for God!' suggests a possible view of cries like 'Jesus is Lord!' and 'Maranatha!' But it does not offer any solution to the theological questions it raises. To a Roman like Pliny it might seem that Christianity was a new religion which had set up the cult of a new god, namely Jesus Christ. However, although early Christian worship included acclamations addressed to Jesus, there is no evidence that it was addressed principally to him, and we can be virtually certain that neither Jesus himself nor his immediate followers had any such thing in mind.

Our analysis so far has suggested some of the complications and difficulties of the assertion that 'Jesus is God'. The ante-Nicene patristic writers inclined towards a subordinationist view of Jesus, interpreting 'Jesus is God' along the lines we have coded as (B2, G3). Few would wish to defend such a view today, for it is not easy to reconcile either with Jesus or with pure monotheism.

Conciliar orthodoxy settled upon a very bold, ingenious and highly-original solution, asserting a distinction of coequal Persons within the One God. It could then be said that Jesus is 'God the Son' as distinct from 'God the Father', which (if one could only comprehend the initial distinction) would certainly give 'Jesus is God' a meaning: Jesus is a Second Person of the One God of monotheism (B2, G2B). But one of the many unpalatable consequences of this theory is that Jesus is not the proper name of an individual man. The theory states that Jesus was generically human but not an individual human being: his humanity was 'impersonal'.

Our earlier discussion suggests that when people began to say this they were changing the logic of the name Jesus. It was ceasing to function primarily as the name of an historical individual, a man, and becoming a technical term in a mythical-dogmatic system of ideas.

The vocabulary of the developed faith is not only very hard to understand, but also very alien to the New Testament, so it is not surprising that many people today wish to dispense with it, while yet hoping to retain the divinity of Jesus in the strong (B2, G2B) sense. And they wish to claim that the idea is taught in the New Testament. Here is an example of the difficulty they get into: in *The Truth of God Incarnate* the editor of that book, Michael Green, writes as follows: 'It would be ridiculous to imagine that

Jesus is God *tout simple*. The New Testament writers do not claim this for him; they know he is very much one of us' (p. 23). So it is clear that, like other theologians, Green does not accept every interpretation of 'Jesus is God'. What is he excluding? He says that it is not the case 'that God Almighty has abdicated in favour of his Son' (p. 23), and we should not suppose that Jesus exhaustively defines or embodies God. We should understand Jesus in a way that leaves room for the Father who sent him (p. 26). Biblical monotheism is to be maintained.

However, elsewhere in Green's text we find the following statements, which are presented as paraphrases of or inferences from the New Testament, and declarations of Green's own faith: Jesus 'takes the place of God Almighty in the Old Testament, as the one to whom every knee will bow' (pp. 22f.); 'he is indentified with Almighty God' (p. 23); 'God ... has disclosed himself as Jesus' (p. 23); 'the Father has openly bestowed upon him the sacred name of God' (p. 24); 'he is God-become-flesh', and the early Christians were 'all convinced of the deity of their Lord Jesus' (p. 24); 'the name of Yahweh is the name of Jesus' (p. 28); 'God has incarnated himself in human flesh' (p. 40); and 'Jesus was metaphysically not metaphorically one with God Almighty' (p. 41). These assertions are connected not merely with the exalted but with the historical Jesus, who 'seems to have accepted worship as his due' (p. 45), and whose theological teaching is 'rampant megalomania ... unless he is indeed God' (quoted from C. S. Lewis, p. 46).

When the New Testament writers say 'God' they normally mean God the Father, Yahweh the God of Israel (G5, G2B) and they do not have any idea of a distinction of coequal Persons within God. So in order to proclaim Jesus' deity Green must virtually reduce him to a theophany of Yahweh like the one recorded in Genesis 3.8, and support this view by leaps in the argument. God was in Christ, therefore Christ was God; the fullness of Deity *indwelt* Christ, therefore the fullness of Deity may be *predicated of* Christ; St Paul *associates* Jesus with God, therefore he *identifies* Jesus with God; St Paul sees all God's action as being mediated through Christ, therefore he regards Christ as connatural with God: Jesus is God's image, therefore Jesus is God; and so on. In the interpretation of Philippians 2 a poem with an ethical-religious meaning is read dogmatically, and the implicit contrast with Adam/Lucifer is suppressed, because it demolishes the argument. For Green's Jesus, like Lucifer, regards worship as his due and snatches at equality or even identity with God.

The correct and traditional appeal to the Old Testament in the interpretation of Jesus sets him firmly in a line of great charismatic men of God. But when Green turns to the question of the *truth* of his claims about Jesus he forgets the Old Testament and argues direct to Jesus' divinity from his authority (p. 42), his moral teaching (pp. 42f;), his obedience (pp. 43f.), his powers of forgiveness and judgment (pp. 45f.), his mighty works (pp. 46ff.), his cross and resurrection (50ff.), and so on. Yet the Bible itself sees these powers, sufferings, and glories as having belonged to many before Jesus, and as becoming general in the future. His death is in a line of such deaths, his power of bestowing divine forgiveness is a power which he transmits to his followers, his resurrection is the beginning of a general eschatological resurrection, and so on. In a word, all his great charismata are seen as having been anticipated in the past and as destined to be generally shared in the future. Is it not strange to argue from Jesus' perfect continuity with his background to his absolute discontinuity?

The difficulties, both of logic and of exegesis, in the traditional doctrine seem to me to be overwhelming. People say, What will you put in its place?; and my answer is, What else but the primitive faith as preserved in the New Testament?

Historically speaking, the most substantial and religiously-valuable descriptive material that we can associate with the name of Jesus is the tradition of his teaching. So all that is said of Jesus must be true to and compatible with the message preserved in his critically-reconstructed sayings and parables.

Here I have to meet the historical objection that we do not have one single certainly-authentic saying of Jesus. Briefly, my reply is that though particular words are uncertain the 'voice' is clear. The voice uses language as a tool for revealing to the hearer the coming, the reality, the claims and the grace of God. The voice precipitates the hearer into a final confrontation with God through which salvation is received. The continuing power of the voice is what is called 'the work of Christ', and what it effects in the hearer is what theologians call 'the eschatological event', or more simply conversion.

Jesus, in short, was a prophet who brought the tradition of prophetic monotheism to completion. In his voice the coming of God in judgment and mercy and the turning of man to God in repentance and faith are perfected, and final salvation arrives in the world.

It is a mistake to think of Jesus as having introduced a special form of religious consciousness, for we do not have historical information adequate to justify such language. And it is misleading to use words like *teaching, message, announcement* and so on, as if Jesus brought information. The voice is in fact religious *action* which still continues. We know little of Jesus' life, though what little we can glimpse is in accord with his voice. The most religiously-substantial thing we can reasonably confidently associate with Jesus is his voice, his peculiar form of saving linguistic action. The primitive faith in him as Lord, Messiah, Saviour and Son of God is a response to that action.

Jesus' voice does not bear witness to himself, but to God: and if anyone is to bear witness to Jesus, it can only be God. Thus Jesus could not see himself, or be seen by his early followers, as divine by nature in his own right. He was seen as exalted precisely in his lowliness, his obedience, his self-forgetfulness, his emptiness, his perfect God-centredness. He was nothing in himself, but owed everything to God. His sonship was not, in the pagan manner, lofty cosmic rank, but the exact opposite: the very highest degree of human piety and obedience. He revealed God not positively, by being so great as to be God-made-flesh, but negatively, by being so little that in him God is all in all. He is Lord – only because in him God is Lord; Messiah – only because in him God is King; Saviour – only because in him God saves; and son of God – because he is the least in the Kingdom of Heaven.

To say all this is to propose a context of Jewish piety and religious values within which both Jesus and the early Christians' response to Jesus can be interpreted. It is, I believe, the only historically-plausible way of understanding Jesus and the rise of Christianity. But what does it leave us saying about the vexed question of the divinity of Jesus?

First, I reject subordinationism. Later theology was right to say that there is no half-way Saviour and no partial salvation. Secondly, Jesus was a man, in whom traditional Jewish faith reached its fulfilment and became universal. Thirdly, it is barely intelligible and looks like a misunderstanding to regard Jesus as coequally divine by nature. But, fourthly, he may with due caution be spoken of as 'divine' by the fullness of God's gracious self-communication, for he is in the Christian view the first of all, the head of the human race and the pioneer of salvation. The triad, the Father, the Son and the Holy Spirit, symbolizes the way to God he introduced.

A (ii)   Jesus and the Meaning of 'God' – A Comment
Nicholas Lash

The logical problems that attend attempts coherently to speak about the 'incarnation' of God in Jesus are undoubtedly of considerable importance for the work of this colloquium. But I am surprised that, in his attempt to 'clarify our current controversies', Don Cupitt has selected for analysis a formulation which, as he says, 'few theologians would accept without qualification'. It would, I think, have been more helpful to have analysed a formula such as: 'Jesus Christ is the Word of God incarnate.'

I welcome the thrust of his remarks in the first section of the paper, and agree with him that a certain style of christological discourse floats dangerously free from the actual historical individual, Jesus of Nazareth.

Where the section on 'God' is concerned, I was puzzled by the fact that he nowhere discusses the unique logical problems which, for centuries, have been thought to arise in any attempt to speak of a God for whom *radical* transcendence is claimed while he is yet confessed to be, at the same time, 'very near'. The countless medieval treatises on the 'naming of God', for example, bear witness to a conviction that the classical expressions of Christian belief give rise to peculiar logical problems of their own.

Which brings me to Don Cupitt's third section, on 'Is'. In this section, he seems to me too sharply to separate the 'is' of identity and the 'is' of predication. Surely the language of 'person' and 'nature', for example, was invoked partly in order to help Christian theology to negotiate the rapids between (straightforward) 'identity' and (mere) 'predication'? The attempts may not have been successful, but they should not be ignored by oversimplification or distorted by caricature. As an example of caricature, consider the statement: 'To say Jesus is God is to say Jesus is divine, for he has the characteristics a thing must have in order to count as being divine' (p. 36). I cannot think of any major theologian who would accept the suggestion that 'divinity' is a 'characteristic' of a 'thing' called 'God'. Quite apart from anything else, this way of putting things begs the crucial question (touched on in my comments on the second section) as to whether there is, in a phrase of Herbert McCabe's, a 'common logical world inhabited in mutual exclusion by God and man'.

Just as I was puzzled by the formula chosen for analysis, so I was surprised to find Canon Michael Green selected as principal 'adversary', because he represents a strand of Christian thought and spirituality so relentlessly antitheoretical as to be deeply suspicious of any serious analysis of the *logical* issues. He is therefore a surprising choice for a paper apparently concerned to explore some of the logical problems to which classical christological formulas give rise.

I have the feeling, however, that Don Cupitt's paper is not quite what it seems to be. He says that 'The difficulties, both of logic and of exegesis, in the traditional doctrine seem to me to be overwhelming' (p. 39). Perhaps. But, since the formula selected for analysis does not, as I have already suggested, represent 'the traditional doctrine', he has certainly not *shown* this to be the case. The apparently 'cool' laying out of the logical issue is, I believe, a tactical device behind which he is presenting his own extremely interesting theological account of the significance of Jesus.

To sum up. The 'incarnation debate' badly needs, as one of its components, a fresh look at the *logical* problems to which classical formulations in christology give rise. I had, perhaps wrongly, expected to find this discussion in the paper and, not finding it, am disappointed.

—

Brian Hebblethwaite's essay, 'The Moral and Religious Value of the Incarnation', is printed below on pp. 87–100. It covers a number of topics, of which the relation of the incarnation to the atonement is the most important. But it also touches on the coherence question in its sub-section I, arguing that (*i*) the kenotic christologies of Weston, Quick and Farrer offer a refined and penetrating basis for belief today, and (*ii*) the onus of proof of incoherence lies on critics from within a church which has been 'undeviatingly trinitarian and incarnational'. The first point is taken up by Don Cupitt in 3B(i), and both points by John Hick in 3B(ii). Similar issues raised by Charles Moule in his first section, printed on pp. 131–34, are then taken up by Michael Goulder in 3B(iii), and by Frances Young in 3B(v); and replies follow, by Hebblethwaite to Cupitt and Goulder in 3B(iv), and by Lash to Young in 3B(vi).

B (i) Mr Hebblethwaite on the Incarnation
Don Cupitt

We are all modernists nowadays, and Mr Hebblethwaite is no exception. In trying to save the doctrine of the incarnation he modifies it considerably, and moves much further away from traditional belief than he realizes, without actually stating a coherent theory.

The classical doctrine states that in the incarnate Lord two perfect natures, divine and human, are conjoined in one divine Person. In the precritical period this doctrine could claim to be empirically based. Some facts about Jesus showed him to be fully human. Other facts about Jesus (his supernatural powers, etc.) showed him to be fully divine. Yet he was no divided being for his life was one perfect supernatural life, the life on earth of a divine person.

This doctrine has now broken down because better understanding of the principles of historical judgment, of Jewish thought, and of the literary character of the gospels has fatally weakened the traditional arguments for Jesus' divinity. Those arguments began from such features of Jesus' life as his fulfilment of prophecy, his miracles, his sinlessless and his claims. But we now recognize that in every case either the factual premiss is too uncertain, or the inference is invalid, or both. The critical historian no longer sees both natures displayed in Jesus' life. He sees a purely human Jesus, a first-century man of God in the Jewish tradition.

I think every theologian who accepts the critical historical method accepts that we can no longer argue, in the old way, that the incarnate Lord's divine nature was empirically manifested during his lifetime. That is why I began by saying that we are all modernists nowadays. So what is to be done with the traditional belief in incarnation?

Mr Hebblethwaite's theory of God in kenosis as Jesus is offered as an answer. The theory of kenosis (or God's self-emptying) is not a theory designed to account for the facts about Jesus, but a theory designed to explain how one can go on believing in the incarnation in a time when the old arguments have broken down. It starts from the question, 'Given that God is incarnate in Jesus, how does it come about that God is so hidden in Jesus that Jesus does not even know he is God incarnate, but is in every respect human as we are?'

That being so, it is clear that kenotic theories presuppose good independent grounds for believing in the incarnation. Only if I already have good reason to think there is someone hidden in this room is it reasonable for me to produce a theory to explain how he has hidden himself. The kenotic theory only purports to show the 'how' of the incarnation; it cannot prove that the incarnation has occurred.

Mr Hebblethwaite's hypothesis is that God (or, as he sometimes says, the eternal Son of God) can exist in two states simultaneously, a state of glory and a state of kenosis, without prejudice to the divine unity. The eternal Son of God incarnate has a dual consciousness of himself in his two states. As God in glory he has the fullness of divine self-knowledge, and as God in kenosis in the form of Jesus he knows himself only as a humble human servant of God.

This theory involves a much more literal conversion of the Godhead into flesh than traditional theology permitted, for the man Jesus is identified with God in kenosis, and Mr Hebblethwaite is clear that God in-kenosis-as-Jesus is very God. In that case a suffering human being is very God, and suffering and humanity can be predicated of God absolutely.

The old doctrine conjoined two natures without confusion. Mr Hebblethwaite replaces the two natures with a new doctrine according to which God, without prejudice to the divine unity, can exist in two states, glory and kenosis. And God in kenosis just is a man.

The first Christian writer to call Jesus God absolutely and to say that in Jesus God suffers was perhaps Ignatius of Antioch (Rom. 6.3; Eph. 1.1), but Ignatius still regarded God in glory as impassible (Poly. 3.2). Mr Hebblethwaite wishes to speak of God in glory as suffering and human, and in so doing breaks with monotheism and produces a theology which Feuerbach's celebrated analysis[1] fits perfectly.

The rise of belief in a suffering God took place between the 1860s and the 1920s. J. K. Mozley's study[2] makes it crystal clear that it was a projection of human religious psychology under certain historical conditions.

Why does Mr Hebblethwaite go so far into anthropomorphism? The answer is clear. A historically-minded age can no longer claim to perceive two distinct compresent natures in Jesus. Jesus is simply human. So if divinity is to be predicated of Jesus, it must be predicated of his humanity. A man is God, God is a man. So Mr Hebblethwaite's theory only confirms my own conviction that those who continue today to affirm a strong doctrine of the incarnation risk destroying belief in God.

Still further difficulties arise over the consciousness of Christ. The theory of kenosis appears to require a triple consciousness in the incarnate Lord. For there is God the Son's divine self-knowledge; there is Jesus' own awareness of himself as a human servant of God; and there is God the Son's awareness of himself in kenosis as being the true subject of Jesus' acts and experiences.

But Mr Hebblethwaite does not allow for this third consciousness. He says there are only God the Son's eternal divine self-knowledge and the human self-consciousness of Jesus, the latter being somehow 'included' within the former.

This metaphor of 'inclusion' covers a difficulty. For how are we to imagine this dual consciousness in God the Son? It is as if a bit of my personality breaks off in such a way that it believes itself from its point of view to be an independent personality and agent. It is unaware of me, but I am aware of it, and I know from my superior vantage point that it is not really independent. So I acknowledge it as me and its acts and experiences as my own.

Mr Hebblethwaite clearly has some such picture in mind. An infinite divine consciousness includes within itself and without prejudice to its own unity a finite consciousness which is a mere human consciousness of God.[3]

But the theory is clearly incoherent. The human Jesus' view of his own acts and experiences as a servant of God logically must be different from God the Son's view of Jesus' acts and experiences as acts and experiences of himself in a state of kenosis. Mr Hebblethwaite's theory leaves no one in the position of being able to say, 'I am God in kenosis, suffering in and for man'; and if no one can say that for himself, how can Mr Hebblethwaite say it of him?

So the theory of kenosis fails. It is not just 'mythological', it is incoherent. And from the point of view of monotheism it is much worse than the classical doctrine that it purports to replace. My own belief is that attempts to prolong the life of incarnational theology are now too costly. It would be much better to go back to Jesus and the New Testament and try to produce a better account.

NOTES

1 E. Feuerbach, *The Essence of Christianity*, 1841, especially ch V.

2. J. K. Mozley, *The Impassibility of God*, Cambridge University Press 1926, ch. 2.

3. Consider the following development of Hebblethwaite's position: God the Son has a dual consciousness. But God the Son is One. Therefore in him a man's consciousness of God must be identical with God's eternal self-knowledge. I think this idea is incoherent, but it does figure in some systems of idealistic metaphysics. Indeed, it probably entered Christianity from idealism. But in that case, why restrict the incarnation to the case of Jesus? Why should not every rational creature be 'included' within the divine in the same sense? If it is possible in one case it is possible in any number of cases.

B (ii)   Is there a Doctrine of the Incarnation?
John Hick

I should like in response to Brian Hebblethwaite's paper to focus attention on the question where the onus of argument or of explanation properly lies in our contemporary christological debate.

Brian claims that the theological status quo, based as it is on a long tradition of trinitarian and incarnational belief, must be presumed by all those calling themselves Christians to be satisfactory, and that it is therefore up to any who have qualms about that tradition to state a case against it.

I think that this is correct in one sense but incorrect in another.

It is undoubtedly true that the idea of divine incarnation in Jesus Christ is one of the fundamental themes or motifs pervading the Christian tradition. But it is as such a very general idea, which people have tried to explicate in a wide variety of ways. What we receive from our tradition is a broad imaginative motif together with a history of attempts to spell it out; and the question before this Colloquium is how it may properly be understood and used today. For I take it that we are Christians – that is, people whose relationship to God has been formed under the impact of the life and teaching of Jesus – who are trying to mediate that impact to the world of our own day. We want the revelation of God which has come to us through Jesus both to continue in our own post-Christian society and also to make its contribution to the wider religious life of mankind.

What we have, then, under the great reverberating term incarnation, is a very general idea together with a variety of different interpretations. The picture of God coming down from heaven to earth and living for a while as a man among men has immense imaginative and emotional power. It helps us to feel that God is with us in our own world. It meets our need for a leader whom we can idealize, projecting every perfection upon him and resting upon his commands and promises without question. And it fills the poetic horizon with the marvellously evocative picture of the holy child at the centre of the archetypal family, and in the margins the star-led wizards from the east and simple shepherds to whom a choir of angels has miraculously appeared out of the night sky. All this has the moving force of a great mythic story; and around it there has been woven over the centuries a rich tapestry of music, painting and sculpture. Indeed a great deal of the art of Europe, until almost the present century, has been a celebration of this myth of divine incarnation in the midst of our human history.

But when we turn from the general motif and its creative elaboration in art, to theological science, we quickly observe that there is nothing that can be called *the* Christian doctrine of the incarnation. Indeed the long history of the christological debates is the story of the church's failure to achieve a clear and agreed spelling out of the broad imaginative conception that God was incarnate in Jesus the Jewish messiah. Consider some of the variant answers to the questions which arise. Was Jesus conscious of being God the Son? The synoptic gospels imply No, and the Fourth Gospel implies Yes. The older theologians, until within about the last hundred years, generally thought Yes, whilst theologians today generally think No. But it makes an enormous difference whether we are talking about a divine incarnation which was conscious and self-proclaimed, and which is accordingly taught on the authority of the incarnate one himself, so that to be his disciple involves believing that he was God incarnate; or whether, as now seems much more likely, the incarnational motif is an idea subsequently seized upon by his followers and projected back upon the historical Jesus. Again, we have the officially adopted metaphysical hypothesis of the two natures, but no accepted account of what it means for an individual to have two natures, one human and the other divine. We have a number of rejected attempts to spell this out, such as Appollinarius' suggestion that Jesus' body (including perhaps his 'animal soul' or $\psi v \chi \acute{\eta}$) was human whilst his rational soul or $vo\hat{v}\varsigma$ was the divine Logos. Leaving aside questions about the animal soul, this was an intelligible hypothesis. It spelled out the incarnational motif in such a way that its implications could be developed and examined. And in seeing what its implications were, the church could see that they were unacceptable. For such a theory denied by implication the genuine humanity of Jesus. But the striking fact, which I want to underline, is that no acceptable alternative spelling out has yet been propounded. We are left with the general conception of divine incarnation, with its perennial appeal to the imagination, but with no agreed account of what it means or amounts to.

I have suggested that the incarnational motif should in fact be understood as a basic metaphor. If this is right, the centuries-long attempt of Christian orthodoxy to turn the metaphor into metaphysics was a cul-de-sac. For the metaphor has always evaded the attempts to convert it into a coherent theory or hypothesis. The history of Christian thought is littered with frustrated attempts, and in the end the creed-writers had to be content simply to declare again the mystery of the incarnation, with only a rudimentary move towards the full spelling of it out. The lesson of this history, I suggest, is that the idea of divine incarnation is a basic metaphor functioning as religious myth, and that it is a category mistake to try to specify it as an hypothesis of theological science.

If one takes this view, one will naturally see the many attempted metaphysical theories – including the classic two natures theory and the modern kenotic theory – as products of human speculative thinking rather than as divinely revealed truths. Seeing them in this way, one will think it proper to probe and criticize them like any other intellectual constructions. This leads Hebblethwaite to complain that some of us do not treat the traditional formulations with sufficient respect. And it may be that some of us do not have the reverence for tradition that we ought to have. Whether or how far this is so must be for others to judge. But let us not entirely forget the opposite danger that we – the Christian community through the centuries – having created a formula which has no literal meaning, should then bow down before it as a divine revelation which is too deep for us to understand and which it is impious to question!

Let me refer finally to the kenotic theory, which emerges more and more as the great hope of those who feel that the incarnational motif, understood literally, must have some clear and definite meaning. Hebblethwaite refers to the theory as it has, he says, been refined and expounded with great care and penetration by such theologians as Bishop Frank Weston, O. C. Quick, and Austin Farrer. I hope that he will draw out from their work some definite hypothesis which can be discussed. I confess that I would myself find it hard to do so from Weston's main exposition of kenoticism in his book *The One Christ*.[1] For he does not seem to me to face the questions which we want to ask today. Nor can I be happy with the corollary which he draws that Christ had two wills. Nor, again, would I find it easy to develop an adequate theory from Quick's discussion in his *Doctrines of the Creed*.[2] I would however commend to contemporary kenoticists Quick's agreement with William Temple that the kenotic idea is mythological. Quick writes, 'In so far as Dr Temple says that the kenotic theory has a mythological appearance, we may indeed not only agree with him, but go further in saying that it is inevitably expressed in terms of myth. For myth is the only language we can use about supramundane realities, in so far as we think and speak of them in the category of action .... [We] tell a myth about them .... And the kenoticist contends that the theologian, if he would express the truth about the incarnation as fully as he can, is bound to tell a myth in order to account for that element or moment in the incarnation which belongs definitely to the sphere of historical fact' (p. 136). This is indeed perhaps the main thing that I also want to say about the kenotic idea: it is a powerful myth, and (I would add) it must not be forced into the mould of a metaphysical theory.

Again, I would not find it easy to base a durable kenotic theory on Farrer's delightful but comparatively slight paper 'Truly God and Truly Man', which has recently been posthumously published.[3]

In short, I feel quite strongly that if kenoticism is to be put forward as the answer to our problems, it needs to be expounded and discussed at first hand. If there is a viable understanding of incarnation here, let someone 'lay it on the table'!

NOTES

1. Frank Weston, *The One Christ*, Longmans 1907.
2. O. C. Quick, *Doctrines of the Creed*, Nisbet 1938.
3. Austin Farrer, *Interpretation and Belief*, ed., Charles Conti, SPCK 1976.

B (iii)   Paradox and Mystification
Michael Goulder

(This was written as the first half of a reply to Professor Moule's 'Three Points of Conflict in the Christological Debate' (pp. 131ff.), and refers to his appeal to the notion of paradox (pp. 134, 140) to resolve the apparent incompatibility of human personality with divine incarnation.)

Paradox is a somewhat loose concept, of which I have not found much serious discussion;[1] and it is important to distinguish it from mystification. The *Shorter Oxford English Dictionary* defines it in its normal meaning (2a) as 'a statement seemingly self-contradictory', (2b) 'often applied to a proposition that is actually self-contradictory'. Sometimes we can resolve the apparent contradiction and sometimes not. Frederick, in the Paradox song in *The Pirates of Penzance*, had 'been born twenty-one years; yet, if we reckon by birthdays, you are only five and a little bit over': this was because he had been born on 29 February. Paul learned that Christ's strength was made perfect in weakness: we all know that we are more moved by a man pursuing good ends under difficulties than without. In both cases the paradoxical proposition is clear, and the resolution of the paradox is clear also. In other cases the paradoxical proposition may be clear, but its resolution a puzzle. In Frances Young's paradox,[2] the electron sometimes behaves as a particle, sometimes as a wave: we expect that science will sooner or later resolve the paradox with a theory that can consistently account for both types of behaviour. (Otherwise we should not call it a paradox but a contradiction.) It is of the nature of the case that many religious paradoxes will be of this kind, their resolution awaiting the hereafter: 'I, yet not I, but the grace of God' (see below p. 134) for one. It is a puzzle why the Christian sometimes behaves as if borne on a wave of divine grace, and at other times like a destructive hail of machine-gun bullets; but it is easy to see that in practice he does so, and he may hope to see the paradox of grace resolved after death. *Pace* R. W. Hepburn, I do not see any reason why traditionally minded Christians should not appeal to unresolved paradox over the incarnation in the way that Professor Moule and Dr Ian Ramsey[3] (and many others) do, provided only that we know what the paradox is; even though its resolution may have to wait till Judgment Day.

The trouble with this line of defence lies in establishing the incarnation as a genuine paradox; for there are also pseudo-paradoxes, or mystifications, in which the proposition asserted is in some radical sense unclear, and upon probing is found not to be capable of being stated at all. The classic mystification is perhaps the case of phlogiston. Stahl, in the eighteenth century, saw fire as the giving off of phlogiston from a substance. Thus, if magnesium was burnt, phlogiston was understood to be lost, and the resultant chemical – what we should call magnesium oxide, but which was known to Stahl as the calx – was magnesium minus phlogiston. The proposition, Magnesium minus Phlogiston yields Calx, appears at first sight to be a problem-free scientific hypothesis, and as such was orthodoxy in the eighteenth century. The trouble arose when the 'calx' was found to be *heavier* than the metal. Ultimately this was explained by Lavoisier on the hypothesis that there was oxygen in the air which combined with the magnesium, so that: Magnesium plus Oxygen yields Magnesium Oxide. At the time the orthodox formulation, Magnesium minus Phlogiston yields Calx, did not seem absurd, for eighteenth-century professors spoke of 'the levity of the matter of fire':[4] but to us the phlogiston theory is not only wrong, because there is no such stuff as phlogiston, but it has become meaningless, because the weighing involves the corollary that phlogiston has negative mass, and negative mass is a notion apparently defying comprehension.[5] The proposition, 'Phlogiston is a substance of negative mass', does not achieve the dignity of a paradox; it is just a mystification. The distinction between real and pseudo-paradox consists in this, that the real paradox raises no problem about meaning, so that our question arises in the form, 'How can we reconcile p with q?', while the pseudo-paradox cannot be stated except in a mystifying way, evoking questions in the form, 'But what can p mean?'.

It is evident that there are theological pseudo-paradoxes or mystifications just as there are scientific ones. D. Sperber[6] tells of the Dorze tribesmen in the Sudan who believe that leopards are Christians. One might infer from this belief that leopards, like Dorze Christians, fast on Fridays; and that it is therefore safe to go near a leopard on a Friday. This conclusion is not however in practice inferred by the Dorze; but nor is it allowed that leopards are undependable in their Christianity, or that they have a dispensation, etc. Thus what at first seemed a paradox ('But surely only human beings can be Christians?') is reduced to a mystification. We simply do not know what the 'belief' is.

Definitions settle nothing, and others may prefer to call the phlogiston theory and the Dorze's view of leopards paradoxes. In that case it becomes important to recognize that some paradoxes are apparent contradictions, while others are apparent nonsense. We can all see that the electron paradox is sense, both the wave and the particle theories being readily comprehensible, but in apparent contradiction; whereas the concept of negative mass, or of non-fasting Christian leopards, is not sense, or at least seems not to be sense unless someone can give content to it. It is also important to recognize that many religious paradoxes are apparent contradictions but perfectly good sense. The claim that God loves us as his children is in stark contradiction with the facts of human suffering, but it is a comprehensible *claim*. The attempt by John Wisdom in 'Gods'[7] and by Anthony Flew in 'Theology and Falsification'[8] to show that no assertion was being made in such a claim had to be answered, or religious belief would have been accepted as vacuous. The religious man cannot allow that under probing his assertions melt away into apparent nonsense, that is, that he has no idea what he is saying. Apparent contradictions are another matter, and seem inevitable in religion, where there is a limit to what we understand about man, as Brian Hebblethwaite says, let alone about God.[9]

Now incarnationalists often seem unaware of this distinction, and of the need to answer the charge that their 'belief' is not a paradox but a mystification, or if a paradox that it is apparent nonsense rather than apparent contradiction. Professor Moule follows a long line of expositors in setting out to give a careful definition of what he means by incarnation. It is 'a unique and distinctive identification of God's "Word" with Jesus ... in Jesus ... the Logos *became* a man of flesh and blood' (pp. 131f. below, Moule's italics). At first sight this looks as straightforward a religious claim as 'Magnesium minus Phlogiston yields Calx' seemed to be a straightforward scientific claim, but probing leaves the reader as mystified by the first as by the second. We are all familiar with statements of the kind, 'The Logos became a man', for we often say 'X became a Zambian citizen', 'Y became a bishop', etc. In these sentences 'became' involves some element of change and some element of continuity, or, in Moule's word, identification. X is no longer English by law, nor Y a don; but both are essentially the same people they were before. In 'the Logos became a man', some differences at least are easy to spell out – the Logos had no flesh-and-blood body, for example, before the incarnation, but after the incarnation it had. The problem lies in understanding the element of continuity or identification, and it is here that we are mystified.

Preachers often follow St Paul's 'though he was rich, yet for your sake he became poor', with the analogy of the prince who became a beggar. The stress is laid upon the difference of honour, income, scope, etc., but the problem of continuity is exactly not touched by such analogies; for the prince and the beggar are *the same man*, and it is not clear what is *the same* between the Logos and Jesus. We might try to mitigate the difficulty by drawing on the fable in which the prince became a frog. Here we think we can understand what is being said. The body is different, but the frog still has the prince's memory, his power of reason, his love of the princess, etc.: it is the same *personality*. But then this doctrine, which is roughly that held by St John, with Jesus remembering what it was like to share the Father's glory before creation, and felling his enemies to the ground with an *Ego eimi* as they come to arrest him, is not that maintained by modern incarnationalists. Moule wants St John's words, 'the Word became flesh', but I take it that he does not want St John's doctrine which gives content to them; and he does not tell us what doctrine he does want. If the prince 'becomes' a frog *completely*, with a frog's mind and individuality, and no memory of princely prior existence, we should say that the prince had been *replaced* by a frog. It is this dilemma which reduces the incarnation to a mystification. All the attempts that have been made to say what the element of continuity is between the Word and Jesus seem to be either implausible or vacuous, and they have in many cases been declared heresy. But unless *some* element of continuity can be alleged, nobody knows what is being stated, and 'the Word became a man of flesh and blood' is apparently not sense. This is the challenge to incarnationalists: *unless some continuity between the Word and Jesus is being asserted, their doctrine is not a paradox but a mystification, not an apparent contradiction but apparent nonsense.* As a belief it goes into inverted commas. In this respect I should not wish to go as far as John Hick in comparing the doctrine to a square circle, i.e. to transparent nonsense: but that it is apparent nonsense seems evident.

The Fathers found the solutions offered to this challenge implausible, and declared them heretical. Modern kenotic theologians, like Professor E. L. Mascall[10] or Fr H. McCabe[11], seem to opt instead for vacuity: Jesus is metaphysically the Word

of God, in his person, in his ego, but his human nature or consciousness is not affected by this. I will return to Mascall shortly,
but perhaps I may make the general point with a parable. Return-
ing from abroad with a friend, I hear that the Vice-Chancellor of
the University of Bedlam is Lord Beaver. 'What!', I say, 'A new
V-C?'. 'No', replies my friend, 'the old V-C, Sir Robert Badger,
must have become a peer'. In the distance Lord Beaver looks like
Sir Robert, and the voice is similar, and the same conspicuous
probity governs all his actions; but on closer acquaintance the
differences seem obvious. 'Oh', says my friend, 'he must have had
a face-lift; and his voice is pitched deeper because of the new
dignity; and he will have had a new central nervous system put in
for the job: but it is the same chap.' Soon I feel driven to ask, 'But
what is in common between the V-C we knew and the V-C we
know?' If I am told, 'Nothing. But metaphysically they are the
same: it is a paradox', two consequences will follow: first, I shall
feel totally mystified, and second, I shall suspect that what began as
a misidentification is being maintained from a reluctance to confess
error.

Is not this very close to the situation over the incarnation? It
looked at first as if Jesus' claims, his miracles, his saving power,
etc., required him to be divine: and the doctrine that he was the
Word made flesh seemed to be God's revelation and therefore
unquestionable. But today all the actions which to the Fathers gave
substance to the incarnation – the miracles, Jesus' memory of pre-
incarnate life with God, 'I and the Father are one', etc. – now find
this-worldly explanations. Furthermore the belief that the Bible is
infallible truth is discredited. But when it is asked, 'What then is in
common between Jesus and God?', the reply advanced by modern
kenoticists is, 'Nothing, so far as Jesus' human nature is concerned:
but metaphysically he is the Word of God'. What this means, and
what grounds there can be for accepting it (other than reluctance
to allow that the church has been in error) remain obscure.

As an example of this obscurity I take Professor Mascall's
statement in *Theology and the Gospel of Christ*, because it is modern, because it is not lacking in subtlety, and because it draws on
the work of a number of continental theologians, and so is not
idiosyncratic. I do not at all wish to saddle Professor Moule with
Professor Mascall's opinions: I merely wish to show that one current attempt to expound his definition ends by increasing the
mystification.

Mascall begins (p. 132) from C. Wessels' speculations on the
manner of the virginal conception, suggesting that the chromo-

somes in Jesus' human body were all provided from a single ovum in Mary, with the exception of the sex chromosome. She conceived by parthenogenesis, but a Y chromosome was miraculously supplied in place of the X chromosome (otherwise Jesus would have been a girl). In this way Jesus was of a completely human *nature*, with a fully human psychology or *consciousness*. What is different about him is that he is a divine *person* or *ego* or relational being: 'what is purely divine is the hypostasis in whom the genetic inheritance inheres' (p. 133). There is no reason why two completely identical natures should not exist, but each would have its own unique personhood (p. 154). So personhood is distinct from consciousness, and is known by a 'pre-conscious or unthematic self-awareness ... distinct from, and antecedent to, the knowledge which it can have of itself as an object in acts of introspection' (pp. 136f.). However absorbed Mascall may be in his thought, he retains 'a pre-conscious awareness that the experience is being undergone by Eric Mascall and not Chairman Mao or Mrs Jacqueline Onassis' (p. 137). Jesus' person had this pre-conscious awareness of being the co-equal Son of the divine Father, taught him by his mother from her memories of his conception and birth (pp. 150f.), and experienced in his relation with the Father. He became fully aware of this relationship in his human consciousness, as is shown by his use of the terms Abba, and whatever was the Aramaic for *Ego eimi* (pp. 162ff.); but the divine consciousness never intrudes into the human consciousness, which would otherwise be modified by it. The human consciousness is aware of the divine ego by intuition, somewhat like the experience of the mystics (p. 166). To be more precise, citing Galot, 'the Incarnation has brought, for the human nature that is assumed, a supernatural ontological elevation which adjusts its activity to the divine ego of the Word. This elevation allows the human activity of consciousness to be set in motion by the divine "I" (*je*) and to perceive reflexively the divine "me" (*moi*)' (p. 167).

We should first note with approval that Mascall does postulate some *action* of God whereby the incarnation is supposed to have taken place, viz. the virginal conception. Jesus cannot *be* the Word unless God took some steps to make him so, and those theologians who confess to scepticism over the gospel birth narratives need to say what act of God they are substituting for them. It is true that Mascall's anti-critical attitude evinced in the earlier part of the book makes his reliance on these biblical traditions quite implausible, especially when he can be perfectly sophisticated in these matters on other occasions. But even if we do posit substantial historical accuracy for either Matthew or Luke, the postulation of a miraculously supplied chromosome or sperm does not seem adequate to provide what is required, an ontological basis for divine personhood. It is here that modern genetics makes an important difference. To a Jew with the ancient world's biological understanding,[12] a man *was* the seed of his father. So, according to Matthew, Jesus was divine, being God's literal son. But this is not so in the modern view. Mascall accepts that Jesus made water wine and restored a man's withered hand: but that does not make the water or the man divine in their being. If the miraculous supply of whatever is needed to give action to the hand does not alter its ontology, why should the miraculous supply of a chromosome or a spermatozoon?

Second, Mascall wishes to draw on modern scientific understanding of what it is to be a man, but he harks back when in doubt to St Thomas: he even tells us (p. 195) that present-day embryologists agree with St Thomas that 'animation' takes place after twenty-eight weeks, 'while using a different vocabulary'. To a modern scientist (or anyone), the fusion of sperm and ovum constitutes a potential new human being, with a slowly developing consciousness reflecting its complement of genes and chromosomes and its environmental experiences. Our genetic knowledge simply leaves us baffled by talk of two consciousnesses in Jesus, or of a divine ego with a (principally) human consciousness, or of the Word 'assuming' a human consciousness. We do not have two consciousnesses ourselves, one 'unthematic' and the other self-conscious. We are persons or egos, conscious of our environment in different modes appropriate to the object. In moments of abstractedness, or perhaps in mystical transport, we may have a very minimal consciousness of ourselves in relation to our thought, or to God: at other times, in reflective prayer or in personal relations, we are very conscious that it is *us* in the relationship.

Third, the divine personhood seems to be metaphysical in the pejorative sense of the word. It is a doctrine which does no work, for Jesus' awareness of a unique filial relationship to God can be easily explained without it. It is like the medieval 'anima' which was first supposed because the foetus seemed to 'quicken' after so many weeks of pregnancy, and later became disreputable, becoming in Locke's disparaging phrase, 'something, I know not what'. The church has a sad record of reluctance to resign such otiose pieces of metaphysical backing, and to recognize that, in Flew's epigram, a fine brash hypothesis has died by inches.

By his use of phrases like 'the human nature assumed by the

Word', and by such discussions as the date at which Jesus received a human soul, Mascall leaves us with the conviction that to be an incarnationalist is to live in the thought-world of the thirteenth century, and not among moderns, who use a different vocabulary for real reasons. Incarnation was not a mystification to Thomas, but the distinctions drawn by Mascall and the French-speaking Thomists whom he cites at length seem to bear no relation to the modern world-view – of which, indeed, he is openly contemptuous. Those who live in such a world seem driven by such an apologia to see his view of the incarnation as apparently not sense.

It is worth saying, as a last if somewhat obvious point, that the present issue is the crucial one. Professor Moule writes as if his 'Three Points . . .' were in some way on a par. The first is perhaps (in his view) a drawn battle, but space can be made for incarnation if allowance is made for paradox. On the second and third point he sees incarnationalism as the clear victor. The experience of the first churches was of a divine, incarnate Lord; and no satisfactory doctrine of salvation is open to us without incarnation. But surely there is no such parity in the matter. The primary question is, 'Can the incarnation doctrine be stated?'; and if it cannot, if its expression always seems to be nonsense, if it is but a mystification, then *it is valueless though Christ himself and all the saints in heaven 'believed' it*. Nor can any satisfactory soteriology be based upon a house of cards. Doctrines of the atonement constructed on incarnational premises are themselves notoriously difficult to state coherently, but if the incarnation cannot be stated either, Professor Moule's (not very fair) decrial of the *Myth*'s salvation doctrine as 'exemplarist' is no more than a lament. Our concern with christology is a concern for truth. If St Paul and St John believed something that we cannot make sense of, that is sad: but so far from settling the matter in favour of their 'belief' because they believed it, it leaves us with the challenge of finding a doctrine which will satisfy our criteria for sense, adequacy and plausibility.

NOTES

1. See I. Ramsey, 'Paradox in Religion', in *Christian Empiricism*, ed. J. H. Gill, Sheldon Press 1974, pp. 96ff.; R. W. Hepburn, *Christianity and Paradox*, Watts 1958. There are no articles with 'paradox' in the title in either *Religious Studies* or *The International Journal of the Philosophy of Religion*.

2. *The Myth*, p. 33: the example is a favourite with theologians, cf. Hepburn p. 17, Ramsey p. 102.

3. Ramsey's paper is baffling. He distinguishes 'avoidable' (resolvable, in my terminology) from 'unavoidable' paradox, and of the latter rejects Barth and Kierkegaard as purveyors of 'logically inaccessible' paradox. The remaining 'logically explorable' paradoxes are then approved, including the Chalcedonian formula: they can be revealing, but leave the 'mapping' of 'God', 'union', 'Person', etc., still on our hands. These words are then said to operate like 'I' in the sentence 'I am running but I am not – it's the new drug that is taking my legs round'. But this is a simple ambiguity: the drug enables the runner to draw on reserves of energy he cannot usually dispose of. Alternatively, the Nuer tribe's belief that a twin *is* a bird is commended (with Evans-Pritchard) as being 'quite sensible, and even true' once it is understood that it means that 'in respect of God, twins and birds have similar characteristics'. Evans-Pritchard says that one needs the Nuer language to make this transition; which seems to be a confession that English enables us to make sense of an apparent primitive contradiction. In the end paradoxes fall into Ramsey's favourite category of being the means of disclosure through models and qualifiers: but my impression is that these days the Chalcedonian definition discloses nothing except its defenders' wish to be orthodox.

4. M. Macquer, *Elements of the Theory and Practice of Chymistry*, ET 1775, I p. 8.

5. For an account of the phlogiston theory and its overturn, cf. J. B. Conant, (ed.), *Harvard Case Histories in Experimental Science*, Harvard 1960, I pp. 65–116.

6. D. Sperber, *Rethinking Symbolism*, Cambridge 1975 (ET).

7. John Wisdom, *Logic and Language*, First Series, ed. A. N. Flew, Oxford 1951.

8. *New Essays in Philosophical Theology*, ed. A. N. Flew and A. MacIntyre, SCM Press 1955.

9. In a Radio interview, 29 September 1977.

10. E. L. Mascall, *Theology and the Gospel of Christ*, SPCK 1977.

11. *New Blackfriars*, December 1977.

12. Cf. Aristotle, *de Gen. Anim*. 1.20.1, and the useful note in the Loeb edition.

B (iv) The Logical Coherence of the Doctrine of the Incarnation
Brian Hebblethwaite

It is certainly difficult, indeed paradoxical, to suppose that a human life lived out within the framework of first-century Jewish consciousness, could actually *be* the incarnate life of God himself in one of the modes of his infinite and eternal being. But this doctrine is not overthrown by setting out travestied versions of it, as Don Cupitt does in his reply, nor is it overthrown by pressing the details of all-too-human analogies, as is done by both Don Cupitt and Michael Goulder.

It is a travesty to suggest that, for kenotic christology, divinity is predicated of Jesus' humanity. That is certainly to confuse the natures. We predicate divinity of Jesus, because we believe his humanity to be the vehicle and expression of the eternal Son. There is no conversion of the Godhead into flesh. To think that is to operate with some crude picture of two kinds of stuff.

Nor is there any reason to postulate three consciousnesses, where God incarnate is concerned. Indeed it is hard to take such playing around with theological concepts seriously. All we need is Jesus' own sense of filial dependence on the one hand, and God's awareness of his (God's) own acts through incarnation on the other.

Notice how Cupitt attacks my metaphor of 'inclusion' – the suggestion that Jesus' human self-consciousness is 'included' within the divine self-consciousness as its vehicle and expression. Cupitt asks how are we to imagine it, as though our talk of God is decided by what we can imagine! He goes on not only anthropomorphically but Cupittomorphically by talking of some hypothetical division of his own personality, as though that were a basis for advance in theological understanding. His objection, generalized, turns out to rest on the highly anthropomorphic picture of two human individuals and the impossibility of our thinking of them as identical. But that is no way to explore the logic of God-talk.

A similar fault appears in Goulder's more careful statement of the objection from alleged incoherence. He tells us a jolly little story about the Vice-Chancellor, changed utterly, so that there is no continuity, by which identity-talk could be justified. But this all-too-human analogy does not begin to meet the case. We are not suggesting that God becomes an utterly changed God, or that Jesus becomes a different man from the man he was before. The continuity in incarnation is quite clear. It is the continuity of God's own act in incarnation, manifesting, in another mode, his steadfast love and limitless grace.

These objections fail because they themselves depend wholly on what we can imagine anthropomorphically. I notice that accusations of anthropomorphism come from critics who themselves, at least in considering their opponents' views, think only anthropomorphically. There is a sense, of course, in which, for the classical Christian tradition, it is true that God anthropomorphises himself in coming amongst us as one of us, but that can only be said when we are operating with a totally unanthropomorphic concept of God, when we train ourselves to think, not in images, but theologically of the eternal and infinite God, who is such as to be able to live out a truly human life on earth for our sake, and to relate himself to himself in an earthly parable of the blessed Trinity.

I said that the doctrine of the incarnation was paradoxical, and so it should be, if human words are to be used to precipitate our minds beyond the natural into thought of the transcendent. This is the function of paradox in religious language, as Ian Ramsey was always keen to show.[1] It is not a matter of rejoicing in straight contradiction at the single mundane level of talk about two human individuals. The paradoxes are a sign that we have to stop thinking anthropomorphically; and they are a tool for thinking theologically about the one who cannot be 'comprehended' with clear-cut univocal terms. We have to learn how to use these tools. It is certainly not the case that 'anything goes' when we begin, as Ramsey encouraged us to do, to explore the logic of irreducible religious paradox. I offer my remarks on kenotic christology as an example of the kind of discrimination that one can at least try to make in this area.

NOTE

1. See his 'Paradox in Religion', now in *Christian Empiricism*, Sheldon Press 1974.

B (v)   Can there be any Evidence?
Frances Young

Among some defenders of the doctrine of incarnation, I discern a
desire to produce *evidence* in support of their claim, (especially
perhaps in the writings of Charles Moule); and I find myself naturally asking the question, what evidence is there suggesting that a
divine incarnation took place in Jesus of Nazareth? Yet any appeal
to evidence immediately implies some element of 'docetism'. Like
many other words in the current debate, this word is obviously
'slippery' in the sense that different people understand it differently; but it is now accepted by the majority of Christian
theologians that Jesus must have been an entirely normal human
being, that any qualification of this implies some element of docetic thinking, and that docetism, however slight, undermines the
reality of the incarnation.

I therefore pose the following conundrum:

*If Jesus was an entirely normal human being, no evidence can be
produced for the incarnation.*

*If no evidence can be produced, there can be no basis on which to
claim that an incarnation took place.*

B (vi)   What sort of Evidence?
Nicholas Lash

1.   Among some defenders of the doctrine of God, I discern a
desire to produce *evidence* in support of their claim; and I find
myself naturally asking the question: What evidence is there suggesting that 'God' is other than a figment of the human imagination?

It is now accepted by the majority of Christian theologians that
confessions of faith in the reality of God are not appropriately
grounded in claims that God appears as a fact in the world.

If God is not a fact in the world, no evidence (according to the
logic of Dr Young's argument) can be produced for his existence.

If no evidence (of the sort she seems to have in mind) can be
produced, there can be (according to her) no basis for claims that
God is other than a figment of our imagination.

Dr Young might care to reconsider what *sort* of evidence, in
support of what kinds of claim, might be appropriate in such matters.

2.   If it is part of the definition of a 'perfectly normal human
being' that there can be no evidence that he embodies and discloses, in his humanity, the presence and character of God, in a
manner and to an extent that most of us do not, then:

either no prophets or holy men are 'perfectly normal human
beings';

or there can be no grounds for reasonably affirming that any
particular individual is a prophet or holy man.

Behind Dr Young's assumption that humanity cannot, without
ceasing to be humanity, be the expression, embodiment, contin-
gent form of God, there lurks unexorcised the demon of the
Feuerbachian 'competitor God'.

C   Myth and Truth in Scientific Enquiry
John Rodwell

I came to *The Myth of God Incarnate* as a practising biologist under a contractual obligation to reflect on the world and produce scientific statements about it and as a priest with a vocational impulse to reflect on the world and foster religious insights into it. I therefore shared with the authors, though from a rather different standpoint, two main concerns. First, at a critical level, I agreed with Maurice Wiles that the type of theological questions asked in the book could be proper and necessary,[1] and indeed with Leslie Houlden that our contemporary intellectual situation demands such an activity from us if we are to maintain our integrity.[2] Second, at a pastoral level, I shared the concern of the authors (not always recognized by their critics) that the richness and creativity of the Christian perspective should be preserved and encouraged in mission.[3] Yet I was greatly disappointed with the result of their reflections. In this and a later contribution I wish to explore why this should be so. To do so it is necessary first to outline some recent developments in thought about the nature of scientific enquiry, chiefly associated with the name of Karl Popper.[4]

The popular view of science is that it comprises a body of established fact garnered by observation and experiment, upon numerous specific examples of which are based general statements or laws. This particular empirical method, induction, is what guarantees the legitimacy and authority of science and distinguishes it from non-science – statements based on other foundations such as prejudice, faith or speculation. Popper early found induction an unsatisfactory criterion of demarcation and his critique of it can best be understood in terms of two strands of development.

First, Popper was asking the question 'What distinguishes science from non-science?' in the context of four major theoretical developments: Einstein's theory of relativity, Marx's theory of history and the psycho-analytical and psychological theories of Freud and Adler. He found himself thrilled by the first but disappointed by the others. What worried him was not that these seemed less truthful or exact but that their sheer explanatory power made verification by further experience inevitable. Einstein's theory was different. The very outrageousness of some of its predictions (that, for example, light, say from a distant star, would be attracted by a heavy body, like our own sun) laid it wide open to refutation, even by a single observation. It thus seemed to Popper that irrefutability was a vice of a theory rather than a virtue and that the true criterion of a scientific statement was its falsifiability.

Second, Popper took up the problem which Hume detected in the nature of the induction process itself, namely that 'even after the observation of the frequent or constant conjunction of objects, we have no reason to draw any inference concerning any object beyond those of which we have had experience',[5] that no number of specific examples of observation or experiment could logically entail a general statement or law. Popper solved the difficulty of reconciling this realization with the need to preserve the empirical nature of science by again invoking falsifiability and doing away altogether with the need for induction: 'only the falsity of a theory can be inferred from empirical evidence and this inference is a purely deductive one.'[6]

The importance of this startlingly simple proposal is best seen against the background of Logical Positivism. Building on the early philosophy of Wittgenstein, the Vienna Circle developed the idea that all genuine (i.e. meaningful) propositions were truth functions of elementary propositions which described facts ascertainable in principle by observation. Verifiability was thus seen as the criterion of demarcation between meaningful and meaningless statements and, further, verifiability and meaningfulness coincided with the definition of science which was the class of all verifiable and meaningful statements.

Popper pointed out that, though specific examples of observation might be empirically verifiable, general statements in science were certainly nót so (because of the flaw in the induction process) and they could not thus be described as truth functions of observation statements. For Popper, the verification principle advocated by the Logical Positivists ranked science with the rest as meaningless. But, in any case, what was needed was not a criterion of meaning between sense and nonsense but a criterion of empiricism between science and non-science. Popper thus uses falsification to draw a line not around but within meaning.

If we turn to the implications of Popper's proposal we can see something of its fruitfulness for this debate. Consider, first, the nature of scientific theory. Most scientists, faced (in so far as they have been) by the logical unjustifiability of induction, have resorted to the idea of probability, the degree of which in any particular theory is raised by each confirming piece of evidence and which therefore provides an adequate working substitute for certainty. But, says Popper, this is an invalid compromise: it is very easy to produce any number of statements whose probability is extremely high. The difficulty with such statements is that they convey next to no information; their information content decreases to the extent that they become more probable until they approach tautologies with a probability of one and an information content of zero. What we should be aiming for are statements with a low probability and a proportionately high information content. Such statements are highly falsifiable and highly testable: good theories prohibit, better theories prohibit more. We should therefore not crave to be right but take risks in our theorizing because, should we turn out to be right, we will have progressed further.

It is thus easy to see why Popper was attracted by the boldness of Einstein's theory and repelled by those of Marx, Freud and Adler. It was formulated unambiguously and so fully open to refutation. What the other theories did was to cope with refutations by adjustment or introduction of some auxiliary assumption in an *ad hoc* fashion so that their adherents never came face to face with contradiction. Indeed, they had modes of understanding the world which grew increasingly powerful in their ability to explain everything that came their way. This tactic (which Popper termed the 'conventionalist twist' or 'conventionalist stratagem') rescued the theories only at the price of destroying their scientific status.

Rather, says Popper, having framed our theories as clearly and audaciously as possible, we should submit them rigorously to the test of falsification against our observational and experimental experience of the world. Should a particular theory be found wanting, it should be abandoned – not lightly if this implied uncritical testing, but not sadly if this implied a desire to avoid refutation. For being refuted means learning that things were not as we thought and this is the first exciting step towards a better theory. This must provide a solution to the reformulated problem (not a reformulated solution to the same problem as in the 'conventionalist twist') by containing the preceding theory in so far as it turned out to be right, by contradicting it in so far as it turned out to be wrong and by being again susceptible to falsification in a renewed round of testing.

It may be asked how, if numerous observations cannot logically lead to the formulation of theories through induction, we frame our theories at all. The answer is, in any way that happens – by dreaming on top of a bus, by a flash of inspiration, through mistakes, or even by generalizing (psychologically not logically) from experience of observations. There is, says Popper, no logic of creation of theories, for

> without waiting, passively, for repetitions to impress or impose regularities upon us, we actively try to impose regularities on the world. We try to discover similarities in it, and to interpret it in terms of laws invented by us. Without waiting for premises, we jump to conclusions.[7]

Hence science is essentially a process of conjecture and refutation.

In general, the response to the question 'Which comes first, the hypothesis or the observation?' is 'An earlier kind of hypothesis' and in the history of science most theories have been arrived at by the modification of existing theories. Indeed, the idea of 'observation' *in vacuo* is absurd. No person can simply 'observe' without a context, a problem. Observations are interpretations in the light of the theories which precede them. More ancient observations may themselves predate these theories, but these are themselves observations within particular frameworks. However long the chain of theory and observation, it is the former which comes first.

We may ask ourselves at this stage how far the activities of the various authors of *The Myth of God Incarnate* meet the methodological requirements imposed by Popper's views. There is, of course, no doubt that the overwhelming tenor of the book is a critical one and, indeed, one senses a certain professional satisfaction in the public exercise of investigative faculties. Well and good, but is it critical in the right way and is the satisfaction misplaced? Only Michael Goulder presents us with a single theory about the possible origin of the traditional incarnation doctrine (pp. 64–86) and one must admire it for its baroque qualities. It appears eminently to fulfil the need of a Popperian hypothesis, teetering on the edge of falsification, and one must commend him for his daring. Whether it is true is, of course, another matter (and one to which Graham Stanton addresses himself in this volume) and one must hope that its author will himself now join in the search for contradictory evidence and not succumb to the desire to modify in a patchwork fashion and thus destroy the scientific integrity of his proposal.

Yet, Michael Goulder clearly wants it both ways for in his other contribution to the book 'Jesus the Man of Universal Destiny' (pp. 48–63), he offers us what is really an exercise in inductive reasoning, moving from what he himself sees to be the case about men of destiny in human history to a new proposition about the status of

Jesus. In this he follows other contributors in seeming to prefer to work from what he knows (or supposes) to be so about the world, to what he proposes to be so about Jesus. But this method of reasoning, though almost universally respected, is hardly the full fruit of our post-Enlightenment heritage and it is certainly not in the spirit of Popper's quest of conjecture and refutation.

Two examples. First, both Frances Young (p. 38) and Leslie Houlden (p. 131) adjure us to abandon 'creeds' in favour of 'a new openness' and 'experience'. Certainly, one would be wise to avoid the acrimony that often accompanies the credal pronouncement of religious commitment and, of course, a wide-eyed appreciation of the present existence is essential for the sensitive articulation of belief, but there is no *a priori* reason why a creed, even one as ornate as the 'Athanasian', should not be accepted as a legitimate starting point and laid open for refutation. It may well be refuted in the light of Christian experience but that does not rule it out at the start. (Whether it can, in fact, be refuted is another matter to which I return below.)

Second, and related to this, it matters not one jot for the legitimacy of a hypothesis how it came to be framed. In his first contribution to the book, Don Cupitt in 'The Christ of Christendom' draws our attention to the backgrounds of the origin of the traditional incarnation doctrine (p. 140) and the kenotic variants of the nineteenth century (p. 137), supposing that to expose the political and social pressures involved in particular bits of theologizing is somehow to discredit their products from the outset. Michael Goulder, in the introduction to his Samaritan hypothesis (p. 65), has similar anxieties about the 'mystery' of inspiration and certainties about how it may be dispelled. I shall return in my second contribution to this volume to the fuller implications of this sort of view but suffice it to say for the moment that, for Popper, all this is of interest as part of the psychology of the creation of theories rather than their logic and of no importance, as such, to their acceptability as starting points for testing.

To speak in this way seems to put a low premium on truth for the sake of a sort of swashbuckling critical adventurism and, indeed, Popper's challenge to scientific orthodoxy has led some to suppose this to be so. Certainly, says Popper, science is not a body of established fact and our knowledge is always provisional. We can never be certain that what we accept at a particular time is true and, moreover, we should not be heartbroken should it be shown to be false. We cannot logically justify our acceptance of a particular theory and are deliberately keyed up for its rejection. What we can do, though, is to justify our preference for one particular theory over another.

Take the case of Newtonian and Einsteinian physics. Both are, in Popperian terms, scientific yet clearly both cannot be true in every respect. Upon confidence in the former was built an entire epoch of human development, yet a time came when the latter yielded a more fruitful understanding by according more fully with the factual observations which followed its appearance. Newton's theories were not an inherent part of the world; they were an inherent part of Newton. Einstein's likewise are of himself and may themselves be superseded by a yet more appropriate statement about physics. For the moment we prefer Einstein's and they take us a step nearer to the truth.

Science thus has to do not so much with establishing theories as secure or certain or probable in themselves as in searching for the truth that they reach out for. Science lays claim to a truth which is still open to debate but which can, ever more closely, be approximated to. Popper thus sees truth as a correspondence with the facts but accepts that it is a regulative idea rather like the notion of accuracy which, with the increasing sophistication of our instrumentation, we might approach ever more closely but which we can never be certain of attaining. 'We do not know,' says Popper, 'we can only guess'[8] and in doing so returns to the idea of science as *anticipatio mentis* which Bacon long ago rejected in favour of the inductive *interpretatio naturae* and further still to a favourite of Popper, the pre-Socratic Xenophanes, for whom truth was 'but a woven web of guesses', *doxa* rather than *epistēmē*.[9]

Yet, for Popper, truth itself is not enough: it must be interesting truth, truth with a high degree of explanatory power, truth with a low probability, truth hard to come by. He quotes with approval a verse by Wilhelm Busch:

> Twice two equals four: 'tis true
> But too empty and too trite
> What I look for is a clue
> To some matters not so light.[10]

For only if it answers some difficult, fertile problem does a truth become relevant to science in the same way that a court, when it demands from a witness the 'whole' truth, expects as much relevant and interesting truth as can be got, rather than true irrelevancies. And thus, if we are faced with two theories which stand up equally well to testing, we should always choose the one with the more informative content to take science and the pursuit of truth forward.

I sense, in a number of authors of *The Myth of God Incarnate*, a misplaced anxiety about the nature of theories or models[11] and a somewhat crude view of truth underlying it. Of the contributors, only Frances Young comes close to a sensitive appreciation of the nature of scientific models. Quoting the familiar example of the particle and wave models of light (p. 33) she clearly sees how these might, despite the apparent inconsistency, both be valuable in accounting for certain physical phenomena. In other words she recognizes the possibility of inaccuracy even in this, the apparently most solid and secure of the sciences. But one could go further still than this acknowledgment by accepting that it is of the nature of all models to be inaccurate. Thus are they models, convenient for daily handling in the exchanges of life, as well as sufficiently representational to hope for a connection with reality. No one supposes, for example, that the colourful pattern of lines on an Underground map of London actually *is* several hundred miles of track with rolling stock and all the paraphernalia of a railway network. Unlike the real thing it is meant to fold into the pocket (hence its inaccuracy), but it will help you get from Baker Street to South Kensington (hence its accuracy). All scientific models and all other models have to have this balance of 'wrongness' and 'rightness' and there should be no qualms about the matter. It is from this sort of realization that Popper's humility about refutation and truth comes.

Other authors do have qualms and a puzzling insensitivity about the nature of truth. Some, for example, contrast 'being' with 'being like'[12] 'literal' with 'metaphysical, poetic, symbolic and mythological'[13] and 'factual and descriptive' with 'analogical'[14] in ways which imply a sharp boundary and mutual exclusivity between the two. John Hick compares the lack of meaning in the traditional incarnation statement with that in describing a circle as a square (p. 178). But few have the benefit of the sort of close head-on appreciation of reality that this implies and many would find the contrast made in this way unimaginative. One could conceive circumstances in which, for example, a circle could look less like one's normal understanding of a circle – it could be to all intents and purposes an ellipse (if viewed from off the vertical), as approaching a straight line (if looked at very obliquely) or a dot (if seen from a great distance). Mathematically, of course, it could all the time really be a polygon with an infinite number of sides but such puzzles are not, one feels, welcome here.[15]

A different manifestation of the same kind of anxiety, much more acute in this case, is exhibited by Don Cupitt who sees a rather large proportion of Christian iconography as so inaccurate as to be blasphemous (pp. 133–147). This, quite apart from its basic misunderstanding of the nature of any kind of representational activity (whether art or science), seems to be a little insensitive to the intention of at least some of the artists of the past 2000 years who have struggled, within the limitations of their materials, not simply to reflect the custom of their age, not 'simply' to provide an analogical statement about reality but actually to express the truth.

The key question here is 'What is the exact relationship between models and the reality which, in necessarily inexact terms, they attempt to portray?' or, as Maurice Wiles puts it (and here we return to a more sensitive analysis) ' . . . what sort of link is there between the myth and the history?' (p. 158). Let us go back for a moment to Popper. We recall that he redrew the line between one class of statements and another on the basis of falsification and that, unlike the Logical Positivists, he made it a line of empiricism and not of meaning. Thus, for Popper, non-scientific statements are not the senseless grunts which the Logical Positivists supposed.

> I thus felt (he says) that if a theory is found to be non-scientific, or 'metaphysical' (as we might say), it is not therefore found to be unimportant, or insignificant, or 'meaningless', or 'nonsensical'.[16]

One of the reasons for this is that the line between science and non-science should not be drawn too sharply. Most scientific theories, after all, originated in myths: the astrological tenet of planetary influence on terrestrial events, long attacked as part of a bundle of myths, was, for example, the historical forerunner of Newton's lunar theory of the tides: the Copernican system was inspired by the Neo-Platonic worship of the Sun as the central noble light, and so on.[17] Myths may develop testable components, becoming fruitful and important for science and it would hardly, says Popper, 'contribute to clarity if we were to say that these theories are nonsensical gibberish in one stage of their development and then suddenly good sense in another'.[18] Thus Popper never dismissed Marxism or the Freudian and Adlerian proposals as valueless and neither should we dismiss non-scientific theological statements.

Maurice Wiles clearly recognizes that this is so. He sees that there may be a sense in which a myth can be said to be true or false (pp. 158–9) that 'misleading' or 'inappropriate' might be suitable terms to express falsity in this sort of case (p. 159) and that myths might be 'mixed' in their ability to have general and particular functions (p. 164). This takes us a good way from the position that myths can have no truth claims and it accords well with Popper's view that myths (and beliefs, attitudes and traditions) can, like scientific hypotheses, help us to orientate ourselves in the world when there are no scientifically testable theories available. It is in this sense that Popper himself can talk of a 'faith', faith of a kind completely unwarranted from the point of view of science, faith without which scientific discovery would be impossible.[19]

The essential distinction between myth and science is, in Popper's view, that the latter is accompanied by a second-order tradition of critical discussion. The statement 'Zeus is angry', invoked to provide orientation during an approaching thunderstorm, can, if it is exposed to something more than uncritical acceptance, take us forward in the direction of science by challenging us to look at things in a fresh way and by making us reformulate our statement in a manner which gives a better account of reality. Thus is the pursuit of the authors of *The Myth of God Incarnate* a noble one, quite acceptable in principle and worthy of more than derision and outrage in the church. All clearly find that the formula 'Jesus is God incarnate' when expressed in its traditional form no longer provides the orientation they require. Yet I feel they have, to varying degrees and in various ways, largely failed us in their own critical discussion. Freeing themselves from an outdated unquestioning approach to theological propositions, they generally adopt a methodology which, though apparently in tune with contemporary scientific attitudes, can itself now be seen to be rigid and unimaginative and, by Popper's standards, mistaken in some of its underlying assumptions. I shall consider, later in this volume, one area where the authors seem to have the edge in subtlety over Popper and examine whether this is a sufficient criticism of his views as to render at least some of my own anxieties unnecessary.

NOTES

1. Maurice Wiles, 'Christianity without Incarnation?', *The Myth of God Incarnate*, ed., John Hick, SCM Press 1977, p. 1.
2. Leslie Houlden, 'The Creed of Experience', *The Myth*, p. 125.
3. E. g. Wiles, *The Myth*, pp. 1, 6; Houlden, pp. 131–2 and his contribution to the present volume; Frances Young, 'A Cloud of Witnesses', *The Myth*, p. 13; Dennis Nineham, 'Epilogue', pp. 201–3.

4. Hardly, therefore, recent except in the belated recognition of their importance, for Popper's *Logik der Forschung* (of which *The Logic of Scientific Discovery* is a translation: see note 18) first appeared in 1934. Apart from the works cited, Popper's *Objective Knowledge*, Oxford University Press 1972, is also relevant. The best introduction to Popper is Bryan Magee, *Popper*, Fontana Modern Masters 1973.

5. David Hume, *Treatise of Human Nature*, Book I, Part III, section vi. Popper's examination of the argument can be seen in *Conjectures and Refutations*, Routledge & Kegan Paul 1972, pp. 42ff.

6. Popper, ibid. p. 55.

7. Ibid. p. 46.

8. Popper, *The Logic of Scientific Discovery*, Hutchinson 1972, p. 278.

9. Popper, *Conjectures and Refutations*, pp. 26, 255.

10. Ibid., p. 230, quoting in translation from Wilhelm Busch's *Schein und Sein*.

11. I introduce the term 'model' with some reluctance but to indicate that a scientific (or other) proposition can be something more than a hypothesis expressed in words.

12. Houlden, *The Myth*, p. 129.

13. Ibid., p. 130.

14. John Hick, 'Jesus and the World Religions', *The Myth*, p. 177.

15. One for whom they were very welcome was Ian Ramsey. See, for example, *Christian Empiricism*, ed., Jerry H. Gill, William B. Eerdmans Publishing Company 1974, especially pp. 98–140 and 159–176.

16. Popper, *Conjectures and Refutations*, p. 38.

17. Popper gives further examples in *The Logic of Scientific Discovery*, p. 278.

18. Popper, *Conjectures and Refutations*, p. 257. See also p. 38 for a note on the interesting case of astrology.

19. See, for example, *The Logic of Scientific Discovery*, p. 32 and Einstein's letter to Popper printed as Appendix xii in the same work, especially p. 458. Popper makes an interesting aside about faith in his 'intellectual autobiography' *Unended Quest*, Fontana 1976, p. 18.

4 · Do All Christian Doctrines Stand or Fall Together?

A (i) Incarnation and Atonement: Evil and Incarnation
John Hick

In reassessing the doctrine of the incarnation we need to weigh carefully its religious value. I propose here to consider this in relation to the problem of evil – meaning by this both sin and suffering. In discussing this we are at the point at which the most desperate realities of life – disease, decay and death; hatred, injustice and cruelty; misfortune, deprivation and tragedy – grate harshly upon our theology. In this area, because our emotions are aroused, rhetoric can easily take over from thought; and yet precisely for this reason it is here that careful thought can most be of use.

The moral evil of sin – consisting centrally in selfishness, lovelessness and cruelty, seen as offences against God – has always been perceived as a more basic problem than suffering. And the traditional Christian answer to it has always been the atonement – the idea that in some way Christ's sacrificial death covers and obliterates human sin in the sight of God, thus enabling man to be forgiven and reconciled with his Maker. There is, however, a simple and familiar fact which sets a question mark over this time-honoured notion. This is the fact that in his own life time, and without any reference to his death, Jesus taught the love of God, and brought men and women into a new and reconciled relationship with him as their heavenly Father. Jesus' parables of divine love, the expectation of forgiveness expressed in the Lord's prayer, and Jesus' own declaration of the heavenly Father's present forgiveness to many, were not made conditional upon his own future death. He was already preaching God's accepting and recreating love as a present reality, and calling men and women to a new and better life as a here-and-now possibility. There is no suggestion in Jesus' teaching that during his ministry his heavenly Father was unloving, alienated, angry, unforgiving or condemnatory towards mankind at large but that this situation was to be dramatically changed by his own death. On the contrary, Jesus told, without any reference to his death, such wonderful stories as the parable of the prodigal son, and declared God's present forgiveness to repentant sinners. He also of course expressed his heavenly Father's condemnation towards evil doers – such as the scribes and Pharisees who would neither enter the Kingdom of Heaven themselves nor allow others to enter it; or those who tithed mint and cummin but neglected the weightier matters of justice and mercy and faith (Matt. 23. 13, 23). But this was not a general condemnation of all mankind; nor was it related to his own future death.

It is true that towards the end of his life Jesus saw martyrdom coming. And there is the saying in Mark (10.45) and Matthew (20.28) that the Son of Man came to give his life as a ransom for many. But although this saying has regularly been treated as a dominical summary of the church's atonement doctrine – the doctrine that man's salvation has been won by the death of Christ as some kind of price or ransom paid, or appeasing sacrifice offered, to deliver mankind from a just condemnation – yet no such universal claim is present in it. It probably expresses the then widespread Jewish belief in the vicarious efficacy of the sufferings of the righteous, evident in the literature of the Maccabean martyrs, on the basis of which John Downing concluded that 'at the time of Jesus, people thought in terms of human beings making atonement for others by means of their sufferings and death'.[1] Jesus could well have applied this idea to his own coming martyrdom. And it is probably this ancient belief that the unjust sufferings of God's servants work for the good of Israel that has been extended and magnified by the church into the claim that Jesus' death was 'a full, perfect, and sufficient sacrifice, oblation, and satisfaction for the sins of the world'. In this salvation myth, painted like a sacred halo around the historical event, Jesus' death came to be seen as a cosmic transaction governing the relations between God and man and determining human salvation from the beginning to the end of time.

The Christian myth of redemption by the blood of Christ has had a rich emotional history and has inspired splendid poetic expressions. No Christian who has ever lived within the evangelical thought-world can read without emotion such lines as Cowper's,

> There is a fountain filled with Blood,
>   Drawn from Emmanuel's veins,
> And sinners plunged beneath that flood
>   Lose all their guilty stains.

But however much we may love this strand of our heritage we must be aware that its attraction is confined to those nurtured within one particular religious tradition. The notion of the salvation of the world by the blood of Christ is highly culture-specific. It comes out of a background of ancient Hebraic conceptions of blood sacrifice; and the church's later attempts to rationalize it reflect the ideas and institutions of various stages of European social history. That man was (according to the 'classic' theory) being delivered from thraldom to the devil; or that (according to the 'satisfaction' theory) the divine honour required an infinite appeasement; or that (according to the 'penal-substitutionary' theory) Jesus was being punished in place of mankind for the sum-total of human sin, are explanatory myths which spoke to people in earlier ages but which have now expired – and I do not believe that we need engage in any heroic attempts at resuscitation. For the idea that the death of Jesus transformed God's relationship to man, and caused or enabled God to accept and love his sinful human children, does not cohere with Jesus' own revelation of the heavenly Father whose love is infinitely greater and deeper than that of an earthly parent.

It is however true that martyrdom gives added force to the message of a great man of God. In Christian theology this fact has been taken up by the 'moral influence' theory of the atonement. This too has generated its own mythic expressions, such as the much told preacher's story of the head-hunting tribe whose loved and respected chief has been converted to Christianity. He tries to persuade his people to give up head-hunting, but fails; for the urge to kill is too strong to be eradicated by rational persuasion. And so when the head-hunting season comes round again, and the men of the tribe begin to prepare for the hunt, he tells them that if they must have another victim they are to lie in wait at a certain clearing outside the village, and when a man comes into view with his head hidden in a coloured blanket they may kill him. They do so, the man appears, is struck down by a dozen arrows, and when the tribesmen rush out to sever his head they discover that they have murdered their own beloved chief. The shock of this realization is such that from that day on they give up head-hunting. By sacrificing his life for his people at their own hands he saves them from their sin. Such a story tells eloquently of a self-sacrificial love whose influence changes and saves people. And when we apply this idea to the death of Jesus we can readily find a sense in which we are all, in principle, responsible for his death – in that it was brought about by the ordinary human sinfulness which we all share – so that in realizing that in our moral blindness we have killed God's Son we may be turned from our wickedness to live.

But this idea, although much more attractive today than the old redemption myths, is no less mythological. We see this when we notice that the story, whilst it makes perfectly good sense when told about a good human being, loses its point when the victim is said to be God himself. For whilst a human being can make the supreme sacrifice by giving his life for others, God cannot. God incarnate would know that his 'death' could only be temporary; for God cannot cease to be God, the eternal source of all life and being; and to speak literally of his death is to speak without meaning. Indeed in earlier theology, to avoid undermining the very idea of God, some clutched at the desperate expedient of saying that *qua* God Jesus was not subject to death and that it was *qua* man that he was killed.[2] But then we sunder the two natures and thereby destroy the idea of incarnation. How was God incarnate as Jesus of Nazareth if God did not undergo what Jesus underwent?

The main alternative, of course, to the traditional Christian myth of the fall of man from grace, and then his salvation by the atoning blood of Christ, is a theology (suggested by the thought of the early Hellenistic Fathers) in which one does not separate creation and redemption but sees our present human existence as a phase in God's gradual creation of finite beings who are to live in conscious filial relationship to him. Having created man through the long evolution of the forms of life on this earth, God is now, through our free responses, fashioning 'children of God' out of human animals. This cannot be accomplished by any kind of quasi-legal transaction but only by the actual transformation of human nature into that which God ultimately intends. And in this long and slow process (which must surely extend beyond the boundaries of our present life) the Christ-event is one of the points at which God has been and still is creatively at work within human life. But to claim that it is the *only* point at which God has been or is acting creatively on earth would be the supreme expression of Christian triumphalism.

Let me now turn, very briefly, from the problem of sin to that of suffering. How might the doctrine of the incarnation help us to meet this immense and agonizing problem? The most hopeful way that I can see would occur within the Irenaean theological framework outlined above, according to which life as we know it is part of the continuing process of God's creative work. This process could not take place in a paradise; for growth comes through challenge and response, and in a paradise there are no challenges. A person-making environment must be one in which real moral decisions are made, and in which there can be real failure as well as success, tragedy and suffering as well as triumph and happiness.

Now it might be suggested that God reconciles us to this painful creative process by coming into the process himself and sharing with us in its stress and suffering. In Christ, it might be said, we meet God himself – or more strictly, God the Son – born as a human child, living a human life, and subjecting himself to the pains and agonies of the world that he has ordained. God loved us enough to become one of us, and thereby to reconcile us to himself and to the pains and pressures of his creative work.

This idea has great imaginative appeal. It is a highly preachable thought that in the incarnation God became our fellow sufferer. But do we not want to say that in his total awareness of and sympathy with his creatures God has *always* participated in every pain and joy, every hope and fear, every feeling and volition, every success and failure of all his human children? Do we not want to say that all the consciousnesses of all his creatures, all their experiences, have always been open to the divine omniscience? If the very hairs of our heads are numbered, and not a sparrow falls without his knowledge, must God not be aware of the entire realm of human experience as it occurs from moment to moment? There is of course a long-standing theological debate as to whether God is utterly impassible and incapable of feeling his creatures' pains and sorrows, or whether he is on the contrary able to feel and sympathize with human suffering through his own immediate awareness of his creation. This debate has important implications for the incarnation doctrine. For on the one hand a strict doctrine of divine impassibility does not permit of incarnation. A God who is in his essential nature impassible cannot become passible; and therefore could not become incarnate and experience human pains and emotions. But on the other hand the contrary doctrine of unceasing divine sympathy and suffering removes this particular need for incarnation, since God is already fully involved in all his creatures' joys and sorrows. A God who knows his creatures through and through, and who participates from the beginning in their joys, feels their sorrows, and grieves at their sins, does not have to become incarnate to do this. Indeed, if his knowledge and understanding of human existence depended upon his having become incarnate on one occasion, at one point in history and at one place in the world, it would be a much less full knowledge and understanding than is possible if he has a total awareness of his creation, including every human thought and feeling. The cross of Christ can indeed powerfully symbolize God's total awareness of and sympathy with his human children. It offers a more vivid and gripping picture than the abstract statement of God's omniscience and sympathy. But the vividness is that of a visible story, not of an additional truth.

Once again, then, as in the case of the atonement, we have (as it seems to me) to say that the idea of the cross transforming God's own nature or state is not theologically viable. But may not the death of Jesus have another kind of relevance to human suffering, more analogous to the moral influence view of its relevance to sin? May we not say that although the cross, and the incarnation as a whole, whilst not exclusively constituting God's co-suffering with humanity, nevertheless *reveals* that co-suffering and so enables us to believe it? Could it not be that God has always suffered with the sufferings of his creatures, and always been hurt by their sins, but that the cross of Christ makes this divine suffering visible as an event in human history?

So far as the considerations which have been before us thus far are concerned, this is indeed possible. But to formulate such a possibility brings yet other problems forward for attention; and I will briefly mention two of them.

First, there is the difficulty involved, from the point of view of this theory, by the historical particularity of the incarnation – its occurrence as an historical event at a particular place and time, influencing mankind through the normal channels of human communication, particularly the spoken and written word. This has meant that the knowledge of God's suffering love, revealed to the eyes of faith in the Christ event, has been propagated as the gospel of one of the world religions. The Christian religion has indeed spread far and wide and has won hundreds of millions of adherents. Nevertheless, it has at no time been received by more than a minority of mankind; nor can there be any assurance that this will cease to be true in the future. And yet the purpose of the incarnation was presumably, on this view, to make God's self-giving love known as rapidly as possible to the entire human race. The question thus arises, for a revelatory understanding of the incarnation and cross, why God has not become man a number of times, within the different civilizations, instead of only once. It has always been firmly assumed in Christian thinking that the incarnation must be unique; but on a revelatory as distinguished from a divine transaction view of its significance there does not seem to be any basis for this assumption. If divine incarnation is possible, it seems proper to ask why it did not take place in, say, the Chinese and in the Indian as well as in the Mediterranean civilization, around the turn of the eras or indeed earlier. In the ancient world communication between these different streams of human life was so slight and so slow that any divine self-communication would have had to occur separately within each of them if it was to reach the then civilized parts of mankind without a delay of centuries – a delay which is indeed today still continuing. It will perhaps be said that if there had been, whether simultaneously or non-simultaneously, more than one divine incarnation on earth these could not have been fully personal divine acts; God could only act in this way once. But is there any real basis for this assumption? It is no doubt true that on a transactional view of the cross only one act of atonement for human sin was necessary or possible: a debt, once paid, cannot be paid again. But on a revelatory understanding of incarnation and cross it seems arbitrary to insist that God could not reveal himself in other lives, for the sake of other sections of mankind, in the way in which he is said to have revealed himself in the life of Jesus. Here, then, is an area of questioning which the incarnational doctrine has yet to face.

The other question that I would mention is whether the idea of God – or more precisely of God the Son, the Second Person of the Trinity – becoming a man is a viable notion at all, and not a sheer self-contradiction. Certainly no school of Christian theology has yet been able to spell it out coherently. If Jesus had two complete natures, one human and the other divine, and yet was one undivided person, how can that one person be said to be genuinely human? Perhaps however there was a divine *kenosis*, and in Jesus the Second Person of the Trinity had emptied himself of his deity? But then, it would seem, the more complete the divine self-emptying the less complete the divine incarnation. Neither the intense christological debates of the centuries leading up to the Council of Chalcedon, nor the renewed christological debates of the nineteenth and twentieth centuries, have succeeded in squaring the circle by making intelligible the claim that one who was genuinely and unambiguously a man was also genuinely and unambiguously God.

The idea of incarnation can however very fruitfully be used as a metaphor. Indeed the metaphor of incarnation is a basic and powerful one. Iago, we say, was malice incarnate. Joan of Arc incarnated, or personified, the resurgent spirit of France. Winston Churchill in 1940 incarnated the defiance of the British people. That is to say, his words and actions were a striking and accepted expression of that defiance. And when someone thus embodies some ideal or idea or attitude or value three-dimensionally, in his life, we can say, in a self-explanatory metaphor, that this ideal is being incarnated in that life. It is in this sense that we can very properly say that the divine love, the divine attitude to mankind, was incarnated in the life of Jesus – that the Logos was made flesh.

In this sense the divine *agape* is incarnated to some degree in every act of self-giving love and thus in every life in so far as it is an embodiment of *agape*. God's love was incarnated to a notable extent, for example, in the life of St Francis of Assisi, and today in the life of Mother Teresa of Calcutta. And it was incarnated to a yet greater, perhaps incomparably greater, extent in the life of Jesus of Nazareth. It would, as Dennis Nineham reminds us in his contribution to *The Myth of God Incarnate*, be a leap beyond the historical evidence to assert that God's love was *perfectly* or *absolutely* embodied in every moment of Jesus' life. But it is entirely possible that the divine *agape* has been more fully incarnated in this life than in any other. At any rate we know that God's gracious and demanding love was embodied in Jesus' love in so powerful a way that we ourselves are grasped by it today, some nineteen centuries later.

Such an idea is not self-contradictory; and if Christianity can reinterpret its concept of incarnation along these lines, so that incarnation (metaphorically understood) becomes a matter of degree, and is no longer confined to the one instance of Jesus of Nazareth, we shall have a doctrine which points clearly to Jesus as a supreme revealer of God's love, and as one in whom God was manifestly at work, but a doctrine which does not claim an exclusive revelation that undermines the validity of the other great world religions.[3]

NOTES

1. John Downing, 'Jesus and Martyrdom', *Journal of Theological Studies*, Vol. XIV, 1963, p. 284.

2. For example, in his *Tome* Leo says, concerning the two natures, that 'the man Jesus Christ was able to die in respect of the one, unable to die in respect of the other' (para. 3). Gregory of Nazianzum wrote of Jesus that 'He was baptized as man, but he remitted sins as God . . . He was tempted as man, but he conquered as God' (*Oration*, XXIX,20). Irenaeus had written, 'For as he became man, that he might be tempted, so was he also the Word that he might be glorified, the Word remaining inactive in his temptation and dishonour and crucifixion and suffering death' (*Against Heresies*, III, 19. 3).

3. In its totality the problem goes beyond the great world religions to include the non-religious ideologies, particularly Marxism and Maoism, under which large sections of mankind live today. But one problem at a time!

A (ii)   Incarnation and Atonement: A Comment on Professor Hick's Critique of Atonement Doctrine

Charles Moule

Professor Hick rightly observes that 'the idea that the death of Jesus transformed God's relationship to man, and caused or enabled God to accept and love his sinful human children, does not cohere with Jesus' own revelation of the heavenly Father whose love is infinitely greater and deeper than that of an earthly parent'. What Professor Hick seems to have overlooked is that this idea not only does not cohere with Jesus' revelation of God, but is not to be found in the New Testament anywhere. It is a travesty of the gospel, and the incarnational christology which he is attacking has nothing whatever to do with it. The New Testament does sometimes use terms derived from the Jewish sacrificial cultus (though less frequently than is often imagined); and it occasionally uses words derived from a Greek root (*hilask–*) normally denoting propitiation. But it is precisely in its use of these words that the novelty of the Christian understanding of God becomes evident. The pagan notion (still found in parts of the Old Testament) is, indeed, that God's relation to man can somehow be transformed: if he is angry, a costly sacrifice may appease him. But this crude, pagan idea is stood on its head by the New Testament. Instead of man's being the subject and God's being the object of propitiation, God becomes the subject of the action and when there is any object the object is sin. Thus, the translator is forced, by the way in which the 'propitiation' word-group is used, into rendering it not by 'propitiate' but by 'expiate': God is seen as himself taking the initiative in expiating sin and transforming *man's* relation to *him*.[1]

Again rightly, Professor Hick observes that 'to claim that it [the Christ-event] is the *only* point at which God has been or is acting creatively on earth would be the supreme expression of Christian triumphalism'. What he seems to have overlooked, however, is that such isolation of the incarnation from the rest of God's creative processes is nowhere to be found in the New Testament. If, as I believe, there are implicit in the New Testament expressions of belief in the supremacy, finality, or uniqueness of what God has done in Christ, it does not in the least follow that this isolates it from everything else that God does, or makes it the only point at which he acts creatively. In the results of natural selection there is both continuity and discontinuity: why should the occurrence of a hitherto non-existent species make it totally discontinuous with the species from which it has become differentiated?

Indeed, on a theistic view, it is impossible not to believe that God's creative work of reconciliation permeates the whole of his creation and all history, so that every act of self-sacrificing service and generous forgiveness by any one at any time is a part of it. But such a belief is not in the least incompatible with the belief that this continuous process comes to complete and perfect expression at a particular point. On the contrary, it is arguable that it is fitting that God's immanence, involvement, and participation in his whole creation should reach its climax at some time and in some place: the 'scandal of particularity' is by no means a denial but rather a confirmation of the ubiquity and continuity of God's activity. Conversely, however, it is highly questionable whether, as Professor Hick asserts, 'the ... doctrine of unceasing divine sympathy and suffering removes this particular need for incarnation'. Besides, it is not what we need but what is the fact that we must try to discover.

Finally, it is a puerile travesty of a doctrine of the finality of the cross to suppose that its logic is that, if so, Christ could not have pronounced forgiveness before his death. Even at his most 'dispensational', Paul believed that Abraham was justified by faith. God has always and eternally been the God of mercy and forgiveness; but this is precisely because he is such a God as, at a particular time and place, becomes absolutely and totally incarnate. Professor Hick asks: 'Could it not be that ... the cross of Christ makes ... divine suffering visible as an event in human history?' and the answer is: 'Yes: visible, and as an event.' This, and not a docetic mime (as Professor Hick seems to think) is what an incarnational christology implies.

NOTE

1. It is true that there are scholars who still adhere to the translation 'propitiate'; but then they are driven to the *reductio ad absurdum* of God's propitiating himself. See L. Morris, *The Apostolic Preaching of the Cross*, Tyndale Press 1955; D. Hill, *Greek Words and Hebrew Meanings*, Cambridge University Press 1967; C. F. D. Moule, 'The Sacrifice of the People of God', *The Parish Communion To-day*, ed., D. M. Paton, SPCK 1962, pp. 78 ff.

A (iii) Incarnation and Atonement: The Moral and Religious Value of the Incarnation

Brian Hebblethwaite

An important factor in the assessment of our contemporary christ-ological debates is the moral and religious value discernible in incarnational christology. It is one factor only and cannot stand by itself. Only if the doctrine of the incarnation is true may we commend it for its moral and religious value. We have no use for Plato's 'noble lie'. But the questions of truth and value are not entirely separate. While it would be improper to urge the value of the doctrine as the sole ground for thinking it true, it is not unreasonable to suppose that its perceived value may be an indication of its truth. In attempting to give a justification of the Chalcedonian formula, Austin Farrer observed: 'Look here: the longer I go on trying to tell you about this, the more I become convinced that the job that really wants doing is to expound the formula rather than to justify it; or, anyhow, that the justification required is identical with exposition.'[1] This may be going a bit far, but certainly part of the justification of the doctrine consists in exposition of its inner rationality, and that includes its moral and religious value. At the very least it may be said that insensitivity to the value of incarnational christology can lead to a somewhat casual attitude to the historical, experiential and rational ground for thinking the doctrine to be true.

It is no easy matter to assess the moral and religious value of different ways of understanding God and his relation to the world. This is a well known problem in the comparative study of religion. Fortunately that is not our primary concern here. Our christological debates are an internal matter of Christian self-understanding, and we do not have to cope directly with the problem of dialogue between radically different value systems. On the other hand, we are concerned with what have traditionally been taken to be the distinctive doctrines of Christianity, which mark it out from other world faiths. And it can be argued that our assessment of the respective strengths and weaknesses of incarnational and non-incarnational christology within the sphere of Christian self-understanding is bound to be affected by our assessment of the

moral and religious value of Christianity among the world religions. So it needs to be said that such comparison and dialogue, for
all their difficulty, are not impossible. A simple example of such
imagined dialogue is to be found in Ninian Smart's *World Religions: A Dialogue*[2] chapters six and seven.

I concentrate here, however, on the discussion internal to Christian self-understanding. I begin rather negatively with some comments on the moral and religious value of what has been said by
recent critics of incarnational christology. I then attempt to bring
out, positively, the moral and religious value of the doctrine of the
incarnation, first in my own words, then with examples both from
popular piety and contemporary theology. I conclude with some
brief remarks about the implications of incarnational belief for
Christian ethics.

I

Critics of incarnational christology from within the Christian
church have no business to be telling us that the onus of proof lies
with defenders of the tradition. Whether they like it or not, they
live in and out of a tradition of faith, expressed in the creeds and
confessions of the church, which is undeviatingly trinitarian and
incarnational in its understanding of God and of Christ. It is up to
them to make out a case against incarnational and for non-
incarnational christology. Since our concern here is with the moral
and religious nature of the incarnation, I say nothing about the
evidence for the doctrine and little about its logical coherence,
except to show in passing that recent critics are much too ready to
cry contradiction.

I begin by asking two related questions: have the critics shown a
proper moral and religious sensitivity to what they are criticizing?
And does the non-incarnational christology which they advocate
possess the moral and religious value which they claim for it?

My first group of worries – about the seriousness with which the
tradition is being taken by those who wish to question it – is liable
to rebound upon my own arguments. For it is only too easy on both
sides of this dispute to set up caricatures of opponents' views in
order to have an easy target for demolition. Yet again I stress that
the onus of proof lies with the attack, not with the defence, if it is
Christian self-understanding that is in question. And one is bound
to say that recent criticism of the doctrine of the incarnation has
shown quite astonishing moral and religious insensitivity to what is
under discussion. What is one to make, for instance, of Michael
Goulder's reference to 'a landing-take-off-and-landing myth'[3], in

respect of the christologies of Paul and John? It is interesting to compare Goulder's treatment of these matters with that of Bultmann. I do not know if there is more or less to be said for Goulder's hypothesis of a Samaritan origin for Christian incarnational doctrine than for Bultmann's hypothesis of a gnostic redeemer myth, but at least Bultmann showed, in his commentary on the Fourth Gospel, a fine sensitivity to the moral and religious value of what came to expression there.

Another example, this time of sheer perversity in moral judgment, is to be found in Don Cupitt's essay in *The Myth*. The burden of his argument is that the Christian doctrine of the incarnation has reinforced the conception of religion as monarchical and authoritarian. 'As the manifest Absolute in history', he writes, 'Christ became the basis of the Christian empire and of political and ecclesiastical power in the present age.' 'Inevitably', he goes on, 'Christianity became, or rather was deliberately made absolutist and authoritarian.'⁴ It is in the claim that this development was inevitable and that these tendencies have an essential connection with the doctrine of the incarnation that the perversity of Cupitt's judgment lies. For it is quite clear from the New Testament and from Christian piety down the ages that what has given Christianity its characteristic moral and religious force is the conviction that its Lord had humbled himself and taken the form of a servant.

A third example – and here we touch on the question of coherence – can be found in the cavalier treatment given to kenotic christology, especially in respect of its insistence on the human limitations of Jesus' self-knowledge. Kenotic christology, although its early versions in German and English theology were justly criticized for metaphysical naivety, has in fact been refined and expounded with great care and penetration in the writings of theologians such as Frank Weston, O. C. Quick and Austin Farrer. In particular, the moral force of the doctrine that God, in becoming man, subjects himself to the conditions of human knowledge and self-knowledge, so that, *qua* human subject, he experiences his identity with God in terms solely of his relation to his heavenly Father (that relation being seen by us as reflecting in God-man terms the inner God-God relations of the blessed Trinity) – the moral force of this doctrine is very great. God is seen here to have humbled himself in order to make himself known and knowable as the one who, out of pure love, comes to us as a servant and loves his own 'unto the end' (John 13.1). Kenotic christology enables us to see that, by incarnation, the humanity of God is that of a particular human being, a first-century Jewish man. As Austin Farrer put it: 'God the Son on earth is a fullness of holy life within the limit of mortality.' But Hick, in his preface to the paperback edition of *God and the Universe of Faiths*, refers dismissively to the 'new paradox of God incarnate who does not know that he is God incarnate'.[5] To refer dismissively to the notion that Jesus was God but was unaware of it is to fail to grasp the point of kenotic christology. It is to assume that there is no alternative between a thoroughly docetic Christ and a purely human Jesus. But in fact the tradition has carefully distinguished what can be said of the human subject, Jesus, from what can be said of the divine subject, God the Son, whose human expression and vehicle, in his incarnate life, the human subject, Jesus, is. (As such, of course, it is, uniquely, not an independent human subject – hence the doctrine of 'anhypostasia'.) Clearly, God, *qua* God, is aware of who he is and what he is doing, but, *qua* man (i.e. as Jesus) his self-awareness is limited to a filial sense of dependence on the Father. For this reason incarnational christology attributes two consciousnesses, not to Jesus, but to God incarnate. This distinction has been carefully mapped by Geach, in his treatment of the logic of what has been called 'reduplicative propositions'.[6] It emerges that much depends on what one sees as the primary subject of christological statements. It is no good suggesting that Jesus, *qua* God, could do this, and, *qua* man, could do that. That would already be to confuse the natures by predicating unlimited divinity of the man instead of predicating real humanity of God incarnate. The primary subject of all christological statements is God. It is God, *qua* God, who cannot die, and it is God incarnate, i.e. God, *qua* man, who suffers and dies for our salvation. Nor is there any question of sundering the natures here, when it is made quite clear that we are not talking of two separate individuals, but of the divine substance, which is such as to include within its own subjectivity, the human subject, Jesus, as the expression and vehicle of God's incarnate life.

Although I regard insensitivity to the scope of classical Christian theism and to the elements of kenoticism which it has shown itself to be capable of embracing as being primarily a theoretical theological fault, I stress here that it has the consequence of rendering these writers incapable of appreciating the value of the incarnation.

When we turn to the question of the moral and religious value of the non-incarnational christologies offered in the place of the classical doctrine of the incarnation, one is bound to say that they look pretty vague and thin. It is very difficult to see why we, in the twentieth century should take the purely human Jesus to be 'the man of universal destiny' (Goulder). The human parallels which Goulder offers have the effect of demoting Jesus to the status of one exemplar of selfless love among others. But the community of love which came into being as a result of the events concerning Jesus is sustained down the centuries by more than the example of his martyrdom.

Cupitt's Jesus is a more austere and less intelligible figure. We are to recapture, it seems, something of his sense of the immediacy of God, and of his eschatological faith. But who can say what this really means? To recapture, across the centuries, an echo of the authentic voice of Jesus can only feed our contemporary faith when it is not divorced from the spiritual and sacramental presence of the risen and ascended Christ.

Leslie Houlden speaks of 'the centrality of Jesus for all that concerns man's understanding of God' and indeed of God's 'deep and intimate involvement'[7] with the world. But what do these words mean when the beliefs that give them some concrete basis are jettisoned in favour of 'experience'?

I have similar difficulties with the suggestion that God's patient love is revealed in the world by the death of martyrs. How, one may ask, does someone else's death reveal *God's* love? And when Frances Young writes, very movingly, that the cross of Jesus constitutes 'above all, a revelation of divine involvement in the suffering and evil of the world',[8] it seems that she is trying to retain the moral and religious value of the traditional doctrine in a context that cannot bear that weight. As Michael Ramsey pointed out, in comment on a radio discussion of these issues, the religious value of the cross for us – in face of suffering and evil in our own lives – consists in our being able to see God there in person (not just by sympathy with someone else).

The sharp polarity between what, following O. C. Quick, one may call the modernist and the liberal elements in current non-incarnational christology is brought out by a consideration of the respective positions of Dennis Nineham in *The Myth* and Geoffrey Lampe in the Bampton Lectures. For Nineham, a combination of historical scepticism and historical relativism makes it impossible to accord to Jesus himself the moral and religious significance that even the other authors of *The Myth* wish still to find in him. Nineham finds the value of Christianity to reside rather in the full and rich relationship to God,[9] which life in the church makes possible for us today. But how can this be, when both the historical basis and doctrinal shape of the church's tradition have been overthrown? At the other pole, Lampe still wishes to speak of Jesus' 'perfect and unbroken response to the Father'[10] as of supreme exemplary significance for his followers ever since. But how, in non-incarnational terms, can one account for such unique perfection at one point in past history, let alone for its continuing import across the centuries? On either view, the supposition that the church, the supposed bearer of moral and religious value down the ages, has radically misconstrued the nature and place of Christ in respect of our knowledge of God, casts grave doubt on the viability of the doctrine of providence involved (a church-centred providence in Nineham's case, a Jesus-centred providence in Lampe's).

In his introductory essay to *The Myth*, Maurice Wiles very properly asks how much of the Christian religion would survive the abandonment of incarnational belief in its strong metaphysical sense. That book's own instances of non-incarnational christology suggest that very little that is distinctive does survive, and that what does so survives only by relying on elements in the tradition which presuppose a fuller incarnational understanding.

I am not arguing that there is absolutely nothing of moral or religious worth in the writings under consideration. We find in them much that expresses a pure faith in God, a maturity of spiritual perception (I think here particularly of the Bampton Lectures), and a conviction of the authenticity and value of religious experience as such. Such elements these Christian writers share with men of all pure ethical monotheistic faiths. But Christianity has claimed to introduce something further, something new and unique into the history of religions. And it is the moral and religious value of this 'something more' that has been lost in non-incarnational christology.

II

What, then, is the moral and religious value of the incarnation? I shall first summarize this under four headings: (a) revelation and personal knowledge of God; (b) trinitarian belief; (c) the problem of evil and the atonement; (d) presence and participation.

(a) In the first place, the moral and religious value of the incarnation lies in the greatly increased potential for human knowledge of God and personal union with God introduced by God's own presence and acts, in human form, this side of the gap between Creator and creature. The character of Christ *is* for us the revealed character of God, and becomes the criterion for our understanding of the nature and will of God. In a sense the humanity of Christ mediates God to us, but in another sense God's love is communicated to us immediately by God's own incarnate presence here in our midst. It is perfectly true that we today are not face to face with God incarnate as the disciples were. But the inevitable limitations of that particularity are overcome, as I shall stress below, by his spiritual and sacramental presence and activity, by means of which God's personal self-revelation in Jesus is universalized. My point here is that the story of Jesus gives that universal activity of God its concrete, particular and utterly personal form.

The humanity of Christ is, of course, for Christian understanding, permanently taken into God. The risen Christ remains the focus and channel of our knowledge of God and the key by which all other experience of God is converted into personal knowledge of the blessed Trinity.

(*b*) The trinitarian implications of christology must be stressed further here, if we are to avoid an excessively individualized Jesus cult. Jesus reveals God to us, not only by his character and acts and passion, but also by his prayers to the Father, by his resurrection, and by the outpouring of the Spirit. But the doctrine of the Trinity has an independent place, as well, in our assessment of the moral and religious value of incarnational christology. For in forcing us to think of God in richer, relational terms, as the fullness of love given and love received within his own being prior to creation, it resolves that impasse in pure monotheism which results from conceiving of God on the analogy of an isolated individual. Lampe claims that there is no need to project relationship into God, since God participates immanently in his creatures' reciprocities.[11] But this makes creation necessary to God, if God is to enjoy the fullness of being as love. This, I submit, is to introduce real incoherence into any religiously and metaphysically satisfying concept of God.

(*c*) Thirdly, the moral and religious value of the incarnation is seen in the way it confronts the world's evil. In happier days, this point was seen by Hick, when he wrote: ' ... it is part of the meaning of christian monotheism that there is an ultimately responsible moral being, who is absolute goodness and love, whom we may trust amid the uncertainties and anxieties of the gradual unfolding of reality to us in time. We are led to this trust by seeing the divine responsibility at work on earth in the life of Christ. For there we see the Love which has ordained the long costly soul-making process entering into it and sharing with us in its inevitable pains and suffering.'[12] As was pointed out above in respect of Frances Young's reference to the cross of Christ, the moral force of this depends on Christ's *being* God. One cannot accept responsibility for the world's ills through someone else. Hick now wishes to stress God's 'participation in every pain . . .' But the manner of this participation makes all the difference. Only if we can say that God has *himself*, on the cross, 'borne our sorrows' can we find him universally present 'in' the sufferings of others. It is not a question of 'awareness' and 'sympathy'. It is, as Whitehead put it, a matter of the 'fellow-sufferer who understands'. This whole dimension of the Christian doctrine of the incarnation, its recognition of the costly nature of God's forgiving love, and its perception that only a suffering God is morally credible, is lost if God's involvement is reduced to a matter of 'awareness' and 'sympathy'.

I come, thus somewhat indirectly, to the doctrine of the atonement, which, of course, has traditionally been held to spell out the chief moral and religious value of the incarnation. As J. K. Mozely emphasized in his excellent essay in *Mysterium Christi* on 'Christology and Soteriology',[13] it is soteriological considerations that require us to think of Jesus as coming to the world from the side of God, and not as the highest stage in religious evolution. And certainly it is only if we can think of Jesus Christ as being divine as well as being human that we can speak of his life and death and resurrection as of universal salvific significance for all men. The objectivity of the atonement consists in its being God's act for all. Unfortunately the manner in which this is so has been spelled out in a variety of theories of the atonement which are themselves open to grave moral objection, and this has led to revulsion from objective theories of the atonement and a failure to perceive the real moral significance of the incarnation. Consequently it needs to be stated quite categorically that God's forgiving love does not depend on the death of Christ, but rather is manifested and enacted in it. It is precisely because the Spirit who converts our hearts and builds up our life in the Spirit is the Spirit of the crucified God that God's forgiveness and our reconciliation have the profoundly moral quality that has been the real inspiration of Christian piety down the ages, despite its often crude forms of expression. The costly and deeply moral nature of God's reconciling work was summarized by Austin Farrer thus: 'What, then, did God do for his people's redemption? He came amongst them, bringing his kingdom, and he let events take their human course. He set the divine life in human neighbourhood. Men discovered it in struggling with it and were captured by it crucifying it.'[14]

(*d*) Fourthly, the religious value of the incarnation is seen in the christological and trinitarian concentration in terms of which present Christian experience, worship and life are to be understood.

As Moule has repeatedly stressed, it is conviction of Christ as a living presence, both spiritually and sacramentally, that differentiates specifically Christian awareness of God from all other. Moreover Christian worship has never been conceived solely as a matter of response, in gratitude and adoration, by creatures to their Creator. It is rather a matter of being caught up into Christ's eternal offering to the Father, and of being indwelt by the Spirit, who, from within, draws us in worship into the inner life of God. Similarly, in the body of Christ, we become, by adoption and grace, instruments in the history of divine action, which is not only a matter of God's movement out towards his creation, but a movement back from creation to God. The specifically Christian insight is that this too, the movement from creation to God, takes place in God, through the humanity of Christ, and derivatively through ourselves, as we are united with Christ, alike in worship and work.

III

Before illustrating these central features of specifically Christian self-understanding from the writings of some contemporary theologians, I should like to indicate the way in which they come to simple, yet profound expression in Christian hymnody.

Fortunately the popular Christmas carols will ensure that Chalcedonian orthodoxy will be remembered long after *The Myth* is forgotten.

> Hark, hark! the wise eternal Word
> Like a weak infant cries;
> In form of servant is the Lord,
> And God in cradle lies.

The Passiontide hymns bring out the saving significance of the incarnation:

> My song is love unknown,
> My Saviour's love to me,
> Love to the loveless shown,
> That they might lovely be.
> O who am I
> That for my sake
> My Lord should take
> Frail flesh and die?

St Patrick's Breastplate and the hymns of Cardinal Newman ensure that trinitarian faith finds expression in Christian worship, and I cannot resist quoting the second verse of F. W. Faber's little sung hymn, 'Most ancient of all mysteries...':

> When heaven and earth were yet unmade,
>   When time was yet unknown,
>   Thou in thy bliss and majesty
>   Didst live and love alone.

The eucharistic hymns preserve, most eloquently, that sense of the presence of the risen Christ by his Spirit which is the essence of living Christian faith:

> Thee we adore, O hidden Saviour, thee,
> Who in thy Sacrament art pleased to be;
> Both flesh and spirit in thy presence fail,
> Yet here thy Presence we devoutly hail.

> And now, O Father, mindful of the love
>   That bought us, once for all, on Calvary's Tree,
> And having with us him that pleads above,
>   We here present, we here spread forth to thee
>   That only Offering perfect in thine eyes,
>   The one true, pure, immortal Sacrifice.

It really is no use saying that this sort of thing still has the power to move as myth; for its moving power consists in the real content of these words, and if all attempts to articulate the doctrinal content of such poetic forms of expression are to be dismissed as incoherent, then the power to move is lost. We are not moved by nonsense.

The moral and religious value of the doctrines of the incarnation and the Trinity comes to more sophisticated expression in much contemporary theology, both Catholic and Protestant. I select four books to illustrate this: Hans Urs von Balthasar's *Love Alone: the Way of Revelation*, T. F. Torrance's *God and Rationality*, Jürgen Moltmann's *The Crucified God*, and Eberhard Jüngel's *Gott als Geheimnis der Welt*.[15]

Von Balthasar's little book presents, in summary form, the main thesis of his so-called 'theological aesthetic', that men are won over into loving contemplation of the trinitarian God, by the revealed glory of God's own act of love in incarnation and the cross. Scripture and doctrine alike are only witnesses to 'the concrete, incarnate God, who interprets himself as the absolute love of God'. Liberal Protestant theology, says von Balthasar, makes 'the revelation of the Cross and Resurrection innocuous by transforming it into a banal "teaching" or parable – instead of accepting the form itself realistically as the dramatic appearance of God's trinitarian love and as the Trinity's loving struggle for mankind'.[16]

Earlier, he has pointed out the way in which God's act of love in incarnation reveals the Trinity. 'The obedient love of the Son for the Father is certainly the model for human love before the majesty of God but more than that, it is the supreme image of divine love itself appearing. For it is precisely in the Kenosis of Christ (and nowhere else) that the *inner* majesty of God's love appears, of God who "is love" (1 John 4.8) and therefore trinity.'[17] He has already emphasized that where 'Christ is referred to as "the image of God", the words are not to be taken as a mythical statement because the world of myth has been for ever left behind since the Incarnation.'[18] Von Balthasar's insistence on the enacted and revealed love of God himself as constituting the source and ground of our response in love and contemplation brings out very clearly the fact that, in this paper, we are talking about the religious value of the incarnation, and only derivatively of the religious value of the *doctrine* of the incarnation.

T. F. Torrance addresses himself to the articulation of a specifically Christian understanding of the relation between God and man with great theological penetration. In a lecture, entitled 'The Word of God and the Response of Man', to be found in *God and Rationality*, he speaks of the 'Word' of God as that 'mode of His Being in which God goes forth to meet man, freely relating His divine Life to him within the conditions of his creaturely nature, and in which He sustains man in his meeting with God, enabling him freely to relate his human life to the majesty of the divine Nature'.[19] At this point I would stress the latter aspect of the doctrine; for it is the incarnation which not only brings God to us, but creates the conditions in which our own response to him can be made. God not only enters our estranged existence 'in order to struggle with the perverse nature of an alienated creation, to meet the full hostility of evil by accepting and bearing it in Himself. . .' God incarnate also himself constitutes the perfect *human* response, by incorporation into which we are enabled to respond. It is this element which is so notably absent in liberal Protestant theology, namely the fact that man's response to God takes place in God – in the Spirit, through incorporation into the body of Christ.

My third example of contemporary theology in which the moral and religious value of the incarnation is seen is Jürgen Moltmann's *The Crucified God*. There is much in that book with which we might well wish to quarrel, but the central chapter, which has the book's own title, constitutes a remarkable attempt to think through what it means for our concept of God to say that Christ's cross is God's cross in our world. 'With the Christian message of the cross of Christ', he writes, 'something new and strange has come into the metaphysical world. For this faith must understand the deity of God from the event of the suffering and death of the Son of God and thus bring about a fundamental change in the orders of being of metaphysical thought and the value tables of religious feeling. It must think of the suffering of Christ as the power of God and the death of Christ as God's potentiality.' An indication of the way in which this is spelled out in terms of its moral and religious value is given in the following quotation: 'If Christian belief thinks in trinitarian terms, it says that forsaken men are already taken up by Christ's forsakenness into the divine history and that we "live in God", because we participate in the eschatological life of God by virtue of the death of Christ. God is, God is in us, God suffers in us, where love suffers. We participate in the trinitarian process of God's history.'[20]

I quote this passage because it points up the folly of suggesting that the suffering of God with all suffering creatures can be affirmed without a doctrine of the incarnation or, even more implausibly, that to affirm God's unique personal presence in the cross of Christ is to make God somehow less present to the whole of suffering humanity. On the contrary God's presence with suffering humanity can only be affirmed on the basis of God's own suffering in the cross of Christ.

My last example of creative incarnational and trinitarian theology is Eberhard Jüngel's *Gott als Geheimnis der Welt*. A first look at this important new book suggests some modification of the trinitarian doctrine so far adumbrated in this paper. While Jüngel makes it absolutely clear that to say that 'God is love' is to posit an internally differentiated, relational deity, he also suggests that the self-sacrificial nature of the divine love is only seen in the love of God for the world, a love that meant for God himself not only the *sending* of the Son, but his passion and death. This is very different from saying that God needs the world in order to love. It is rather to insist that God's inner nature as lover and beloved is enacted and manifested in creation and the cross.

In mentioning these four books, I can do little more than hint at the possibilities in theological exploration of the moral and religious value of the incarnation. But a factor of considerable importance for our present debate emerges from a study of these writings. It is clear that these authors stand firmly within the tradition of incarnational and trinitarian orthodoxy, and yet break with at least the most powerful strand in the tradition over both the impassibility of God and the degree to which an element of kenoticism is to be welcomed and embraced within a broadly orthodox position. It is, of course, a matter of judgment whether these developments (both, it should be stressed, of great moral and religious significance) constitute a break with the tradition of comparable dimensions to that proposed in non-incarnational christology. I am bound to say that to my mind there is no comparison. The developments regarding our understanding of the suffering of God and of the human limitations of Jesus' self-consciousness are quite legitimate developments within incarnational and trinitarian theology, while the rejection of the doctrines of the incarnation and the Trinity marks a decisive break with the faith of the Christian church.

The appeal to the over-arching authority of the incarnational and trinitarian tradition is not, it should be emphasized, a bare appeal to authority. The authority of the tradition lies fairly and squarely in its content, in the way it commends itself to historical judgment, to rational comprehension and to experiential authentication. In particular, as has been urged in this paper, its authority lies in the moral and religious value to be found in it.

I append a note on the implications of incarnational belief for Christian ethics. It has often been pointed out that a number of ethical consequences follow from belief that God's love is enacted and made manifest in the incarnation and the cross.

In the first place it is suggested that this shows that the material is not alien to the spiritual, but that body is to be seen as the vehicle of the spirit. This is spelled out further in Christian sacramental theology, and often generalized into a sacramental view of the universe.

In the second place, the incarnation has been taken as the pattern of Christian ministry, as a matter of involvement and service in every area of human life.

This includes what may be singled out as a third implication, namely, involvement in the communal and political structures of human life. On this basis, political theology is a valid deduction from the gospel of the incarnation. If it is argued that the recorded teaching of Jesus hardly bears this out, the reply must be given that Christian social ethics are based on principles drawn from the whole event and action of the incarnation.

No doubt I shall be told that these general principles of sacramental life, involved service, and political commitment do not depend on the truth of incarnational christology, but can be argued for and commended irrespective of Christian doctrine. No doubt they can. That is why the bulk of this paper was argued on other grounds. But the question remains an open one, whether other systems of religious or indeed non-religious belief have in fact fostered and have in fact had it in them to sustain such incarnational practice.

NOTES

1. Austin Farrer, 'Very God and very Man' in *Interpretation and Belief*, SPCK 1976, p. 128.

2. Ninian Smart, *World Religions: A Dialogue*, Penguin Books 1966.

3. Michael Goulder in *The Myth*, p. 80.

4. Don Cupitt, *The Myth*, p. 141.

5. John Hick, *God and the Universe of Faiths*, Fount 1977, p. xvii.

6. See Peter Geach, *Providence and Evil*, Cambridge University Press 1977, pp. 24-8.

7. Houlden, *The Myth*, pp. 131-2.

8. Frances Young, *The Myth*, p. 30.

9. Nineham, *The Myth*, p. 202.

10. G. W. H. Lampe, *God as Spirit*, Oxford University Press 1977, p. 111.

11. Ibid., p. 139.

12. Hick, *God and the Universe of Faiths*, pp. 69f.

13. J. K. Mozley, 'Christology and Soteriology' in *Mysterium Christi*, ed., G. K. A. Bell and A. Deissmann, Longmans Green 1930.

14. Austin Farrer, *Saving Belief*, p. 99.

15. Hans Urs von Balthasar, *Love Alone: the Way of Revelation,* Burns & Oates 1968; T. F. Torrance, *God and Rationality*, Oxford University Press 1971; Jürgen Moltmann, *The Crucified God*, SCM Press 1974; Eberhard Jüngel, *Gott als Geheimnis der Welt*, Mohr, Tübingen 1977.

16. *Love Alone: the Way of Revelation*, p. 120.

17. Ibid., p. 71.

18. Ibid., p. 66.

19. *The Crucified God*, p. 215.

20. Ibid., p. 255.

A (iv) Incarnation and Atonement: God Suffered and Died

Frances Young

In spite of its obvious difficulties, the statement 'In Jesus, God suffered and died' is recognizably a characteristic affirmation of Christianity – although it is not in fact to be found in scripture or creed in so many words, and patristic theories of incarnation were quite incapable of doing justice to the truth which was affirmed in the beloved rhetorical paradoxes of their preaching.

'In Jesus, God suffered and died' has been taken to imply certain central Christian claims:

1. In Jesus, God bore our sins, took atonement upon himself and so made forgiveness available to his rebellious creatures.

2. In Jesus, God took responsibility for the evil and suffering which is a constituent part of the world he has created. The traditional form of this statement would be in terms of victory over the powers of evil; more recently, the focus has shifted to the reality of God's involvement in our experiences of suffering and death.

No Christian theologian can afford to sit lightly to these affirmations. The moral and religious heart of Christianity lies at this point, and I would agree with Brian Hebblethwaite that 'only a suffering God is morally credible' in the face of the world's ills. But in the context of the present debate, the following points should be considered:

1. 'God suffered and died' is a particularly striking example of the problems posed by religious language. On the one hand, there is a sense in which the death of God is an obvious nonsense, so that, however complex the difficulties of precisely distinguishing between literal, metaphorical, analogical and other kinds of language, all would agree that the statement 'God died' cannot be straightforwardly and literally true. On the other hand, to attempt an explanation (e.g. that God *qua* God cannot die whereas God *qua* man can), or indeed to try to state the 'core belief' conveyed in these 'mythological' terms (e.g. that it simply expresses graphically God's sympathetic involvement in his creation – though, of course it does mean at least that) is immediately to undermine its impact and (I suspect) to reduce its essential meaning.

It seems to me that theology is on a false path when it attempts to give definition to this kind of language. Ultimately truth about God is not open to analysis and investigation in the same way as items in the created universe. The Fathers who insisted that God is inexpressible and incomprehensible, that all knowledge of God and language about him is indirect, were at least saved from the kind of theological fundamentalism which imagines that we are dealing with truths that can be precisely stated, with meanings that can be fully elucidated. In this area language to which we can give no 'literal' content may well contain and convey a truth otherwise inexpressible.

So 'God suffered and died' is not to be emptied of content or explained away, but is to be affirmed together with the acknowledgment that it cannot be regarded as a simple statement of precisely what was the case. We are using the language of 'religious myth' which conveys a truth whose mystery is beyond human understanding and incommunicable through any mode of expression other than the parabolic.

2. It is often stated that the person who can help a sufferer is someone who has experienced a similar kind of suffering and come through it. The impact of the story that God suffered and died has depended upon its implication that God is like such a person, a conviction which has undoubtedly had a profound psychological effect upon suffering believers who have felt that God could understand their predicament.

Yet there are many forms of suffering which Jesus of Nazareth (i.e., in terms of this account, God-in-Christ) did not experience; and if this and no more is what the story implies, it may tend to reduce God to a 'sympathetic ear'.

It seems to me that the story acquires much greater significance and far more direct relevance to particular instances of human suffering in the present, if Jesus' humanity is taken totally seriously and the cross is regarded as the 'classic case' of God's presence in the midst of human sin, suffering and death – that is to say, the mode of God's presence there is seen as potentially the mode of his presence in other desperate situations. God not only suffered and died, but suffers and dies, in and with human beings.

3. According to the Marcan account, part of Jesus' desolation on the cross could be described as God-forsakenness; i.e. Christian faith affirms the presence of God in what was experienced as his absence. (Whether or not this was historically Jesus' actual experience is not the question here; it has become part of the 'myth' and is highly significant in this context.) This paradox is undermined by

identifying the subject of the experience with God incarnate. The tragedy of Jesus is revelatory of God's presence in the world's tragedy only if it is an entirely human story.

4. To adopt such a view is not to reduce the presence of God to 'mere sympathy'. We have to take the meaning of the *sympatheia* – suffering-together-with – in its fullest sense, recognizing that God's involvement in his world must be far more intense and intimate – indeed of a quite different order from the most intense human *sympatheia*. God in his immanence really shares in, participates in, identifies himself with particular instances of human tragedy. The cross particularizes this involvement for us and saves it from being a rather vague, general and therefore somewhat 'unreal' truth about God. But this particularization should not be allowed to imply that God was really present there in a way quite different from anywhere else; for on such a view the reality of God's involvement in other instances of profound tragedy may be overshadowed by the story of the cross rather than illuminated by it.

5. Cross and resurrection are inseparable motifs, but if resurrection becomes the proof that Jesus was divine or that God was incarnate in him, it immediately reduces the reality of crucifixion and death. It is hard to avoid docetism and do justice to the cross (patristic convolutions make this apparent to us), and it is all the more difficult if there is something inevitable about its reversal in the resurrection, or if the resolution of the tragedy is found through the triumphant act of a *deus ex machina*. If the death is taken really seriously, then God's power to transform may be discerned *within* the tragic situation, not merely in miraculously wafting away the consequences. Thus the cross becomes a dramatic presentation of the fact that the way to overcome evil is not to escape from it, but to bear it creatively in the presence and power of God.

B   A Wider Framework
Leslie Houlden

The charge most generally levelled against the authors of *The Myth of God Incarnate* is irresponsibility. Even among those in broad agreement with their proposals many have felt that it was inappropriate to present them with fanfares: too damaging to the faithful, too boat-rocking. Experience suggests that such critics were being over-protective, inclined to underestimate the toughness of some of those for whom they were concerned and insufficiently solicitous for others who, in various ways, shared the puzzles which set off the essay-writers and were ready to be helped by their attempts to solve them. Anyway, in the long run it is important that the truth should be out, and it can only be elucidated by discussion at many levels.

But in another sense the charge may stick. The decision to write essays on christology was determined by considerations arising within the world of professional theology – the subject was in the air. Yet publishing with fanfares implies the intention to discuss questions close to the needs and interests of a wider public, not skilled in theology but concerned about faith and its intelligibility. That would direct attention to problems of method, questions of presupposition, and theological issues more fundamental than christology which necessarily depends for its concepts and its language on ideas concerning the being and nature of God.

It is then a matter of how to place christology in these wider contexts. Some critics of *The Myth* have themselves proceeded by suggesting that the styles of christology put forward in the essays lose any force they might possess if set in some ampler framework. The purpose of this essay is to select a number of these suggestions in order to see how far their claim may be upheld, and then to sketch an alternative ampler framework which hopes to recognize the justice of some of the complaints against the original book and to begin to meet them in a more satisfactory way.

The resurrection
Some of the suggestions offered amount to a protest against the isolation of the idea of incarnation from other related aspects of

Christian doctrine. The claim is that once that isolation is ended, dissatisfaction with the traditional doctrine of incarnation is much less justified and may indeed be removed. The doctrine does not stand alone and can only be fairly judged in the light of the whole traditional belief about Christ, most clearly in the light of his resurrection.

Thus, in a long review of *The Myth*,[1] John Baker concluded with the claim that if only the writers had taken account of the resurrection, their findings would have been different: 'the affirmation from which the Christian faith and life began, and which apparently the contributors to this volume could not bring themselves to take seriously – the Resurrection of Jesus.' The same point is made by John Coventry, as part of a broader case, to other aspects of which I shall return:[2] 'whatever we may think our faith rests on, and however we may think it works, the resurrection is a constitutive part of its object and is not to be regarded as part of the apparatus of human interpretation of that object, defined as the historical Jesus.'

Yet neither critic gives any argument to show how this could be so, or even tells exactly what he means by 'the resurrection' – or explains why the resurrection of Jesus is to be differentiated in its theological meaning from other alleged resurrections, all matters which need unravelling if their point is to be made effectively. They both come near to leading one to echo Stevie Smith's exasperated and haunting protest: 'Oh Christianity, Christianity, why do you not answer our difficulties? . . . Oh what do you mean, what do you mean? You never answer our questions.'[3]

The following considerations are immediately relevant: first, the 'event' of the resurrection is problematical – what 'event' is alleged and how is it identified? Is it the same as exaltation (and what is that?) and is a bodily element required for the doctrine to do the work required of it? Second, what kind of link between 'event' and theological interpretation is supposed? How precisely does the *resurrection* of Jesus (as distinct from other claims about him), whether spiritual or bodily, lead to the affirmations made on the basis of it, such as 'victory over death'? In some senses of that term, no one possesses any such thing; but if it is taken in other senses, then how exactly is that victory either assured or guaranteed in a particular way by the resurrection of Jesus? The path of argument, linking the one to the other, is not without snags. To approach the same ground another way, how tied is such an interpretation of the resurrection to a package of late Jewish concepts, so that if we do not share them (and manifestly in the main we do not), it is not immediately clear how the interpretation, put in those terms, can stand?

Third, it is far from obvious why Jesus' resurrection should have a significance denied to his survival of death, which is after all, at the level of ordinary Christian hope, what his followers may expect to share with him. Resurrection is a term which inextricably mixes event and religious meaning; when the word is used about the Christian hope, how much is it done with the intention of conveying aspects of religious meaning felt to be lacking in talk of survival and not to speak significantly about 'event' at all? In the absence of, or at any rate the decline of, almost all traditional eschatology, can the idea of sharing resurrection be other than metaphor, however evocative and powerful? Then what is it a metaphor *for*?

The reply may come that the question is improper: metaphor is self-sufficient and self-commending, it conveys its own truth. Indeed. But then, claiming the benefits of metaphor, a statement may have to forgo the benefits of more literal modes of speech. Would this then distinguish talk of resurrection from talk of survival? And would the aim of talk of resurrection be to evoke a sense of the universal and inclusive nature of Christ? And must we then be content to allow such a sense to be evoked in us and do its poetic work? And admitting that, would we do better, when engaging in more dogmatic statement about the universal presence and activity of the divine, to speak in terms of 'God'? For certainly, at that level, talk of the universal or the inclusive Christ involves fearsome difficulties: is one not being asked to envisage unimaginable extensions to a known historical person, Jesus? Persons are precisely individual, particular, related to time and place. To universalize is to depersonalize – at any level that looks like the literal and claims its benefits. So, no, it is metaphor: let it then be content with the great benefits of poetic speech – and admit it.

Moreover, it remains to be shown how Jesus' resurrection corroborates precisely the classical doctrine of his person, rather than, for example, a belief in his centrality in God's purposes. In so far as it is put forward as a corroboration of the classical doctrine, then undoubtedly the form of that doctrine which it most naturally and helpfully supports is one now widely felt to be least helpful in other ways – one that sees Jesus' humanity as impersonal and so universal, 'including' ours. Yet what problems of implied docetism and sheer unintelligibility now face such a teaching!

In other words, hope raised by placing incarnation in this wider doctrinal picture is quickly dashed; first, because the attempt to elucidate one area which is problematic, by setting it alongside another area which is equally problematic, makes only for a deeper darkness. Second, because even if the bringing in of the resurrection somewhat widens the discussion concerning Jesus, we are still detaching him from the Christian faith as a whole; and only on the basis of fully satisfactory assumptions about the nature and working of that whole faith can we speak satisfactorily about him. We need to dig deeper, into conceptual and historical roots, if we are to discover the level at which incarnation and resurrection find their spring as diverse aspects of the witness to Jesus.

The presence of Christ

Discussion of the resurrection sometimes (perhaps in the cases of the critics referred to above) seems to mean not so much the occurrence itself as its consequences: the lordship of Christ, or, more broadly still, his continued living presence. Other writers have raised this matter more explicitly.[4] But here again, I miss consideration of clearly urgent questions, and once more the debate seems to lack candour with regard to method and assumptions.

A first question concerns the pedigree of these terms. No one in the present debate disagrees about the need to understand the words (titles such as Messiah or Son of Man) by which the first Christians expressed their convictions about Jesus in the light of the times, if we are to enter into their feelings and convictions. But the sense is sometimes conveyed that ideas such as Christ's presence, or even his lordship, which feel more immediately accessible, can dispense with such exposition. But they too go back to our origins; they are integral with the greater whole and equally require us both to exercise interpretative skill and to make an imaginative leap if we are to see what they saw. Like other more clearly technical expressions, these terms cannot be drawn to our use without consideration of the shift from one thought-world to another.

But talk of Christ's living presence functions chiefly to bridge the gap between the origins and the continuing story of Christian life. If it is to achieve this satisfactorily, do not certain matters need to be clarified? For example, how can a person of later times identify his experience as experience of Christ? Only surely by some mode of reference to the historically identifiable Jesus. How then can such an identification either bypass or sit light to historical scholarship and so to historical uncertainty about Jesus? How can it fail to reckon with both the ultimate opaqueness of all historical figures whom we may seek to 'know' and the conditions attendant upon the exercise of the imagination by which we seek to encroach upon that opaqueness?

Next, how can 'presence' talk fail to seek ways of welcoming and not begrudging the fact that Jesus lies not only in but behind the gospels and that, even if reporting and describing him accurately, they are responses to him and evaluations of him, made in the light of the writers' diverse cultural, social and Christian circumstances? Jesus is visible to us and distinguishable from other figures of the past through those early reactions to him and to the powerful impressions he made; and both the strength and variety of the reactions is itself a testimony to the power exerted by him. He is then both conveyed and obscured by those reactions; and the two aspects necessarily co-exist, providing us with both opportunities and limitations. But how can present experience possibly do away with these conditions? And if present experience offers directness, must not the terms of that directness, in the light of the conditions, be carefully stated and qualified? How else can we avoid the subjectivity which has attached the label 'Jesus' to any and every aspiration of his followers, many of which are good and worthy, deriving inspiration from and having a line of correspondence with the historical Jesus, but some of them patent travesties, whether harmless or malign?

Then, how can a person, given any awareness of *homo religiosus*, fail to reflect on the fact that while Protestant Christians experience Christ, Catholic Christians may experience Mary and Buddhists the Buddha, and not immediately ask himself questions about projection and subjectivity and conditioning? In other words, where are tests which we can apply, or must we accept any and every mere assertion? Clearly one important kind of testing comes from the consensus of the Christian community. While in some ways easing the problem, that approach also extends it, taking to the corporate level the difficulties raised above.

My contention is that acceptance of these questions as both legitimate and inevitable is not a perilous and unfortunate burden, courting the diminishing of faith, but the hopeful path to fundamental matters of method and assumption whose treatment can alone lead to a satisfactory account of the questions concerning Jesus from which the enquiry began.

Theology versus historical criticism

In the article already referred to, John Coventry has raised a criticism, applying more to some authors of *The Myth* than to others, which brings us to the level of method. It is that historical enquiry, in this case into the life of Jesus and Christian origins, is one thing, systematic theology is another, and that the writers of *The Myth* have confused them. The former is properly conducted according to the canons of general historical scholarship and makes no assumptions concerning faith, the other from within the church and on the basis of faith. The former seeks to discover the unknown, the latter to elucidate and expound the given. The essayists erred in allowing history to dictate their theology.

It may well be argued that it is precisely the pressing of this distinction (or often its complacent assumption) in the period of historical criticism which has led to the failure of the church to receive its manifest fruits except by a series of tantrums and gulps, leading to continued indigestion even after the swallowing is ostensibly accomplished. A more placid, less painful digestive process might well have brought us to a position where the faith found it easier to commend itself in the intellectual forum of the West and did not seem to so many to possess only the attractions of the esoteric and the mysteriously 'other'.

To leave aside such hypothetical historical judgments: while the distinction has obvious truth and value, in pointing to two distinct objectives and safeguarding two distinct tasks, it also has severe inadequacies, in terms of both theology and practical procedures, and may cut at the roots of the tree it is designed to protect. (There is also the irony that the distinction is itself a product of that modern style of analysis and objectivizing whose conclusions it wishes to isolate and keep at bay.) First, it implies a disjunction between historical happenings and divine revelation which Christianity has always sought to avoid. On the contrary, precisely because it has meshed them together, Christianity has never been simply a spiritual theory or an abstract doctrine but has accepted mutual dependence between the two. Indeed, during most of its history, it has pointed to a multitude of historical happenings with complete and untroubled confidence as among its principal supports. But the mutual dependence means that historical enquiry cannot be a matter of indifference to theological statement and the latter is bound to be affected by its patent conclusions.

Moreover, it is not as if historical criticism were a method which confined its attentions to Christian origins, though systematic theologians often write as if this were the case. It is precisely its application to the development of Christian doctrine, throughout its history, which has inevitably put the classical doctrinal formulations in a new light. Once we have been 'taken behind the scenes' and made aware of the cultural and ecclesiastical circumstances in which the formulations arose, and once we unravel the tale of their diverse meanings in successive circles of Christians, we can no longer see them as part of an autonomous body of truths, demanding only our elucidation and exegesis. Exegesis and historical enquiry cannot but go hand in hand. The sympathetic historian, entering into the beliefs and ideas of his subjects, shades into the theologian, expounding those ideas as part of a developing body of doctrine.

Finally, the implications of such a distinction for any confident belief in a creator God, who speaks to us through any and every authentic perception of truth and not merely through an isolable stream of theological truth, are grievous to consider. It makes for distortion at a fundamental level of belief, and leads in turn to further distortion and imbalance in the more peripheral areas of faith. It promotes educational procedures which produce intolerable tensions in the handling of evidence. It gives rise to the temptation to squeeze evidence into moulds provided by doctrine or to the transformation of Christianity into a doctrine withdrawn from and immune from the uncertainties of history – quite as radical a departure from traditional Christianity as any that John Coventry discerns in the authors of *The Myth*. Is it not clear that historical enquiry cannot be so easily sent into its corner by theology and instructed to mind its own business; that the rise of historical enquiry is one of those recurring transformations of sensibility which theology must learn to welcome, not keep at arm's length; and that the whole shape of the matter has been so altered that to think in terms of such a distinction in order to achieve the purposes here desired is scarcely possible? Of course it is true that historical study cannot of itself prompt affirmations of faith: it can only place danger signs at certain paths and leave others open. But along those others the man of faith has all the space he needs.

The community of faith

John Coventry writes: 'The basis of Christian faith in particular is the experience of encountering the risen Christ as God's self-gift, dwelling in his Body the Church.'[5] He writes further of the wrongheadedness of a faith which depends too much, too exclusively on Christian origins and sets out to discover their present relevance: 'it entirely bypasses the believing community that has existed in the intervening centuries and that exists to-day.' 'The criterion of his (i.e. the systematic theologian's) operation ... must always be the faith of the community.'

As a protest against dictatorship of the church by its theologians (a remote enough contingency one might feel), this is salutary: theology – the orderly statement of religious truth – is neither the heart nor the whole of the matter. Still, in the Christian religion at least, it is always part of it – and either a welcome light on the path or an obstacle to be navigated. It is itself part of the activity of the Christian community, not something imposed upon it from without. Moreover that community is not a monolithic structure, content with its past, unalterable in its perception of Christian truth, but mobile, dynamic, and often keen to press into new developments. Nor is it isolated from truth perceived in society at large: it maintains open links, of many kinds and degrees of sophistication, among its laity more than among its clergy. The appeal to the Christian community as part of the setting for theology entails recognition of these features which are to be seen both throughout its history and today.

To draw attention to this wider framework is then wholly desirable; but it does not lead unambiguously in a preservative direction. The community of faith is a sound and demanding base from which to meet new questions with new answers, as it is for the deep appreciation of the whole Christian past. But the direction of its influence is neither foreseeable nor for that matter beyond testing according to other criteria of Christian truth.

From a number of angles, critics have suggested a widening of the frame within which the traditional doctrine of the incarnation should be seen. Such a widening would, they felt, strengthen its cogency and make a more adequate theological statement possible. Reasons have been given for thinking that none of these suggestions achieves its aim. The failure comes from taking too narrow a perspective and refusing to dig deep enough into matters of method and presupposition. We cannot solve the problems attending one item of the theological agenda by appealing to another, equally problematical. We cannot, on the basis of the Christian experience of God, come to detailed conclusions about the person of Jesus or predetermine the ways in which he brings about that experience. We cannot appeal to Christian theology (Christian theology of all theologies) as if it were unaffected by historical enquiry. We cannot appeal to the community of the faithful as if it stood unitedly and deliberately foursquare on the platform of an unchanging tradition.

We can, however, appeal, without fear of diluting faith, to the religious as well as the historical and human realities behind all these things, just as we appeal to the same realities behind 'the incarnation'. The historical and human realities have been investigated both in *The Myth* and in the present volume. The religious realities have not been ignored but have received less attention.

The starting- and finishing-point of Christian faith is belief in God – along the path opened up by and as a result of Jesus, and then by all that has flowed from him. It is neither more, nor less than this. As Frances Young has shown in her essay in this volume, to force the earliest Christians' conviction about Jesus into an incarnational mould, in the classical sense, is unfair to their sense of his finality and centrality, categories which do more justice to their thought. That way of describing their belief – and certainly they looked to him as men of their time looked to no other – meets the evidence – and is more satisfactory religiously. If it had been maintained (as the Christians of the succeeding period were unable, for wholly explicable reasons, to maintain it), it would have steered away from docetism and led towards a clearer conviction of that primary and genuine fruit of the faith in Jesus – a belief in a moral creator God who is utterly at one with all of us in our sufferings and failures: truly God our saviour.

Some of the critics of the traditional doctrine have perhaps been over-sharp in their judgments: if now it can be made to seem incoherent or morally or historically inadequate, that need not lead to a lack of understanding of its former appropriateness. A benefit of living in a historically-minded culture is the enjoyment of the capacity to enter with sympathy into other periods than one's own. There is no reason for the critics of the classical statements of the doctrine to deny that in certain quite different circumstances it was the necessary and inevitable way of answering the questions posed. But sympathy is not such a finally obligatory virtue as adherence to the truth that is given.

Undoubtedly the style of faith which now seems to present itself is more consciously theocentric than some of the more christocentric styles which have abounded. In response to the caution engendered by historical enquiry, this style has the advantage of drawing into the concept 'God', with its inbuilt brake on idolatry and over-ambitious picture-making, all in Christian understanding that relates to 'the other'. By contrast, strongly christocentric faith contains the tendency to overemphasize the icon 'Christ' and to overestimate the degree of fixity which it is able to bear (in whatever form it may be seen), at the same time underrating its dependence on transient features of human culture.

Moreover, theocentric religion makes sure that the decision of faith is placed nakedly at the point where it always belongs and receives no spurious aid from the support of a Jesus who in truth leaves that decision still open, still to be made – and whose own message seems to have been exactly to put that decision starkly before us without any such aids. The pure sovereignty of God remains the message, with Jesus its impelling messenger and its embodiment, continually presented to our hearts with ever-recurring refreshment.[6]

The religious realities beneath some of the doctrinal 'labels' we have examined can, it seems, bear and profit from other forms of verbal expression than the labels themselves. If we dig below the level at which the critics seek to engage us, we discover the religious realities of Christian faith – what Jesus gave and impelled – springing abundantly and vigorously into life. It does indeed falsify if we treat 'incarnation' as a topic in itself and if we isolate theology from Christian life as a whole. But interaction between areas of theology and areas of Christian expression most candidly and most fruitfully occurs at the deeper level, where the kinds of enquiry now made possible for us are taken with full seriousness.

In this essay, there has been much reference to matters of method. Here too attention to the deeper level affords its benefits, for questions of method and approach affect our treatment of all areas of theology and our way of expressing Christian life. I conclude by listing some of the questions in mind. I believe that work on these matters would set the present conflict between traditional and so-called radical formulations concerning Jesus in new lights and enable them to find common ground. And Jesus, far from being displaced, would return again to perform new work in the heart and imagination.

1. The analysis of the movement from Jesus' influence, via the experience of those who knew him to the various expressions of that experience in words.

2. The analysis of the forms and varieties of religious language, of its metaphorical nature, and so of the styles of its effectiveness.

3. The analysis of the transference of hallowed formulas from one cultural context to another and their role in both perpetuating and shifting religious awareness; the senses in which continuing identity of faith is a reality and those in which it is fantasy.

4. The analysis of the conditions under which translation of religious statements occurs in their movement from one group or person to others, and the implications for religious truth.

NOTES

1. *Journal of Theological Studies*, xxix, 1978, pp. 291–97.
2. 'The Myth and the Method' in *Theology*, lxxxi, 1978, pp. 252–61.
3. *Collected Poems*, Allen Lane, 1975, pp. 416f.
4. Notably C. F. D. Moule in *Theology*, lxxx, 1977, pp. 30–36; lxxxi, 1978, pp. 164–72; cf. also letter by Alan Bill in *Theology*, lxxx, 1977, pp. 206f.
5. Art. cit., p. 260.
6. For a fuller account of the approach sketched very briefly here, see my *Patterns of Faith*, SCM Press 1977, and *Explorations in Theology 3*, SCM Press 1978. In both works, its implications for a range of doctrinal questions are examined, and the attempt is made to show some of the positive results of a candid acceptance of historical criticism for the doctrinal agenda. It amounts to a programme for reviewing doctrine in the light of a fundamental reassessment of method.

C The Incarnation as the Foundation of the Church

Stephen Sykes

(NOTE. The following essay, it will be readily seen, was not written in the first instance for the colloquium arranged by Dr Goulder for the authors of *The Myth of God Incarnate* and certain critics, to which I was kindly invited. Its inclusion in the present volume, despite its apparently tangential character, is entirely due to the pressing insistence of Dr Goulder. Nonetheless the author fully accepts his share of the responsibility for believing that it is relevant to the discussion which the original book initiated, and offers the following reasons for this view:

(*i*) The essay challenges the assumption, which the authors of *The Myth of God Incarnate* all make, that there is such a thing as 'the traditional doctrine of the incarnation' (Hick, p. xi), 'the classical doctrine of the incarnation' (Cupitt, p.134), 'traditional incarnational belief' (Wiles, p. 162), 'the idea that Jesus was God incarnate, as that idea has traditionally been understood' (Nineham, p. 201). The argument of this essay is that the place of the incarnation in catholic orthodoxy is, in the first instance, in the form of a story. That this story clearly had doctrinal implications was realized very early in the Christian church, and numerous attempts have been made from the first century to our own to cope with its inherent problems. But that there is any one doctrine of the incarnation universally admitted to be orthodox I deny. I am therefore unmoved by the suggestion that the last defender of 'full orthodoxy' was a man whose views no one could today defend (so Cupitt, p. 137) – that is the classical, straw-man tactic; the actual history of theology reveals a more interesting and sophisticated picture of variety.

(*ii*) The essay also implies an alternative view on the significance of the perennial problem of the 'culturally determined' character of ancient theology. No theology of any degree of theoretical sophistication can fail to show the marks of the intellectual milieu in which it was developed; we learn from the ancients not by ossifying their work into 'orthodoxy', and then triumphantly proving its culturally conditioned character, but by enquiring what problems they were trying to solve. In the event, it turns out, I believe, that the problems of incarnational theologies are perennial. They are eased, no doubt, if it is simply denied that God identifies himself in an utterly costly way in Jesus's sacrificial life and death and in such a manner as finally to achieve man's salvation. But if some such thing is to be affirmed in the belief that it affords the sole means for identifying the nature of God's love, then the problem of time and eternity is unavoidable. The language of the story is irreplaceably and necessarily temporal and sequential; but it is not, for that reason, as a whole mythological or poetic or metaphorical, nor can the logic of the Fathers' speech about eternity be satisfactorily dismissed as obsolete metaphysics. (This point has been made in a penetrating review-article by Professor Eric Osborn, *Prudentia* X, 1 May 1978, pp. 27–47.)

(*iii*) It will be seen that I regard the burden of proof as lying so heavily on the shoulders of those who seek to make Christianity without incarnation plausible, that I almost make it a presupposition of my essay. In this sense it may very well be asked whether I have considered the force of the objections of the essayists at all. To this I believe that I can truthfully answer that, although my own contribution was not written with the opinions and judgments made in the book specifically in mind, most of my own convictions were reached after careful consideration of the very similar opinions and judgments of a host of modern theologians. My method is to offer not a point by point refutation, but to illustrate what any counter-achievement would try to take into account. If I do not face the arguments directly, that is not intended as a discourtesy. But it is an indication that I believe that the present situation in theology, if I understand it aright, requires a very different kind of direction and method from the one which seems to have imposed itself on the authors of *The Myth*.

(*iv*) It will be obvious that there is a close relationship between my use of 'story' and Professor Wiles' discussion of 'myth' in theology (chapter 8 of *The Myth of God Incarnate*). To put the requisite discussion in as brief and acute a form as possible, my view would be that his treatment of the theme goes wrong on page 161. Here the question of understanding myth is treated as a matter of finding some corresponding ontological truth. But in this case the myth, of course, becomes disposable; once we have the ontological truth (what, incidentally, is the force of 'ontological' here? Would anything be lost if the word were omitted?) the myth is naturally subordinated to it. My own view is that the story, including the event of incarnation, which identifies the character of

God, is primary and irreplaceable. The story is also true, in as much as *this* story and no other identifies the nature of the love of God; and it follows that the church's task, including that of theological enquiry, is defined by and dependent upon that truth. As I read Wiles' article (and also that of Dr Young) I can find individual sentences with which I very much agree; at the same time my approach as a whole is different, as I believe the following will demonstrate.)

Introduction

The purpose of this paper is to show how, in treating of the incarnation, one is dealing with a foundational reality for the whole Christian church. This is not as obvious a question as it seems. It seems as if, since the Christian church claims to teach what is true, the only question to be resolved is whether the doctrine of the incarnation is true, and if so how it is related to other truths also taught by the church. But that is a superficial approach to the question, which proposes a merely external relation between the church's teachers and what is taught. The truth of the matter is, rather, as Sir Edwyn Hoskyns perceived, that '*Quid vobis videtur de Ecclesia*, What think ye of the Church? is not merely as pertinent a question as *Quid vobis videtur de Christo*, What think ye of Christ?: it is but the same question differently formulated'.[1] The reason for this is obvious enough. The church itself is not a voluntary human association for the pursuit of certain human ends. It is, rather, called into existence by God to do his work, and its fidelity to its task can only be measured by its obedience to the specific nature of God's call. How God has addressed and addresses man is, therefore, constitutive of the church's very being. On this account of the matter, a teacher in the church is not externally related to a series of possibilities from which he may select the most plausible, or the one open to the least objections. He is himself antecedently defined, and the nature of his task is predetermined, by the way God himself has acted. Christology is not merely a theory about Jesus Christ; it specifies what sort of a reality the Christian church is, in the context of which the theologian is speaking about Jesus Christ.

The purpose of this paper is accordingly to attempt, yet again, to show how the two realities are related, the reality of the incarnation and the reality of the church. Only by an account which shows how the two are interconnected is the theologian's position clarified. Otherwise he appears on the scene as an extraneous factor, ignored unless he attacks cherished convictions; and in this case he will be seen merely as deploying a superior kind of articulateness, or a tyrant with a monopolist's grip upon the sources of knowledge. By contrast his proper rôle as an interpreter of the reality of the church to its members needs to be constantly illustrated, a rôle which contains ample scope both for criticism (as Schleiermacher maintained),[2] and for originality.

The importance of emphasis upon the ecclesial context of any attempt to speak about Jesus Christ lies not in any presuppositions about 'the defence of orthodoxy', although there is a place for considerations relating to continuity in the Christian tradition. Rather it consists in the necessity of relating such speech to concrete events in time and space, things said and done in buildings throughout the world, books of common worship, laws and constitutions, and the way men and women structure their lives in families, social groups and nations. The church is compelled in all these ways to be rooted in what actually is the case. It persists as a complex, multi-dimension phenomenal *reality*; not as a system of ideas promulgated in lecture rooms. As such a reality it is embodied in, and lives by, myth, ritual and by forms of social organization, as much as by an intellectually developed corpus of doctrinal and ethical teaching. The major problem for the Christian theologian is to discern what it is that binds this incredibly complex reality together, the *Anziehungsprinzip*, or principle of adhesion, to refer to Schleiermacher again.[3] He has to offer an interpretation of the church's catholicity, a catholicity which is not that of a purely mental construction, but one which has taken root in many places and is being realized. It is this inclination towards factuality which makes certain forms of theoretical reformulation of Christian doctrine incredible. Whatever their alleged theoretical merits, they so discredit the faith by which the church actually has lived and lives, that they amount to an admission of divine incompetence. The real struggle in theology, by contrast, and the source of most of the internal disagreements between theologians, lies in the diversity of attempts to make intelligible the church's catholicity. It is this which is at stake in a discussion of christology, or in any attempt to relate incarnational theology to the theology of the cross.

I

I am prepared to take, therefore, an Anglican stance, at least as a starting-point for the discussion. I say *an* Anglican stance, since although the doctrine of the incarnation has repeatedly been defended by certain Anglican theologians as constituting the basic Christian doctrine since the mid-nineteenth century,[4] there are no grounds in the basic documents of the Anglican reformation by which the doctrine of the incarnation might be thought to be established in a more central position than, say, the theology of the cross.

To take an Anglican stance as a starting-point simply means to take seriously Hoskyns' proposal that speaking of the church and speaking of Christ are different formulations of the same subject matter. To be an Anglican means to belong to a church in which the story of the incarnation is repeatedly rehearsed and implied, in its liturgies, including its most recent revised service books, in the official catechisms and in its Canon Law (for example, in the Church of England, in the use of the doctrine of the Trinity as a criterion for the admission of members of other churches to Holy Communion).[5] The public use of authorized forms of service alone is enforced in the Church of England,[6] and other churches of the Anglican Communion. The daily use of Morning and Evening Prayer, either privately or openly, is enjoined on every bishop, priest and deacon. Although these regulations are by no means literally or universally obeyed, the ethos of the Anglican communion is substantially determined by what is both explicitly professed and implicitly reinforced in its liturgical practice. Liturgy is the matrix in which Anglicans are taught the Christian faith; there is every reason, therefore, for investigating the widely-held belief that in some special way the doctrine of the incarnation is central to the characteristically Anglican theological stance.

The traditional justification in the Anglican communion for maintaining the doctrine of the incarnation is that it belongs to that corpus of doctrines which the undivided church maintained as the apostolic gospel from the first. 'The visible Church of Jesus Christ is therefore one', says Hooker, 'in outward profession of those things, which supernaturally pertain to the very essence of Christianity, and are necessarily required in every Christian man.'[8] Of these, the naming of Christ as Lord, and the embracing of the faith which Christ proclaimed, together with baptism, are the chief elements; and Hooker explicitly refers to the rule or summary of faith, maintained by Irenaeus and Tertullian, as containing the essential or fundamental doctrines. The idea of the unique authority of these 'fundamental articles' and of the pre-eminence of the first four general councils provided the dogmatic basis for Anglican theology from the sixteenth to the nineteenth century.[9]

There are, however, serious and radical objections to this tradition of apologetic:

(*i*) It belongs to the pre-critical period of Christian theology, when classicist notions of a single universal culture were everywhere assumed, and the idea of a permanent and invariable corpus of theoretical knowledge truly possessed by the enlightened was the natural way in which to interpret the intellectual content of the Christian faith.

(*ii*) The distinction between what is said to be fundamental and what non-fundamental is highly variable, and the content of the *regula fidei* can be shown to lack what must be admitted to be exceedingly important matters of belief, for example concerning the eucharist.

(*iii*) Historical research has demonstrated that the unitary concept of 'the apostolic gospel' conceals both the variety of belief and the conflicts which were part of the experience of the apostolic communities.

(*iv*) It is profoundly arbitrary and unhistorical to assume that what was defined by the church in the first five (or six, seven or eight) centuries is authoritative, but that subsequent decisions have no authority. It is also arbitrary to select certain parts of the faith professed in those centuries and to ignore other parts.

These objections are decisive against any simple repetition of the standard Anglican apologetic, which must be abandoned. Profound consequences follow for the Anglican tradition of theology and theological education, which has relied on historical study of basic sources, especially of the Bible and the Fathers, to provide the fundamental terms of its basic apologia. A defence of the view that the incarnation is the foundation of the church cannot now proceed by, for example, a demonstration that the gospel of John has a historical foundation, or that incarnational orthodoxy predated Athanasius. Although historical scholarship reveals the subtlety or lack of subtlety with which theologians of the past wrestled with the problem of the eternal in the midst of time, there is no escape from the act of theological analysis and evaluation of the nature of the faith by which the catholic church lives. For this analysis there are no agreed criteria. The criteria are recognized in the act of analysis itself, and the success of any analysis lies in its ability to illuminate the catholicity of the church.

Accordingly what is to be attempted here is the outline of a way of seeing how the incarnation functions in the life of the church.

II

There are, and always have been, many gods in the world in which the Christian gospel is preached. Crucial to that message, therefore, is the content of that knowledge of God which the gospel brings.

Knowledge of God, in the Christian gospel, is of one upon whose undeviating goodness men may rely, and whose will is subject to no merely arbitrary variation. God is not thought of as partial in his regard for, and treatment of, different persons.

Knowledge of who God is is, moreover, correlative to knowledge of the kind of world in which we are alive. The appearance of the world process, which is sometimes devastatingly unequal in its apportionment of good and ill to particular persons, does not express the ultimate intentions of the deity. Whatever the changes and chances of human life, the divine compassion and judgment is believed to be steady and true. Accordingly it is of the utmost importance for the terms on which human life is lived that what is said about God should be reliable.

The same is true for knowledge of others and of oneself. In Christian faith men know both others and themselves as the living subjects of the love of God, of his goodness and of his judgment. Without such knowledge the structure of human relationships is open to a fundamentally different interpretation. Accordingly it is again vital for the way life is lived that what is said about God should be reliable.

'As a rule men are polytheists';[10] they are such in the sense that consistency in the ordering of the direction of their lives is rarely achieved, and if attempted is a matter of great internal struggle. The reception of the Christian gospel throws a man directly into the midst of that struggle, of which the doctrine of the one, undeviatingly good God is both the cause and means of conquest. Necessarily the Christian gospel is concerned with the quality of the response to the undeviatingness of God, and the ultimate reason for such continuity as the handing on of the Christian tradition requires is that human response to God should be response to the one God.

If it be granted that who God is is crucial to the Christian gospel, then precision in the manner of speech about God is crucial to the authenticity of the pattern of human response. Who God is may be spoken of abstractly or concretely. Abstractly, his nature or character can be referred to in a traditional list of character adjectives and nouns, such as righteous/righteousness, holy/holiness, love/lovingkindness, and so forth.

But abstract speech is always necessarily dependent upon concrete speech. Righteousness, holiness and lovingkindness are not identifiable apart from stories which exemplify or illustrate what is being referred to. To speak of who God is with the precision required for the ordering of human response to him entails telling a story or stories in which who he is is exemplified or illustrated.

But the abstract language in which God's character is rendered, has, inevitably, a range of human associations and stories. Human life knows the use of the same character adjectives and nouns (especially, of course, love), and tells a variety of stories exemplifying and illustrating it. The stories and their meanings are implicit in the structure of social relations characteristic of any given society, and within societies may be subject to individual or familial variations. Thus what 'love' is in a given society may be rendered in sets of archetypal 'love stories' and their interpretation, and is implicitly qualified or reinforced by purely individual experiences of love (made up into story-type recollections) at the hands of parents, siblings or a mate.

If the range of possible meanings of character adjectives and nouns derived from the culture or human life is plural and diverse, so also are the meanings derivable from biblical stories in which God is characterized. The use of scripture as a means of identifying who God is is entailed in the very concept of 'scripture'.[11] Here, then, is an authoritative source, but one which has led to a series of construals of the character of God which have most certainly varied. Even if the story of Jesus (which itself contains a variety of events and stories (parables) within stories) is taken as of central significance for construing the character of God, the impact of the sheer variety of other stories is not suppressed. The use of the scriptures in the church guarantees and perpetuates a plurality of renderings of who God is. This is the background against which understanding the function of speaking of the incarnation must be seen.

III

The incarnation is, in the first instance, an event in a story which renders who God is in concrete form. It is not a story which illustrates something which we otherwise already know, nor is it a story which is archetypal in the human consciousness. Rather it is a story whose meaning cannot be rendered otherwise than by the narration. It is, literally, indispensable.[12]

A story is, essentially, character and event in interaction. The story in the context of which incarnation is an event, contains all the elements of story grammar; a setting, a theme, a plot and a resolution. The setting is human history, the theme is the rescue of mankind from destruction, the plot is the entry of God into the contest, and the resolution is man's judgment and final redemption. In the case of the incarnation the setting involves statements about the characters involved in the story (God himself, Mary and Joseph, Jesus and his contemporaries). The theme is implicit in the intention expressed by the sending or coming of the Son of God. The plot connects the birth with the life, death, resurrection and ascension of Jesus. The resolution is the final nature of human destiny, and is the outcome of this particular story, not of any other possible story.

Both the rendering of who God is in story form, and the telling of this particular story are indispensable to speaking of God. The form of a story is indispensable not simply because it is a vivid and pedagogically effective means of communication, though that is of great significance in the task of Christian instruction to wise and simple alike. It is indispensable because it is in the end by means of stories that human identity is patterned. For a child, consciousness of time itself is rooted in the rehearsal and memorization of events which link him or her with, in the first place the mother, or mother-substitute, and in due course with the family. These are stories of primary existential import, whose rehearsal undergirds the effort which every human being makes to derive a sense of meaning from his immediate environment, in and through the passage of time.

Accordingly, the story-form in which incarnation is told is not an illustrative device for saying something about God which could be told more clearly in another form. It is, in essence and intention, a story of primary existential import, whose rehearsal contains the meaning of the individual's life. It is an inclusive story in the sense that in the entry of the Son of God into the world, the nature of my own origins as a fleshly reality is given its significance; in his death, my own death is included; in his resurrection, God's power to raise me from death is told.

Moreover, it is the telling of *this* story which is vital, not any story which might illustrate love or costly forgiveness or triumph over adversity. The incarnation means the coming into flesh of one who stands in a unique relation to God. The 'coming' or 'sending' of Jesus is a uniquely costly act by God himself, who identifies himself utterly in what Jesus does and suffers. This mission of

Jesus, as the parable of the vineyard tenants in Mark 12. 1–9 illustrates, is distinct from the sending of prophets who do not stand in the same relation to God himself. The essential point of the parable in its Markan form is the treatment meted out to one than whom there could be no one closer and more loved by the vineyard owner himself. The probable fate of the unworthy tenants, as hinted in the final question, 'what will the owner of the vineyard do?', merely underlines the critical, eschatological character of the moment of the coming of the beloved. Here the character of God as at once loving and judging mankind is told in concrete form. The parable hints that the crisis of a man who contemplates the person of Jesus may be like that of the tenants faced by the owner's son. The story of the incarnation affirms that that hint has the ultimate and irreplaceable security of revealing how God has, in reality, entered the human condition.

The significance of this story for the Christian tradition is that it has become the paradigm for construing who God is in the other scriptural stories in which God figures. This paradigm provides the interpreter with a standard for saying whether or not what God is said to have done elsewhere in the scriptures is 'in character'.

Moreover it creates a hierarchy in the possible ways of construing God's attitude towards the world. In this hierarchy certain attributes attain a status which provides a means of interpreting other attributes also attributed to God. The anthropomorphic nature of this method of 'character-portraiture' is literally unavoidable, but is a source of great confusion in theology. The notion of divine transcendence, the tradition of the *via negativa* and the very act of worship itself are the means whereby gross anthropomorphism is constantly subjected to criticism and correction.

IV

The basic form in which the incarnation is spoken of in Christian proclamation is not, therefore, in the form of doctrine but in the form of story. It is a story which in the first instance tells of Jesus, his deeds, his teaching, his death and resurrection. This story is told in a context, initially of eschatology which relates the event of Jesus to the events of the divine judgment at the end-time, and in due course of the whole of God's dealings with humanity. The decisive matter is not whether the doctrine of the incarnation is early or late, but whether the story of the incarnation is how the character of God is identified.[13] The investigation of the historical origins of incarnational theology provides neither confirmation nor refutation of this theological assertion. As an interpretative paradigm, the incarnation is neither true because it is early and Palestinian, nor false because it is late and Hellenistic. There are no good grounds for requiring that a developed form of incarnational theology be found, *expressis verbis*, in the teaching either of Jesus or of the apostles.

Rather, the argument that concludes that incarnation is an indispensable category for Christian theology deploys all the considerations relevant to supposing that it is by means of this, and no other story, that God desires that he shall be identified. One major element in any such set of considerations is the contention that only such a view makes the church's catholicity intelligible; that is, the way in which the constant narration of this story has lodged itself in the church's teaching and worship must constitute a *prima facie* reason for supposing that in the form of this story God himself has addressed man.

Certain consequences follow from seeing the incarnation in this way. In the first place, what is identifiable as 'incarnational theology' (of which the Johannine prologue is the first, early beginnings) is not the primary datum for treating the reality of the incarnation. There is sufficient evidence that John himself realized the severity of the theological problem of a Sonship which was at once one with its Father, and yet wholly subordinate.[14] There has never been any final, or single resolution of this difficulty. Rather what the history of Christian doctrine reveals is a series of attempts, of greater or lesser sophistication and degrees of success, at mitigating the inherent difficulties. Under circumstances of acute controversy, decisions were made which validated certain forms of language and anathematized certain propositions (Nicaea). Also, certain expository documents were authorized (at Chalcedon), which provide a degree of guidance. But neither the Nicene creed, nor the Chalcedonian definition, nor the authorized documents, constitute one single orthodox doctrine of the incarnation. Incarnational theology continues to consist of a variety of different articulations of the incarnation, whose primary form is the story of God's self-identification with the human condition.

A second consequence relates to another of the dimensions in which the church actualizes itself, that is, in its worship. When the congregation assembles, it assembles 'in Christ'. That is not the same thing as saying that the church is the extension of the incarnation. Rather, the unique and unrepeatable incarnation of the Son of God becomes the basis of the text and of the offering of the liturgy, by the experience of the common contextualizing of diverse personal backgrounds and intentions in a jointly under-taken liturgical act. 'In Christ' there is an experience of harmony and unity, such that in the liturgical act the community, in its fellowship with the whole body of the church, is a sacrament of Christ himself. The story of the church sacramentally *is* his story; again the inclusiveness of the story of the incarnation is apparent.

Finally, it is evident that attaching to the celebration of the eucharist there is a unique rehearsal and recollection of the story. Here is affirmed in the most realistic manner the inclusion of our humanity in the humanity of the one who offered himself to God. The very story of Jesus itself contains a hierarchy of stories, in which the story of the night on which Jesus was betrayed provides the interpretative canon for the terms on which communion with God is possible. No false dichotomy between theologies of the incarnation and theologies of the cross is possible. We are not fused to God by the inclusive humanity of the incarnate, as though the death of Jesus were merely an unfortunate prelude to his resur-rection and ascension. Nor, on the other hand, are we delivered from false pride by the cross, as though the character and being of the crucified were irrelevant to the stark act of his crucifixion. Rather the whole context of the death of Christ in the story of God's self-identification with man is rehearsed as integral to the understanding of the power of the cross; and the story of the cross as integral to the understanding of the costliness of God's self-identification with man. In the liturgical act of eucharist, accord-ingly, the church is most true to its own identity.

V

This paper has attempted to show in outline how the incarnation functions in the life of the church. It sets out the case for seeing in the incarnation the 'principle of adhesion' by which the complex elements which comprise the reality of the church's life belong to one thing, namely the realization of the purposes of God in the world. In the first place it was acknowledged that the standard, Anglican apologetic for the 'fundamental' character of the incarna-tion was open to devastating objections. In its place a theological analysis was undertaken which attempted to show the integral character of the story of the incarnation to speech about God. Knowledge of God was said to imply conditions by which the true God might be distinguished from false gods. Such conditions were fulfilled only by concrete speech in which God's character is identified in a series of actions, collectively comprising a story. This story is indispensable; and within it the incarnation is an event which is paradigmatic for all other possible stories in which God figures. Finally it was argued that this story has lodged itself in the teaching and worship of the church in such a way that in its rehearsal and realization of the story the church's own identity is proclaimed as included in that of its Lord.

Accordingly the incarnation may be spoken of as the foundation of the church and incarnational theology as the foundation of theology.

NOTES

1. E. C. Hoskyns, 'The Christ of the Synoptic Gospels', *Essays Catholic and Critical*, SPCK 1926, p. 153.

2. On the importance of polemics see F. D. E. Schleiermacher, *Kurze Darstellung des Theologischen Studiums*, ed., H. Scholz, Wissenschaftliche Buchgesellschaft 1969, pp. 17ff.

3. *Reden über die Religion*, G. C. B. Pünjer (ed.), Schwetschke 1879, p. 249.

4. See, e.g. R. C. Moberly, 'The Incarnation as the Basis of Dogma', in *Lux Mundi*, ed., C. Gore, John Murray 1889.

5. Canon B 15A 1(b) of the Canons of the Church of England.

6. Canon C 15.

7. Canon C 26.

8. *Laws of Ecclesiastical Polity*, Book III, i, 4.

9. On the importance of fundamental articles see P. E. More, 'The Spirit of Anglicanism' in *Anglicanism*, P. E. More and F. L. Cross, SPCK 1935, pp. xxiv ff. On ecumenical councils see S. L. Greenslade, 'The English Reformers and the Councils of the Church', *Oecumenica*, Gerd Mohn 1967, pp. 95–113, and H. Chadwick's article in *The Heritage of the Early Church: Essays in Honour of Georges Fiorovsky*, Orientalia Christiana Analecta 195, 1973, pp. 393–408.

10. H. R. Niebuhr, *The Meaning of Revelation*, Macmillan, New York 1941, p. 77.

11. For the argument on this point, see D. H. Kelsey, *The Uses of Scripture in Recent Theology*, SCM Press 1975, pp. 97ff.

12. On the indispensability of realistic narrative see H. W. Frei, *The Eclipse of Biblical Narrative*, Yale University Press 1974, pp. 13ff.

13. On the 'story-relative' identification of God, see R. H. King, *The Meaning of God*, SCM Press 1974, ch. 5.

14. See C. K. Barrett, 'The Father is greater than I' (John 14.28): Subordinationist Christology in the New Testament', in *Neues Testament und Kirche*, ed. J. Guilke, Freiburg 1975, pp. 144–159.

Nicholas Lash's 'Christology and the Future of Truth' could have been included either here or under 7: 'Can *We* Believe in the Incarnation?' It is an affirmative answer to the latter question, but it turns on the interdependence of the doctrines of salvation (especially), of resurrection, of God, and of creation. The reader is also referred to the discussion by Basil Mitchell in the Summing-up Essay.

5 · Is the New Testament Evidence Clear or Ambiguous?

Professor Moule discusses three topics, of which the first is set out above in 3B – including some comments of my own on the essay following – and the third in 4A. It has seemed best to leave his essay in its original form and include it here.

A (i)   Three points of Conflict in the Christological Debate

Charles Moule

Although this essay might be deemed anything but eirenic, the writer hopes that the attempt to locate and identify three points at which the two sides in the debate come into conflict with each other may itself be some aid to mutual understanding, and so may promote the study of their common subject.

The debate is an old one, and has kept on recurring ever since the christological controversies of the fourth and fifth centuries. Changing circumstances have, of course, given each successive recurrence of it a new angle. Today, for instance, the influx of people of other faiths into Britain lends a new urgency to the question of the relation of Christianity to those faiths. But even this is an old and long-debated question which has been carefully thought out long since by responsible theologians; and basically the issues are always the same; and so are the points of conflict. However, to attempt once more to bring these into sharp focus may be of value; and, as a step in this direction, three such points are described in this essay.

(i) *The claim that incarnational language constitutes a threat to personal values*

Broadly speaking, it seems that alike the contributors to *The Myth of God Incarnate* and Professor G. W. H. Lampe, in his Bampton Lectures for 1976, *God as Spirit*, agree in believing that the language of incarnation, if used in a fully distinctive way, is not only unsatisfactory but actually fatal to a realistic and fully personal account of Jesus. In order to understand this, the term incarnation needs to be carefully defined. It must be understood that, in this context, what is meant by incarnation (the Latin for 'enflesh-ing' – Greek, *ensarkōsis*) is a unique and distinctive identification of God's 'Word' – his *Logos* or self-expression – with Jesus. Inspiration is not the same. Inspiration denotes God's breathing into a person – the entry of the divine Spirit into a human being. But inspiration, even if raised to the highest degree, is not synonymous with incarnation as that word has been technically used in christological debate. Into prophets and seers – and, for that matter, into poets and artists – God may enter as Spirit or as Wisdom or as *Logos*. But in Jesus, if we use the language of incarnation technically, the *Logos became* a man of flesh and blood. It is true that John 1.13 claims for all alike who received 'the true light' that they were begotten, not just by physical processes, but by God. Thus, they all, so to speak, had a divine origin. So, too, Nicodemus is told, in John 3, that, to see the Kingdom of God at all, one needs to be 'born of the Spirit', 'born again' or 'born from above'. But in John 1.14 comes the statement that 'the Word became flesh'; and this has traditionally been interpreted as describing something distinct and different and unique. No doubt, etymologically incarnation could mean much the same as inspiration: it could denote the entry of the divine into the human (into 'flesh-and-blood'), as in any inspired person. But the word has been appropriated to mean what might less ambiguously be called 'fleshment' simply (*carnatio*, rather than *incarnatio* – Greek *sarkōsis*). It is not just the *entering* a man, but the *becoming* a man of flesh and blood, the becoming a mortal. It stands for the very antithesis of a docetic view of Jesus.[1] It means that, so far from merely disguising itself in human garb, the utterance of God, his *Logos*, became human.

Now, to use this language of incarnation (say these writers in effect) is to use essentially self-contradictory terms. A divine, pre-existent Being could not conceivably become a man without destroying that man's humanity – destroying that infinitely precious reality which we call his personality. It would be an impossibly chimerical union. None of the heretical attempts to explain the alleged phenomenon in the early controversies worked. Neither Arius nor Apollinarius nor Nestorius nor Eutyches offered any plausible solution. And the *homoousios* formula – that Christ is 'of the same substance' as both God and man – though ultimately agreed upon, was only a confession of defeat – simply the making of a self-contradictory assertion.

Even inspiration *can* be depersonalized, and one needs to discriminate between different conceptions of inspiration. Thus, judged by the direction of biblical theology as a whole, the notion of inspiration as 'possession' – that is, as tyrannous invasion of the human person by the divine – is retrograde. The utterance of the Delphic oracle may be represented as due to the possession and overpowering of the Pythian priestess by a power not her own, which makes her a mere mouthpiece or plays her like a flute. Jewish and Christian writers, too, have sometimes so represented inspiration. But the higher levels of biblical understanding do not think of inspiration in such terms. Rather, the approach of God to man by inspiration is to be thought of as essentially the heightening of the person's own powers by the divine companionship: the making him more of a person, not less.[2]

Accordingly, the language of inspiration needs careful safeguarding, for it can be devalued. Nevertheless, it can be used on a high level, and can serve personal values, whereas to speak of incarnation – it is urged – is necessarily retrograde; for to say that the divine became human, as though there were divine and human 'essences', is to replace terms of a fully personal approach of God to man by sub-personal terms suggesting the mechanical or chemical combination of these two essences or 'stuffs'.

If it is really so, that any 'ontological' language (that is, the language of the Greek philosophical tradition of the early centuries which referred to divine and human 'being' or 'essence'[3]) is necessarily depersonalizing, then it follows that, in order to preserve personal values intact, the language of ontology, including, in effect, incarnation also, must be renounced. There is no difficulty in speaking of Jesus as inspired, provided the meaning is safeguarded. Let us even make it a supreme and superlative degree of inspiration. But to use the language of 'essence' or 'being' (as in incarnational language) is – it is urged – a misconceived attempt to set up a barrier between Jesus and other human beings, and represents a retrograde step towards sub-personal categories. The second conflict-point is –

(ii) The claim that 'ontological' christology is due to fantasy

It was a so-called 'high' christology, reckoning Jesus as uniquely one with God, or, in short, divine, that came ultimately to be expressed in this allegedly undesirable ontological language, because there seems to be no other sort of language that firmly 'pegs' this sort of christology. But (say these writers) the development of a 'high' christology can be explained away. It can be explained as the result merely of processes of divinization in the enthusiastic but mistaken imagination of disciples and devotees – processes which are easily intelligible and can be paralleled in the history of other religions: in antiquity, the elevation, for instance, of a Heracles to the level of a cult deity; and in our own day, a similar phenomenon with some of the nationalist leaders in Africa who have been virtually deified. Thus, it is alleged, we may explain and discount – explain away – the doctrinal elaborations of the years following the death of Jesus.[4] It is a simple progress of the imagination, from a real man of history to a fictitiously divine figure.

Here, then, are two conflict-points in the debate. The position represented by *The Myth* repudiates incarnational language as depersonalizing and unrealistic; and holds that, in any case, claims for Jesus which led to the use of such language can be shown to be unjustified. Before the third is named, here are some reflections on these two.

The first point represents an undeniably attractive position. It is not unlike that of Theodore of Mopsuestia, in the fourth century, when he proposed to describe the union of God and man in terms of Christ's total pleasingness to God, and his constant choice of God's will. It is similar, too, to what was so appealing about D. M. Baillie's book thirty years ago, *God was in Christ*.[5] Its answer to the question, How can God be in Christ? was in terms of 'the paradox of grace'. By this, Donald Baillie meant St Paul's paradox, 'I, yet not I, but the grace of God' (I Cor. 15.10). What Christ, as a fully human person, did of his own volition, turns out to have been done equally by the divine gift (or *charis*) of God within him. Professor Lampe's Bampton Lectures seem to lie very much in the same direction.

But for all its attractiveness, one needs to ask whether this non-'ontological' account of Jesus does not represent an over simplification, and whether it really matches up to the implications of the impact made by Christ both before and after the crucifixion. It is suspiciously like a mere rehabilitation of an old-fashioned (and, many would say, discredited) Liberal Protestantism which drove a wedge between that 'before' and 'after', and entertained such slogans as, 'Let us be rid of Paul! Let us get back to Christ!'[6] Does it match up to the data? For, although 'the paradox of grace' comes from Paul, it is not he who applies it to Christ. Paul uses it of himself. His description of Christ is different: it is in terms of a 'high' christology which, in certain respects, makes Christ distinctive. And it is false to the earliest evidence of the meaning of Christ to ignore this phenomenon. Language which seems to recognize in Christ both the human and the divine may seem to constitute a threat to a fully personal conception of the relation of God to man; but if the data seem positively to require the recognition of a transcendent figure in Paul's experience, and the identification of this transcendent figure with the historical Jesus, it may be that the paradox has to be accepted.

This brings us to the second point, namely, the claim made by those who want to eliminate incarnational language that what points to incarnational language is the result of imaginary attributes bestowed on Jesus by enthusiastic followers as time passed and their grasp on the real, historical figure was weakened. This, however, is contrary to the evidence. There is not space in this essay to set it out in detail; but consider such evidence as the following.

(a) It is a widely held but unexamined assumption that each of the synoptic gospels was intended to present the christology entertained by its author. If this were so, then it might be possible to take the view that the 'high' christology of the Pauline epistles may be counterbalanced by a much less explicit christology read out of the synoptics. It has been claimed[7] that Mark's christology is authoritative and as much a part of the New Testament as Paul's, and that one is justified in choosing Mark rather than Paul. But this is to skate over the question, What was Mark's intention? What is the gospel meant to do? Was he trying to present a fully Christian christology – the christology he himself entertained – or was he, rather, supplementing the sort of christology he and Paul entertained by an account of what Jesus' ministry looked like before the Easter-faith was reached? A strong case can be made for the latter supposition.[8] In the first place, it stands to reason that any preacher presenting such claims for Christ as are reflected (for instance) in the accounts of preaching in the Acts would be open to questions from the audience, such as, Who is this Jesus whom you preach? If he was such as you say, why did he collide with the religious people in his own nation? Why was he crucified? On what grounds do you claim that it was all 'according to the scriptures', that is, in keeping with God's design?

There is no need, for the present argument, to debate whether or not the Acts correctly represents the early preaching. Even without its evidence, the allusions in the Pauline epistles to the original preaching, the primary evangelizing of Paul, endorse enough of the Acts outline for the present purpose. The point is, simply, that any 'post-resurrection' and distinctively Christian preaching of Jesus as crucified and raised, and as Messiah and Fulfiller of scripture, would demand precisely the sort of pre-resurrection explanatory narrative that is offered by the synoptic gospels. This is not to say that their narrative is never anachronous and that post-Easter attitudes are never read back into it. But it is to question whether the assumption is correct that they were meant to present the full christological position of their writers who themselves stood in the post-resurrection era. That they were intended to be ancillary to the apostolic preaching and to provide an account of Jesus preliminary to the Easter-confession is *a priori* a more reasonable assumption.

But there is more than merely *a priori* evidence. If Luke and Acts are by the same author, here is objective evidence that, in his gospel, the author was deliberately refraining from making explicit the very christology which he himself entertained. It is true that Luke, unlike the other synoptists, already calls Jesus Lord (*Kurios*) in the gospel. But he does so only when he is himself, as narrator, referring to Jesus. He refuses, with only the rarest exceptions, to represent the title 'Lord' as used by one of the participants in the story *until the resurrection*. Then, in chapter 24, they say 'The Lord really has risen'. And in the post-resurrection narrative of the Acts, the title is on the lips of Christians frequently. But, until then, Luke's *dramatis personae* do not give him this title. The *vocative, Kurie*, must be ignored for this purpose. All three synoptists represent Jesus' contemporaries as using the vocative *Kurie*, in address to Jesus; and, although in certain contexts it does seem to imply an unusual degree of regard, if not reverence, it is such a common Greek idiom of polite address to any respected human person that it cannot be ranked as a special 'title'. (In this respect it is comparable to the English 'Sir!' which, in the vocative, does not imply a knighthood.) The only exceptions in Luke's gospel narrative (over and above the vocative use) are on the lips of Elizabeth (1.43), on the lips of an angelic messenger (2.11), and, possibly, on the lips of Jesus himself (19.31, cf. verse 34: but this may mean 'the owner' of the colt). Thus it is demonstrable, without the need to raise any questions of historicity, that the author of Luke-Acts regarded the christology expressed by Jesus' own contemporaries in the pre-crucifixion ministry of Jesus as less explicit than that which was entertained after the resurrection. Not that, after the resurrection, the human aspects of Christ (descended from David, etc.) were not prominent. The point is simply that, in Luke's own narrative, he is acclaimed as 'Lord' after but not before. And this means that the two cannot be claimed as alternative and equally valid expressions of christology.[9] It is the Easter acclamation of Jesus as Lord that constitutes the explicitly Christian confession.

As a matter of fact, even the christologies of the synoptists, Mark not excepted, are far too mysterious and pregnant to be interpreted in simple, human terms. The implications, even of those reticent, pre-resurrection estimates are much deeper than can be satisfied by such formulae. As Henry Scott Holland perceived,[10] there is a sense in which the synoptists need an explicit christology such as that of St John (and it would be equally true of

St Paul) to 'solve' the problem which they imply. Thus, Martin Kähler, long ago, was justified in claiming that the Liberal Protestants' re-constructed, rationally intelligible, human Jesus was only a 'so-called historical Jesus', whereas the only Jesus really derivable from the traditions is something more mysterious.[11] Hoskyns and Davey said something similar in *The Riddle of the New Testament*.[12] Even in the synoptic story before the cross, a Jesus who is hailed by some as simply a Davidic messiah is nevertheless shown also as one in whose presence God's sovereignty is realized in an unparalleled way, and as one who assumes an authority such as no prophet had ever dared to assume. Explicit claims for himself are of doubtful authenticity; but the traditions about his authoritative words and acts are good.

(*b*) But if it is not legitimate to claim an apparently 'reduced' christology from (say) Mark – though the reduction even here is more apparent than real – as equally valid with a Pauline 'high' christology, neither is it legitimate to assume that a 'high' christology is the final result of an evolutionary process of pious embroidering due to the lapse of time and to borrowing from saviour-cults and other influences alien to the beginnings of the Christian movement. This point is debated in detail in my book, *The Origin of Christology*. There is not space in a short essay to repeat the argument. It must suffice to say here that some of the 'highest' christology in the New Testament is already present, by implication at least, in the earliest datable documents of the New Testament, that is the earlier epistles of Paul. It is not even necessary to appeal to the so-called 'titles' of Jesus, though these do appear, as a matter of fact, to be rooted firmly in the earliest understandings of him – in some cases, even in his own sayings. But, apart from any titles, the experience of Jesus reflected in the earliest epistles as an inclusive divine presence, as personal indeed but more than individual, and as closely associated with God himself in the bestowal of spiritual blessings, gives the lie absolutely to any theory that relies on the lapse of time and on evolutionary mutations to produce a 'high' christology from the original impact of Jesus. For although Paul uses of Jesus language borrowed from descriptions of ideal humanity – Israel-language and Adam-language – the way he uses it makes it clear that Jesus is recognized as transcending the bounds of humanity. No other figure of recent history was ever identified, in his own generation and by his own contemporaries, as the climax and consummation of all that Israel collectively and mankind as a whole was meant to be. The Qumran documents contain nothing comparable in their references to their teacher.

The second Adam is on the Creator's side of the division between God and man: he is not just a living creature, but a life-giving spirit (I Cor. 15.45). He is mentioned in the same breath with God as the source of spiritual blessings, in the greetings and farewells of the New Testament epistles. *Kurios*, 'Lord', is applied both to Christ and to God, and scriptures relating to the *Kurios* God are boldly applied to the *Kurios* Jesus.

(*c*) Implied in this last phenomenon is a further datum which must not be overlooked. This is the consistent recognition of Jesus as the mediator between God and man. Christians might well be expected to have seen Jesus as no more than a great teacher and a great example. This would have been perfectly in keeping with Jewish traditions beginning with the basic Jewish attitude to Moses himself. Christians could very easily have claimed that because of Jesus – because of what he had taught them and because of what he had shown them by his life and example – they were enabled with new insight and new faith and a new effectiveness to grasp and enter into the presence of God as Spirit. This, moreover, would have brought them none of the stigma of dangerous innovation, and would have made unnecessary their expulsion from the synagogue and their being banned by the Jews as heretics, their being persecuted and martyred. But this eminently reasonable attitude was not adopted. Instead of using the intelligible formula, 'because of Jesus', they insisted on saying that it was *'through Jesus'*, as a mediator always present, that they drew near to God and God drew near to them. This is the more remarkable in that, in Greek, the difference is only the difference between the accusative and the genitive. *Dia* with the accusative means 'because of'; with the genitive, it means 'through'. They adopted the latter.[13] The fact that Mariolatry, in certain limited circles of much later church life, has claimed a comparable mediatorial presence for the Virgin does nothing to negate the uniqueness of this understanding of Christ's presence, which has been a universal feature of Christian liturgy and confession from the earliest days until now. Nor are the apparitions of saints or other departed human beings comparable with this settled doctrinal conviction of the mediatorial presence of the risen Christ.

Evidence of this kind in no way depends on so uncertain a matter as the alleged claims of Jesus nor upon question-begging theories of scriptural authority. It springs simply from the impact made by Jesus on the first generations of the Christian movement. And it indicates something which, as has already been said, seems to require ontological language, including the language of incarnation, to safeguard it. The language of the Chalcedonian formula was not intended to explain, but only to 'peg' certain convictions about Christ. If there is some other language that can safeguard these, without the disadvantages attaching to the Chalcedonian language, by all means let it be used. But until it is discovered, merely to jettison incarnational language without replacing it seems to do less than justice to the phenomena. As a matter of fact, incarnational language is perfectly capable of being used in such a way as not to clash with personal values; but in any case, it is difficult to see how it could be dispensed with without the loss of certain convictions reflected in the most authentic documents of the Christian movement.

(iii) *The soteriological issue*

There is a third conflict-point, which it would be impossible to discuss even cursorily without overstepping the limits of a short essay, but which may simply be named. This is the old, familiar question of the 'soteriological test' of christology – the question 'Can such a Christ be a Saviour?' The contributors to *The Myth* are wide awake to this question, and their answer is that the Christ whom their position implies can be a Saviour and that he does show us that God is redemptively involved in the world's travail. Some would argue, indeed, that to claim any greater degree of assurance for this would be to indulge an illegitimate 'triumphalism' (as it has come to be called). But it has to be confessed that their interpretation of the work of Christ, like every 'exemplarist' interpretation, makes it difficult to explain how the Christian movement was generated just when it was, and why a merely idealistic notion of human destiny (which is what is implied) did not create a 'church' long before (say, as a church of Jeremiah or of the Suffering Servant). It leaves us with a purely individualistic appeal – the appeal of truth and nobility to the best in each individual – and without any gospel of the remaking of man, and, ultimately, without a church and without sacraments. For an ideology and a merely memorialist ritual has nothing to say to man in his weakness and need of a Saviour. The Jesus we are left with by this revival of Liberal Protestantism is a supremely inspired man; but he cannot be said in any distinctive way to have been raised to life through his death or to raise us, except by the persuasion of a sympathetic example: if he was raised, it is only in the sense in which it may be hoped that already all great men and women live on in the sight of God. Still less can he be spoken of as pre-existent.[14] And if, on these terms, we speak of the divinity of Jesus, we must speak also and equally of the inherent divinity of all men, rather than of the divinization of man through Christ. Christ thus becomes no longer the creator, the initiator of the new humanity, but only the supreme example of what man has it in him to become.

But this is a very long story which cannot be pursued here. In the last analysis, this conflict concerns the question whether a fully theistic position does not necessitate a decisive distinction between the Creator and the created, and whether (despite this) the evidence from the beginnings of Christianity does not necessitate a Christ who, paradoxically, is on both sides of that distinction. It is a painful conflict. The logical conclusion of the position occupied by the contributors to *The Myth* is, it seems, Unitarianism, without any distinctively Christian doctrine. And if it be retorted that the logical conclusion of the opposite position is polytheism, the answer lies, perhaps, precisely in the balance of a trinitarian doctrine and in a carefully maintained paradox. True, there is no merit in paradox for its own sake. True, paradox is sometimes grandly invoked when straight nonsense ought to be admitted to. It is a sacred duty for any thinking person to try to eliminate paradox. But if the data refuse to let us escape a paradox, it may be necessary to entertain it.[15] The earliest reflections of the impact made by Christ on his followers show the conviction that the transcendent Person in whom they found new life was continuous with the Jesus of Nazareth who had been crucified. This is what incarnational language struggles to 'peg' or 'fasten' and hold together. Is it not too hasty to call this no true paradox but nonsense? By all means, let us see whether we can reformulate it in some way more acceptable to the philosophical presuppositions of today; but let us not evade it by uncritically cutting the Gordian knot.

NOTES

1. When E. Käsemann argues that St John's gospel is essentially docetic, he has to regard the statement in John 1.14 as secondary to the main thrust of the gospel. See his *Jesu letzter Wille nach Johannes 17*, Tübingen: J. C. B. Mohr 1967, p. 82; ET, *The Testament of Jesus*, SCM Press 1968, p. 44.

2. See, especially, Ch. II of G. W. H. Lampe's *God as Spirit*.

3. For a magisterial examination of this terminology see G. C. Stead, *Divine Substance*, Clarendon Press 1977 – a book too seldom noticed in the furore of 1977.

4. See, e.g., J. Hick, pp. 173–176 of *The Myth of God Incarnate*.

5. D. M. Baillie, *God was in Christ*, Faber & Faber 1948.

6. See F. Prat's summary of this attitude in *The Theology of Saint Paul* ET, Burns, Oates and Washbourne, vol. i, 1945, pp. 22 ff.

7. See, for instance, D. Cupitt, 'The divine Christ – or the real Jesus?', in *The Times*, 17 September 1977.

8. See my essay, 'The Intention of the Evangelists' in *New Testament Essays; Studies in Memory of T. W. Manson*, ed., A. J. B. Higgins, Manchester University Press 1959, pp. 165 ff.

9. See my essay, 'The Christology of Acts', in *Studies in Luke-Acts*: Essays presented to Paul Schubert, ed., L. E. Keck and J. L. Martyn, Nashville/New York: Abingdon Press 1966, London: SPCK 1968, pp. 159 ff. The Lucan phenomenon is, in the main, found also in John.

10. See E. C. Hoskyns (ed. F. N. Davey), *The Fourth Gospel*, Faber & Faber 1947, 45.

11. *Der sogenannte historische Jesus und der geschichtliche, biblische Christus*, Leipzig: A. Deichert 1896; ET (of part) and edition by C. A. Braaten, *The So-called Historical Jesus and the Historic Biblical Christ*, Philadelphia: Fortress Press 1964.

12. E. C. Hoskyns and F. N. Davey, *The Riddle of the New Testament*, Faber & Faber 1931.

13. See my articles, '"Through Jesus Christ our Lord": Some Questions about the Use of Scripture', *Theology* 80.673, January 1977, pp. 30 ff., and 'The Christ of Experience and the Christ of History', ib. 81.681, May 1978, pp. 164 ff.

14. See G. W. H. Lampe, *God as Spirit*, Chs. V and VI, and (e.g.) p. 208.

15. For just criticism of false appeals to paradox, see R. W. Hepburn, *Christianity and Paradox*, Watts 1958; but for the necessity of paradox, see my essay 'The Manhood of Jesus in the New Testament', in *Christ, Faith and History, Cambridge Studies in Christology*, ed., S. W. Sykes and J. P. Clayton, Cambridge University Press 1972, pp. 95 ff.; and for the logical consequences of a reduced christology, see E. L. Mascall's summary in his *Theology and the Gospel of Christ*, SPCK 1977, pp. 206 f.

A (ii) Incarnation or Eschatology?
Michael Goulder

On the scriptural issue, Professor Moule makes three points; of which I take the second first, as he has discussed it at length in *The Origin of Christology*. In this detailed and well-received study he develops two principal arguments to which he refers here, one from Jesus' titles, the other from the church's experience of him as 'an inclusive divine presence'. It is a happy accident that in a controversial area I happen to accept a great deal of his argument, and the reader is thus spared dispute over many technical questions: indeed in *The Myth* I had independently argued for Jesus' application to himself of the terms 'the Son of Man', 'Christ', and 'the Son of God'. Nevertheless it does not seem to me that Moule's argument carries his conclusion, but mine. The point at issue is whether the titles of Jesus, the corporate personality concept and other elements in the New Testament imply *divinity*, and it is at this crucial fence that each of his horses falls.

1. 'The Son of Man', we are agreed, was a title coined by Jesus primarily on the basis of the 'one like unto a son of man' in Daniel 7, who stands for the suffering loyal people of God, whom he will vindicate and entrust with his judgment over the nations, symbolized by the beasts: it had secondary echoes in the Psalms, especially in Psalm 80 where the Israelite king is spoken of as 'the man of your right hand, the son of man you made strong for yourself'. Professor G. B. Caird's words are cited as 'masterly'[1]: the title enabled Jesus 'without actually claiming to be Messiah, to indicate his essential unity with mankind, and above all with the weak and humble, and also his special function as predestined representative of the new Israel and bearer of God's judgment and kingdom'. Moule enthusiastically seconds a further point by Caird that 'the Son of Man' has 'strongly corporate overtones ... (constituting) an invitation to others to join him in the destiny he had accepted'. We agree similarly on 'the old-fashioned belief' that Jesus thought of himself as Messiah (Christ), while rejecting the normal political overtones of the title, and re-interpreting it in a creative and spiritual manner.

'The Son of God', we are similarly agreed, is also a title by which Jesus thought of himself. The title is one of the characteristics of Messiah, as is shown by the Psalms (2;80;89) and II Samuel 7 – these passages being messianically understood in Qumran and rabbinic sources (p. 28). Jesus did not take the title formally, as seems to have been the case with the Israelite kings, but experienced God as his Father in a personal sense, and saw his filial vocation as to obedience and suffering.

Finally, we are agreed that the term 'Lord' (*mare', kyrios*) is one which had both a human and a divine overtone in Aramaic as well as Greek; that it was used both as an invocation (*Marana tha*, 'Our Lord, come') and as a confession ('Jesus is Lord') in the pre-Pauline church; and that it was available as a bridge between an eschatological and an incarnational understanding of Jesus.

So much, then, is agreed: but what seems to be lacking in Moule's argument is any evidence of his claim that Jesus' *divinity* was implicit in these titles from the beginning. He concedes, 'In itself, therefore, the claim that Jesus was "the Son of God" is not necessarily a claim to transcendental status' (p. 28), but argues (in a very compressed, and to me obscure, passage, pp. 28–31, much of it in footnote 33) that Jesus' sonship is so closely associated with the Spirit and baptism as to constitute a high christology. I do not see the force of the argument here, quite apart from wishing to dispute, along with other critics, that many of the texts cited do not go back to Jesus (e.g. Mark 10.38; Matt. 4.1–11; 11.25f.; Luke 2.49).

The truth is that Jewish sources never think of Messiah as divine or pre-existent[2] – in mainstream Judaism he is the descendant of David covenanted in II Samuel 7, 'I will set up thy seed after thee ... I will establish his kingdom for ever'. If Jesus thought of himself as Messiah it is this human figure that he had in mind, with the traditional terms 'the Son of God', 'the Son of Man', 'lord' – all used of human Jewish kings in the Psalter (2.7; 80.18; 110.1 etc.) – re-interpreted and spiritualized. Being a monotheist, Jesus cannot have thought of himself sanely as being Yahweh; and in the more primitive traditions he always speaks of himself in the human, messianic categories discussed by Moule. It is precisely in the later developments that the transcendent vocabulary of the Word of God, the Wisdom of God and the pre-existent cosmic 'beginning' first occur. The titles argument therefore goes against Moule's 'high christology' thesis, not for it: they cohere happily and without exception with the human Messiah view which we find in the Jewish sources, and also in the revealing passage Romans 1.3f., so widely taken as primitive, ' . . .his Son, who was born of the seed of David according to the flesh . . .'.

2. Moule's second argument is from the Pauline sense of Jesus as a *corporate* personality, 'in' whom Christians are, being members of his body and partakers of his Spirit. This 'being in Christ' was an experience as well as an understanding (pp. 47f.), and as such unparalleled in ancient thought (pp. 51f.). The phrases 'in Christ', 'in the Lord' are in a number of instances clear evidence of such a view of incorporation in a transcendent Christ, and at least the 'body of Christ' texts in I Corinthians 6 and 12 view him as 'an inclusive Person, a Body to be joined to which was to become part of him' (p. 81). One can 'put on' Christ, and collective figures like Israel and Adam are applied to him. The argument is crucial for Moule – he devotes more than a quarter of *The Origin of Christology* to it, and returns to it above – 'Paul was led to conceive of Christ as any theist conceives of God: personal indeed but transcending the individual category. Christ is like the omnipresent deity "in whom we live and move and have our being"' (p. 95).

One can have nothing but admiration for the learning and care with which Moule expounds his texts, but surely they do not prove his case. Paul does not speak of *God* as he does of Christ; but rather of *Adam*. Notoriously the phrases 'in God', 'God in us' are almost missing from the Pauline epistles, so that Paul does *not* conceive of Christ as he does of God. Moule's 'in him we live . . .' is Epimenides and Luke, not Paul at all. It is only when Christ has attained a fully divine status, in the Johannine writings, that the language about God and Christ becomes interchangeable. No: there is a hidden leap in the argument from 'transcending the individual' to 'God', which is quite unjustified. The early Christians thought that the last times had begun, the Kingdom of God, the final age; and they accepted the current view that the *Endzeit* was a mirror of the *Urzeit*. Paul's own exposition in Romans 5 and I Corinthians 15 is an antithesis between Adam as 'transcending the individual category' and Christ. Adam, and Abraham, Israel and the Danielic Son of Man, are all *human* corporate personalities which Moule notes himself: but to Paul the primary one is Adam. Moule is right that incorporation is primarily not a concept but an experience, and for this experience we must look to the phenomena of the Spirit described in I Corinthians 12 and elsewhere. But for an explanation of Paul's conceptualizing we are pointed unwaveringly to Adam; to eschatological, not divine categories. The first Adam is balanced by the last Adam. 'As in Adam all die' (as is obvious) 'so in Christ' (here is the good news, already tasted in the Spirit) 'shall all be made alive'.[3]

Moule appeals to the earlier epistles of Paul, and for matters like the corporate personality of Jesus such appeal is justified; and so it is for the greetings of grace and peace from 'God the Father and the Lord Jesus Christ' in I Thessalonians 1.1 and elsewhere. Such close association of Jesus with God is not so very remarkable however. Even so modern an author as Archbishop Cranmer continually uses the phrase 'God and the King' in his letters: 'it was rare indeed for Cranmer, except in his liturgical writings, to write the name of the Almighty without bracketing it with that of Henry VIII.'[4] How much more is this bound to have been the case when the King was God's own Christ, his viceroy, his Son, now raised from death and enthroned in heaven at God's right hand! Paul believed that Jesus was in heaven governing the church through his Spirit till his return: it would be unimaginable for him to greet the church with blessings from God and not from the Lord Jesus Christ, and he invariably brackets the two. But his reign was under God the Father: the time would come when he would deliver the kingdom to God the Father (I Cor. 15.24).[5]

For other matters, though, Moule refers to later letters, such as Philippians, where the *kyrios* of Isaiah 45.23 is God, but in Paul's version Jesus. The theory I proposed in *The Myth* is that incarnational ideas were developed in debate with the other missionaries referred to in the Corinthian letters; and it is not answered by showing that in letters after that Paul thought Jesus was divine – indeed he says as much in Philippians 2.6. The same goes for 'the life-giving spirit' of I Corinthians 15.45. The incorporation of Christians in Christ is there from the beginning, and is an eschatological idea; that the second man was from heaven, or was the rock in the desert, are ideas developed in the dialectic of the 50s at Ephesus.

The two new points, (*a*) and (*c*), which Moule adduces in this book, are less important. It is possible to discriminate a simpler, more Jewish christology both in the gospels and in the early preaching in Acts 2 and 13; and also in some of Paul's own writings, especially Romans 1.3f. and Galatians 3. Moule says that Jesus' unparalleled authority in the synoptic traditions requires the higher Pauline view; the instances commonly urged in this connection are Jesus' claim to transcend the Law, as no prophet had done, or to forgive sins. But again there is a leap in the argument: more than a prophet, he must be divine. But the gospel provides the category of thought which bridges the gap. Jesus did not think that he was a prophet, but that he was the Messiah/the Son of Man; not that he was God, but that he was God's viceroy. It is the Son of Man who has power on earth to forgive sins (Mark 2.12). It is the Son of Man who is lord even of the sabbath (Mark 2.28). Hoskyns' riddle does not require Paul's developed solution. Nor does Jesus' mediatorship take us to incarnationalism. Exactly the same objections apply. It is the bias of orthodoxy constantly to overlook middle terms. The earliest church saw Jesus neither as its great Teacher and example nor as God the Son, but as the man whom God raised up and gave him the Holy Spirit to pour out upon the church (Acts 2.33).

So it seems to me that Moule cannot prove his biblical case any more than he can overcome the primary difficulty of saying what the traditional doctrine is. The evidence is that till the 50s Jesus was thought of as Messiah, who had initiated the last days and formed a new body of salvation, to which men could be transferred from the body of death in Adam. I do not repent of my proposal that it was through the adherence of Samaritan converts that the church of the 50s came to think of him as pre-existent and divine; though I do repent of trying to expound so novel a view in twenty-five pages in a controversial best-seller. But even if Moule's case were conclusive, it would still avail nothing unless he can say what the case is meant to assert. The biblical discussion is really secondary – pegs in the game of Peggotty.

NOTES

1. *The Origin of Christology*, p. 20.
2. The *name* of Messiah is created before the world according to rabbinic traditions (b Pes.54a, Ned.39b etc.), but that is a very different thing from Messiah's own pre-existence. See G. F. Moore, *Judaism*, Cambridge 1927, I p. 526, II pp. 344, 348.
3. Cf. C. K. Barrett, *From First Adam to Last*, A. & C. Black 1962, R. Scroggs, *The Last Adam*, Oxford University Press 1966.
4. J. Ridley, *Thomas Cranmer*, Oxford University Press 1962, p. 257.
5. For a rabbinic parallel to the exaltation of a human Jesus to a throne alongside God, cf. bHag. 14a, where R. Akiba interprets the 'throne' of Dan. 7.9 as 'one for Him and one for David'.

A (iii) A Comment
Charles Moule

I believe that Dr Goulder in his critique of my statements in *The Origin of Christology* and in my essay here interprets the data with an unjustified simplicity in several respects. There is his *divide et impera* technique, taking the data separately one by one and ignoring the evidence of their cumulative force. There is his over-tidy treatment of each datum, turning a blind eye to the rebellious bits of it which refuse to conform to his interpretation. And there is his doctrinal simplification, allowing in effect no alternatives but the interpretation of Jesus as no more than human and the assumption (false, as both Dr Goulder and I believe) that he went about saying 'I am God', and that 'Jesus is God' is an adequate doctrinal statement. Moreover, although at times Dr Goulder remembers that my book is an attempt to interpret the impact made by Jesus on his own and the next generation, he finds it difficult not to lapse into believing that my argument depends on recovering the *ipsissima verba Iesu* – which it does not.

And now some notes on his piecemeal criticisms.

(*i*) 'Son of God' is a role associated with a purely human Messiah, he says. Agreed, of course! But messianic sonship implies status, protection by Yahweh, 'success'. What is implied by the traditions about Jesus' filial consciousness is something not messianic at all, but deeper: immediacy of approach, insight into and complete unity with God's character and will – 'a vocation to obedience and suffering', as Dr Goulder rightly puts it. And in Romans 1.3f., which he adduces, the Davidic tradition, so far from negating everything but his humanity, is deliberately contrasted though still held together with the transcendental sonship which his resurrection declared. I would be slower than Dr Goulder to call 'Son of God' 'a title by which Jesus thought of himself'. Certainly we are agreed that he did not go about saying, 'I am God's Son'. But his exceptional filial consciousness is attested (whether or not 'many of the texts do not go back to Jesus') by the impression left on the traditions concerning his actions and words; and (a point which Dr Goulder says he failed to follow) the fact that the nexus between Spirit, sonship, death, and life appears both in the gospels and the epistles, and yet in such a way as to suggest no direct copying of one from the other but a derivation from what Jesus was and did, is itself further evidence in the same direction. The lustral rites so common in religions generally were given an unusual and special content in Christian baptism – filial obedience even to death, accompanied by Spirit and life, all derived from the death and aliveness of Jesus. This is difficult to dismiss as evidence of nothing but a messianic type of sonship in Jesus.

(*ii*) I do not, as Dr Goulder seems to think that I do, regard the words *mare* and *kurios* as forming a bridge from an eschatological to an incarnational estimate of Jesus. I do not use the category 'eschatological' anyway. I merely point out that a *linguistic* bridge exists from the Semitic words *mare* and *âdōn* to the Greek *kurios*, which means that as a title for Jesus *kurios* need not be derived from Hellenistic saviour-cults. Once again, moreover, Dr Goulder is over-simplifying when he dismisses *kurios* as a merely messianic category. Whatever Psalm 110 may originally have meant, its Christian use is expressly designed to recognize something more than messianic in *kurios*, as, of course, are early Christian uses of scriptures where '*kurios* = Yahweh' becomes '*kurios* = Jesus'. Dr Goulder's attempt to show that this represents a declension away from the realities after AD 50 is highly speculative.

(*iii*) About 'incorporation' language: I said that certain instances of the Pauline *en Christō(i)* (or *en kuriō(i)*, etc.) are such as to suggest that Paul found himself in the same sort of relation to Christ as that in which many a theist (including Paul) finds himself to God. Dr Goulder replies that phrases using *en* with God are lacking (or almost lacking) from Paul himself. It is not Paul, he points out, but Epimenides, placed by Luke on the lips of Paul, who talks about men as living and moving and having their being in God. Dr Goulder's 'almost' is correct; but he does not specify the exception to which it alludes. The fact is that Paul does use *en theō(i)* (side by side with (*en*) *kuriō(i) Iesou Christō(i)*, too) in I Thessalonians 1.1 and (if it is Pauline) also in II Thessalonians 1.1. It is precisely in his earliest phase, or one of his earliest phases, that Paul does use the two phrases together. Dr Goulder sheds that tell-tale 'almost' as he goes on to develop his point. However, let that pass. My argument would still stand, even if Paul had not used the phrase 'in God', for 'being in God' remains a theistic idea, and 'being in Christ' presents a striking analogy to it. It is not true, moreover, that I make a leap from the use of incorporative language in descriptions of a relation to Christ which suggest that he transcends individuality to the conclusion that he is God. My conclusion is that Paul's experience of Jesus is like an experience of God and unlike the experience of a mere human individual. Again, it is one more over-simplification to say that because Adam means Man, and because 'in Adam' and 'in Christ' are parallel phrases, *ergo* Paul is calling Christ simply human, not divine. I would be tempted, were it not a cheap debating point, to ask whether Dr Goulder thinks that Ezekiel's God was but a man because of Ezekiel 1.26. One has to ask about contrasts as well as parallels. Is it evidence of a no more than human estimate when an individual of recent history is spoken of in these inclusive, generic terms? And is it the function of a merely human person to bestow life? Is creation a normal human function? Or the bestowal of Spirit? As for Cranmer's coupling of the name of God with the name of a still living sovereign, the superficiality of the comparison hardly requires to be pointed out. And if the coupling of God and a former human leader is so natural that 'it would be unimaginable for [Paul] to greet the church with blessings from God and not from the Lord Jesus Christ', why do Jews not couple God and Moses in the same role?

(*iv*) About the christology of the synoptic gospels, I claim that the christology represented by the *dramatis personae* of the synoptic gospels must not be assumed to be the evangelists' own christology so that a simpler (say, a Marcan) christology may be claimed as more primitive, more Jewish, nearer to reality than Paul's. This point – that the so-called 'primitive' christologies are reconstructions of what obtained *before* the essential Christian realization of the resurrection – Dr Goulder ignores, thus dodging the question 'What precipitated the earliest post-crucifixion christologies?' Instead, he concentrates on the other side of my claim for the synoptic gospels, namely that as a matter of fact, despite their reticence, they do reflect something more than a man – for instance, in the unparalleled authority of Jesus. He assumes that by this I mean claims to transcend the Law and to forgive sins. But neither of these would I adduce. What I mean is something deeper: the quietly assumed and exhibited presence of God's sovereignty where Jesus was.

(*v*) Finally, Dr Goulder protests that he does not understand what my interpretation of the evidence is meant to assert. It is meant to assert that the impact made by Jesus on his own and the next generation was such as precludes an estimate of him as no more than a man. This is what led to the christological controversies of the early church and ultimately to the framing of a formula designed to exclude both polytheism and unitarianism – a formula which, whatever its shortcomings, seems to me a more subtle and faithful attempt to catch the puzzling phenomena than a simplistic 'either-or' – either that Jesus was nothing more than a man or that he was 'God' without further qualification. Serious Christian theology has never tolerated such over-simplification.

B (i)   Incarnational Christology in the New Testament
Graham Stanton

The essays gathered together in *The Myth of God Incarnate* raise a number of inter-related issues. Two of them are of particular interest to the student of the New Testament. The contributors share the conviction that unless the New Testament documents are read in the light of much later doctrinal statements, the traditional doctrine of the incarnation is less easy to find in its pages than is usually supposed. Several of the essayists insist that the origin and development of incarnational language was culturally conditioned, both in the New Testament period and in christological reflection and controversies in the following three hundred years.

Some readers may be surprised that I have not seized immediately on the word 'myth', the word which provoked the rather frenzied reaction to the publication of the essays. I should not be unhappy to refer to the incarnation as 'myth', since 'myth' can be defined carefully with a positive sense which allows room for a historical element. However 'myth' is a word I should prefer to avoid with reference to the incarnation since it is used in very varied ways and is often taken (even by theologians) to mean 'untrue' or 'delusive'.[1] In recent decades 'demythologizing' has been discussed frequently by New Testament scholars and many have attempted (not always successfully) to draw a distinction between functional and ontological language. Further questions concerning the nature of christological language have not received the attention they deserve. Metaphor, analogy, symbol, parable, story and myth are all found in the earliest christological confessions, acclamations and statements. What is the significance of this? Why are some christological expressions used in particular contexts, but not in others? To what extent is there a difference between language about God and language about Christ?

Before progress can be made in that direction it is important to consider as carefully as possible the *theological principles* which are being expressed by New Testament writers who do use what may be called incipiently incarnational language. The phrase 'theological principles' has been chosen deliberately. To ask whether the doctrine of the incarnation is to be found in the New Testament is to ask the wrong question. For one is then bound to argue *either* that the New Testament evidence is in line with, *or* that it is out of line with the classic christological formulations of the Patristic period. The first-century evidence will be read in the light of one's own convictions about Chalcedon.

Some of the christological emphases of the New Testament writers were not central in the later debates and some of the later concerns were of little interest within the New Testament period. Judged by later standards parts of the New Testament may seem to reflect a very 'low' christology, but in a first-century Jewish context those same affirmations about Jesus may have been extremely bold and even quite unprecedented. One could well argue that some of the christological expressions which seem to be most closely related to later incarnational christology, were, in a first-century context, not necessarily among the most 'far-reaching' and 'radical' christological claims. The pre-existence of Jesus, which seems to us to be a difficult notion, is perhaps a good example : given first-century presuppositions, it was not an unnatural affirmation for some of the first Christians to make. New Testament writings must be considered as thoroughly and sensitively as possible against the background of the varied Jewish and Hellenistic currents of the first century. They must not be pressed for answers to later questions and problems.

An insistence on reading the New Testament writings in their first-century context raises immediately the question of cultural conditioning. Of course the earliest christological claims about Jesus were culturally conditioned! How could the earliest followers of Jesus have expressed their convictions about him without drawing on the categories with which they (and their hearers and readers) were familiar? If they had not done this, expression and communication of their claims would have been impossible. This is such an obvious point that it is surprising that so much space is taken up in *The Myth of God Incarnate* demonstrating that incarnational language used by Christians in the first and later centuries was culturally conditioned. The much more significant point (which is scarcely made in *The Myth*) is that when New Testament 'incarnational' christology is examined carefully with the tools of historical criticism, it frequently runs *against* first-century Jewish and Hellenistic religious currents. Available categories are used, but *always* with qualification. No one category is ever taken over and used on its own; each category is always profoundly modified by being set in juxtaposition with one or more other categories.

The earliest Christians frequently stole the clothes of those to whom they were seeking to say something about Jesus, but the clothes had to be redesigned before they could be of use.

I am prepared to follow the lead of first-century Christians. Their clothes may have to be refurbished, but I am not prepared to throw them away. Even if it is an exaggeration, Gerhard Ebeling's hermeneutical dictum must be taken seriously : 'The *same word* can be said to another time only by being said differently.'[2] The traditional doctrine of the incarnation may need restatement, but the theological principles being expressed by New Testament writers can and must still be taken seriously.

In the pages which follow we shall not lose sight of the question of cultural conditioning, but we shall concentrate on some New Testament passages which refer to the 'sending' of Jesus by God. Although the phraseology of the various passages differs, they all stress the initiative of God in the 'sending' of Jesus. They are certainly incipiently incarnational, even though they were not always at the centre of later christological discussion.

Our starting point is one of the most striking passages in the Pauline epistles, Galatians 4.4f.: 'When the time had fully come, God sent forth his Son, born of a woman, born under the law, to redeem those who were under the law, so that we might receive adoption as sons.' Paul uses 'Son of God' much less frequently than 'Lord', but statistics are often misleading. 'Son of God' is found in a number of passages in which carefully phrased theological statements concerning the relationship of Jesus to God are being used. It is no coincidence that 'Son of God', or, more often, 'his Son' is nearly always used immediately after a reference to God.

Paul's letters do not lead us to suppose that a 'Son of God' christology is being advanced for the first time, as Paul assumes that his readers are familiar with the phrase from initial missionary preaching. In several passages there are good reasons for supposing that Paul is quoting an earlier 'formula'; though this cannot be established conclusively. A 'Son of God' christology is certainly found within a very few years of the crucifixion. It is not a late development which arose as a result of contact with the Hellenistic world or with Samaritan views.[3]

What christological affirmation is intended by 'God sent his Son'? Within the Old Testament and later Jewish writings, as well as in the New Testament itself, there are many references to the sending by God of prophets, wise men, scribes, messengers and other men. Could 'his Son' in Galatians 4.4. be taken as a reference to Jesus as a prophet? After all, both Israel and the king are referred to as 'Son of God' in the Old Testament.

For Paul, Jesus is 'Son of God' in a *unique* sense. The opening phrase of Galatians 4.4, 'in the fullness of time' reflects Paul's eschatology which is so central in his theology. The sending of Jesus is both the fulfilment of God's promises and the inauguration of a new humanity. The purpose of the sending is redemptive; Jesus is not merely a herald of salvation, for God's sending of him is itself God's redemptive act. While the phrase 'his Son' does not necessarily imply the pre-existence of Jesus, there are a number of passages in Paul's writings in which it is implied, so we may assume that this is the case here.

The Son's humanity is stressed : he is born and lives as a Jew of his time. Side by side with this, but without a hint of an uncomfortable juxtaposition, the Son sent in the fullness of time is, for Paul, pre-existent. Here we have the elements of an incarnational christology, but the accent is not on the incarnation *as such*, or on the Son as a heavenly teacher or revealer (as in some later incarnational christologies), but on God's initiative in redemption by sending Jesus at a particular point in time. In this passage Paul's eschatology, his soteriology and his christology merge together. Indeed, we can go further, for the following verses speak of God's sending of the Spirit whereby Christians (as adopted sons) are enabled to cry 'Abba Father!' The opening section of Galatians 4 contains one of the most important tap-roots not only of incarnational christology, but also of trinitarian theology.

The pre-existence of the Son is found in Paul, but it is rarely developed. What is its background? The closest parallels are to be found in Hellenistic Jewish writings which refer to the sending of God's power, wisdom or logos, and to the logos as God's Son. The background of Galatians 4.4 (and further confirmation that pre-existence is implied) is probably to be found in Wisdom of Solomon 9.10 and 17.[4] Here the sending of Wisdom from heaven and the sending of God's Spirit from heaven are set alongside each other, just as the sending of the Son and of the Spirit are in Galatians 4. Solomon prays to God: 'Send her (Wisdom) forth from the holy heavens ... so that she may labour at my side and I may learn what pleases thee ... Whoever learnt to know thy purposes, unless thou hadst given him wisdom and sent thy holy spirit down from heaven on high?' Here Wisdom is a guide or teacher. In Galatians, however, the sending of the Son is not a timelessly valid statement, but a unique and definitive act. There is no parallel in

Hellenistic Judaism to the sending of the Son as one who had died a shameful death just a few years earlier. In Galatians, but not in the Wisdom of Solomon we have an eschatological and soteriological note. The parallel passage from Wisdom provides a good example of cultural conditioning, but also of Paul's modification and qualification of notions which were to hand.

Earlier in Galatians there are two important passages which shed further light on the 'sending of the Son'. At 3.13f. redemption and the gift of the Spirit, which are so central at the beginning of chapter 4, are both mentioned. But in this section of his letter Paul insists that the one who overcomes the curse of the Law is Abraham's heir. In other words, however unique and decisive the sending of the Son is, that sending is to be related to God's acts in the history of Israel. In the second passage (Gal. 2.20), it is not God who sends forth his Son, but the Son of God who takes the initiative himself and 'gives' himself : ' . . . I live by faith in the Son of God, who loved me and gave himself for me.' Galatians 2.20 and 4.4f. provide an example of actions and intentions being shared by God and Jesus, or transferred from one to the other. Galatians 2.20 also confirms just how closely the 'sending' of Jesus is related to the crucifixion for the immediate context of this verse suggests that here Paul has in mind the death of Jesus rather than his coming into the world. The same verb, 'give' or 'give up', is used at Romans 8.32, where there is a clear allusion to the sacrifice of Isaac: 'God did not spare his own Son but gave him up for us all . . . ' Here the initiative is God's and the 'giving up' includes the cross. At Romans 8.3 God's sending of his Son into the world and the death of Jesus are probably both in mind.

In all these passages the 'sending' or 'giving' of the Son is soteriological. There is no speculation or emphasis on pre-existence. Paul's concern is with the saving activity of God. This is confined neither to the 'sending' of the Son into the world (the 'incarnation') nor to the crucifixion, for both are in view. For Paul the *sending*, as well as the death and the raising of Jesus, mark the dawn of the eschatological time of salvation.[5]

Paul affirms both that the Son was sent in the fullness of time for us and that Jesus has been vindicated and is now exalted as Lord. How are these two quite different kinds of christological statement related to one another?

The 'kyrios' christology expresses the authority of the Lord over the individual and the Christian community and it is often related to ethical statements. The 'Son of God' christology expresses the close relationship between God and Jesus and the initiative of God in redemption.[6] These two christologies are used in different contexts and are very rarely brought together by Paul. This should cause us to hesitate before attempting to decide which of the two is chronologically prior.

There is, however, one passage where the two christologies are brought together quite deliberately. At Romans 1.3f. Paul quotes an early credal formula in which the designation of Jesus as 'Son of God' is linked with the resurrection. This is quite unlike the use of 'Son of God' in the other Pauline passages. But right at the beginning of the credal formula Paul's favourite phrase 'his Son' is used[7] and it is linked closely to the gospel of *God* : Paul, ... set apart for the gospel of God ... the gospel concerning his Son ...' A few verses later Paul refers again to the 'gospel of his Son' (1.9) and at 1.16 the nature of the gospel is clarified : it is the power of God for salvation to every one who has faith. 'Gospel', 'Son' and 'salvation' are closely related and in each case 'God' is the subject. In this emphasis on the redemptive activity of God through his Son we are very close to Galatians 4.4f. In Romans 1.3f. the initial reference to 'his Son' is characteristically Pauline, but the reference to Son of God in the clauses which follow ('*declared Son of God ... by his resurrection* from the dead') is not found elsewhere in Paul : for this and other reasons it is taken by most scholars to be a quotation of an earlier credal formula. Paul *modifies* the traditional statement by prefixing 'his Son' in a way which alters the accent of the formula which follows. He wishes to say more about Jesus than the credal formula's statement that Jesus was a prophet (or Messiah) of David's line who was raised from the dead: it was *God's Son* who was descended from David according to the flesh and *declared Son of God* in power ... *by his resurrection* from the dead. The result may be clumsy : its very awkwardness confirms that here we have two different christologies which are not fully integrated.

For Paul a 'kyrios' christology and a 'Son of God' christology are complementary. If either were taken in isolation, the underlying conception would move too close to well-known Jewish or Hellenistic categories. The Son of God is not merely a heavenly revealer; Jesus is not merely a human being exalted as Lord and given an authority 'independent' of God. In Romans 1, as in Romans 8.3 and 32 and Galatians 4.4f., the 'sending' of the Son is soteriological; it is a unique and decisive event which marks God's fulfilment of his promises. The sending and crucifixion of the Son and the resurrection/exaltation of Jesus as Lord are inseparable in Paul's thinking, even though they are rarely (and then only awkwardly) brought together.

The so-called christological hymn at Philippians 2.6–11 is an exception. Here the two forms of christology we have been discussing are found side by side.[8] Although Son of God is not used, it would not have been inappropriate, for the opening phrases into which so much is packed so tersely must surely be taken as incipiently incarnational.

In a number of Pauline passages (not all of which have we referred to) we find the beginnings of an incarnational christology. But Paul is often silent just at the point where his readers in later centuries have craved for more explicit statements. What Paul does *not* say is almost as important as what he does say. Very little is said about the pre-existence of Jesus and little about the precise relationship of Jesus to God. On the one hand, it is not the sending of the Son into the world which *per se* is redemptive. On the other hand, the death of Jesus is never important just because the Son is pre-existent.[9] The incarnational elements in Paul's christology are eschatological and soteriological; the sending of the Son is not an epiphany, for the humanity of Jesus is never lost sight of.

Did Paul consider Jesus to be 'divine'? The answer would appear to be clear: Jesus stood in the closest possible relationship to God, for his favourite phrase 'his Son' points to the similarity, as it were, of God and Jesus, rather than to their 'difference'. But this raises the question of 'cultural conditioning' in an even more acute way. For the most important influence of all on Paul was the Old Testament. How could Paul square his convictions about Jesus with the strong monotheistic teaching of the scriptures?

While the scriptures spoke freely of theophanies, of angels and even of intermediaries, this was never at the expense of monotheism. The strength of this conviction can hardly be over-estimated. Within the varied currents of first-century Judaism, with their increased interest in God's angels, helpers or intermediaries, there was always resistance to binitarian or ditheistic thinking.

Some of the boldest steps were taken by Philo. He can speak of the 'second God' (*deuteros Theos*) who is the logos of the Most High One. But Philo rebuts any possible charge that he is compromising monotheism by insisting that the 'second God' is only the visible emanation of the High, ever-existing God.[10]

Philo was not alone. In apocalyptic traditions which are roughly contemporary with the first decades of Christianity and in Jewish mystical traditions, some of which may go back to the same period, there is no shortage of speculation on angels and mediators. At times these traditions come within a hair's breadth of positing a 'power' in heaven independent of God. But such traditions do not seem to have aroused the ire of more 'orthodox' Jews, presumably because they were not felt to compromise monotheism.

There are a number of rabbinic traditions in which sects which did posit 'two powers in heaven' are attacked as heretical. These polemical traditions, which have often baffled scholars, have recently been studied with more refined historical methods and dated confidently to Palestine in the early second century, though the polemic may well be much older.[11] The rabbis did not object to heavenly beings, but they were particularly scrupulous to avoid the suggestion that any heavenly being could exercise independent authority. Whom were they attacking? In all the earliest traditions the second figure is seen as a complementary figure, a divine helper; it is clear that in many cases Christians are in view.[12]

It is impossible to trace a direct line from this Jewish polemic against Christians back to Paul. But we may be confident that Paul was aware of the danger that his christological statements could be taken to compromise monotheism. It is for this reason that Paul is reluctant to call Jesus *Theos*. God is one.[13] This particular 'cultural conditioning' must be borne strongly in mind in discussion of Paul's christology. It is quite likely that Paul chose to speak of Jesus as God's *Son* in some of his most carefully measured theological statements because he wished to stress as clearly as possible the 'closeness' of the relationship between Jesus and God as well as the humanity of Jesus. But Paul did not play into the hands of his Jewish opponents by portraying Jesus as an independent authority in heaven who descended to earth on his own initiative to disclose to men the knowledge of their redemption.

Paul's rich and varied christological expressions do include elements which can be called incarnational. Of these, one of the most important is his use of 'Son of God'. This is undoubtedly 'culturally conditioned', but as we have seen, the closest parallel in Hellenistic Judaism serves to underline distinctive and important features in Paul's thinking about Jesus. God's sending of his Son is a unique and decisive act of redemption; it is wholly 'new', but it is in continuity with God's relationship with Israel and marks its fulfilment. Redemption and reconciliation are on God's initiative, not man's discovery. With a nice turn of phrase Frances Young contrasts Arius and Athanasius : 'Where Arius severed the mediator from God, Athanasius severed him from the world.'[14] Paul held both together tenaciously and insisted both that God sent forth his Son into the world to redeem men, and that Jesus was born of a woman, born under the law.

In the Johannine writings there are close parallels to the Pauline 'sending' passages.[15] John 3.17 and Galatians 4.4 are strikingly similar in structure, even though the wording is not identical:

> God sent the Son into the world ... in order that the world might be saved through him.

> God sent forth his Son ... in order that he might redeem those who were under the law.

Since there is no question of direct dependence of the fourth evangelist on Paul's epistles, many scholars have concluded that John and Paul are drawing independently on an early christological 'formula'. This seems very probable. John and Paul certainly share several important convictions about Jesus. But does the fourth evangelist move far beyond Paul in his incarnational theology? In particular, has Paul's 'born of a woman' been lost sight of, so that the earthly life of Jesus is an epiphany? Does the incarnation *in itself* have redemptive significance?

E. Käsemann's famous dispute with Bultmann over the interpretation of Johannine christology has sharpened up the issues at stake. Käsemann quotes two passages from Bultmann's commentary which summarize Bultmann's position :

> If the glory had not been there, there could be no talk of revelation. But this is precisely the paradox, which runs through the whole Gospel; the *doxa* is not to be seen alongside the *sarx* or through it, as through something which is transparent, yet it is to be seen nowhere else than in the *sarx* and our regard must continually and firmly be fixed on the *sarx* and never allow itself to be drawn away, if its desire is to see the *doxa*. Revelation is therefore present in a peculiar hiddenness.

> But it is man and only man who is immediately accessible and not the *Logos*; that this man is the *Logos*, I can in any event know only outside of and alongside my knowledge of him as man. But this means that, in any such understanding of the *Logos*, becoming man is never seen as the decisive event of revelation. Thus the Johannine portrayal of the Revealer who has become flesh has no trace of immediate accessibility; to meet him is to be faced with a question, not to be persuaded of something.

Käsemann maintains emphatically that he who has become flesh does not cease to exist as a heavenly being; that he undergoes no 'transformation'.[16] Incarnation for John is really epiphany. For Käsemann the centre of gravity in the evangelist's christology is not, 'the Logos became flesh', but, 'we saw his glory'.

At this point, at least, Bultmann is correct. Käsemann believes that it is not without reason that two millenia have loved the

Fourth Gospel because it portrayed Jesus as the God who walked the earth. There are parts of the Fourth Gospel which could easily be misconstrued in this direction, but there are many passages which clearly run in the other direction.[17] For example, the signs are not open proof that the *Logos* has become flesh. They do not compel belief. The first sign at Cana concludes: 'and his disciples believed in him', but nothing is said about the response of others who witnessed what happened. In the following verses Jesus is asked by the Jews for a sign to *support* his extraordinary conduct in 'cleansing' the Temple (2.18). The Jews want, but are denied, open proof. In this passage not even the disciples understand the words of Jesus; only after the resurrection did they believe the scripture and the word which Jesus had spoken. At 12.37, which, according to C. H. Dodd's analysis, opens the epilogue to the Book of Signs, the evangelist himself carefully points out that signs do *not* necessarily lead to faith.

There is a 'secret' in the Fourth Gospel which the opponents of Jesus are unable to unravel : they may speak with Jesus and see his actions and fail to discern anything significant. Morna Hooker has observed that in every debate between Jesus and the Jews where the teaching of Jesus is rejected, the point at issue is the question of Jesus' origin : those who reject him fail to recognize that he is 'from above'. The 'secret' which is hidden from the crowd is not the mystery of the kingdom, not the messianic identity of Jesus, but the glory spoken of in the Prologue.[18]

'We have seen his glory' (1.14) does not mean that John's Jesus is God striding the earth with feet which barely touch the ground. There are passages which, taken in isolation, might seem to suggest this, but they are exceptions which prove the rule. One such passage is 18.6, where those sent to arrest Jesus fall back to the ground when Jesus says '*Ego eimi*; I am'. Nonetheless Jesus does not escape arrest and the evangelist quickly repeats the unwitting prophecy of Caiaphas, 'it is expedient that one man should die for the people' (18.14). In this way the evangelist draws particular attention to the purpose for which the Son was sent into the world : he died not for the nation alone, but to gather together the scattered children of God (11.52).

In one of the most dramatic statements in the gospel Jesus proclaims, 'I and the Father are one' (10.30). This might seem to support Käsemann's position, but there are passages which expound that statement in another direction. For example, at 12.44–50, where the evangelist carefully summarizes the themes of the preceding discourses, Jesus says, 'He who believes in me, believes not in me, but in him who sent me ... I have not spoken on my own authority; the Father who sent me has himself given me commandment what to say and what to speak.'

The evangelist may well have been aware of Jewish polemic against those who believed that there were 'two authorities in heaven'. Jewish opposition to the Johannine community would have echoed the words of 10.33, 'We stone you for no good work but for blasphemy, because you, being a man, make yourself God'. But the evangelist takes great pains to stress in passages such as 10.36ff. and 8.29 that Jesus, the Son of God, is sent by *the Father* and does not speak or act independently.

Käsemann has exaggerated the difference between Johannine Christianity and other strands of early Christianity. The heart of 'incarnation' christology in the Fourth Gospel, as in Paul, lies in the sending of the Son, who was born of a woman, the Logos who became flesh. 'We saw his glory' (1.14) and 'We have received grace ...' (1.16) are the cries of the believing community in the light of the crucifixion/exaltation of Jesus; the 'glory' is never displayed except to the eyes of faith.

In the Fourth Gospel the 'incarnation' is not to be separated from the passion. There is a sense in which the whole work is a 'passion gospel', for the proclamation of Jesus' death is at least as prominent in the gospel's first half as in the second. With respect to allusions to the crucifixion, there is no turning point in John comparable with Mark 8.[19]

There are, then, important theological principles which Paul and John share. Neither has a doctrine of the incarnation in the sense that the incarnation has significance independent of the crucifixion and resurrection/exaltation of Jesus. This happens for the first time in Ignatius, and is found frequently in later Christian writers.[20] But both Paul and John have 'incarnational' elements in their christologies. Both insist that the sending of the Son is God's redemptive act: it is God's initiative, not man's discovery. For both there is a sense in which the significance of Jesus as the Son sent by the Father is a response of faith: the earthly life of Jesus is not an open epiphany, it does not provide proof.

There is one further passage in which the sending of the Son is prominent. In the parable of the vineyard and the tenants, which is found in Matthew, Mark and Luke, as well as in the Gospel of Thomas, various servants are sent to collect from the tenants the owner's share of the produce : some are treated violently, others killed. Finally the owner of the vineyard sends his own dear son, but he is recognized as the heir, is killed and his body is flung out of the vineyard.

The evangelists clearly intended the parable to be treated allegorically: the servants are the rejected prophets and the one sent finally as God's own dear Son is Jesus. The sending of Jesus to God's people is related to the sending of the prophets, but the evangelists all take pains to distinguish Jesus from the prophets : Jesus is not merely the final messenger, he is sent as God's Son.

In what sense did Mark understand Jesus to be God's Son?[20] The phrase used in the parable, 'my beloved Son' (Mark 12.6) recalls the words of the voice from heaven at the baptism of Jesus (Mark 1.11) and again at the transfiguration (Mark 9.7). In the former passage Sonship is associated closely with the gift of the Spirit (just as it is, with reference to Christian believers, in Gal. 4.6f.). The verses which follow the transfiguration are notoriously difficult, but the passage does stress that Sonship involves suffering and death. This latter theme becomes even more explicit at Mark 14.36 where in Gethsemane Jesus addresses God directly as Abba, Father; to be God's Son is to be dedicated unconditionally to God's will, even to the point of death.

The evangelist, then, uses the parable to express in a different *genre* the same themes found in other passages in the gospel which speak of the Sonship of Jesus. Although the parable is also concerned with Israel's rejection of Jesus, it expounds, in an indirect but powerful way, the significance of the death of Jesus : the death of Jesus involved God, for it is the Son sent by God who was crucified.

Although the pre-existence of the Son is not even hinted at[21] and although the redemptive significance of the death of Jesus does not become explicit in the parable, the parallel with the 'sending' passages in Paul and in the Fourth Gospel is striking. Whatever may be the origin of the parable (and in all probability an earlier form goes back to Jesus himself),[22] Mark, like Paul and John, emphasizes that the sending of the Son is on God's initiative and is inextricably related to the cross. The sending of the Son is not a demonstration of 'divine power' in the usually accepted sense, for it involves rejection and death, and, above all, obedience to God's will.

The precise sense which the evangelist and his readers would have attached to 'Son of God' is much disputed, but it is clear that while for Mark Jesus is a messianic prophet, he is more than this, for his full significance is seen only in the cross and resurrection. If 'Son of God' did suggest to Hellenistic readers in the first century a 'divine' wonder worker (and this is in fact very doubtful), this notion has also been drastically redefined; for Mark the Sonship of Jesus involves obedience, rejection, suffering and death. It is Jesus' cry 'Abba, Father' in Mark 14.36, his acceptance of the cup of suffering and his obedience to God which most clearly spell out the meaning of Sonship.

The incipiently incarnational christology which is found in the New Testament is culturally conditioned. Wherever there are similarities to first-century Jewish or Hellenistic religious expressions, there are also profound changes. No one category by itself is used to express the significance of Jesus. Modification and juxtaposition of several categories always go hand in hand.

The cultural conditioning runs at an even deeper level. New Testament writers were expressing the significance of Jesus within the context of varied currents within Judaism which held resolutely to monotheism and within a Hellenistic environment in which there were many 'gods' and 'lords', as Paul acknowledges in I Corinthians 8.5. Some of their claims could easily have been said to undermine monotheism, but those same claims in a different setting could well have been dismissed as those of religious hucksters.

In studying the origin and development of early christology one cannot rest content with tracing 'parallels' and 'influences'. Pannenberg is surely correct when he reminds us that 'in the history of ideas nothing is clarified and understood by the phrase: this or that has 'influenced' something or other.... In order for an 'influence' of alien concepts to be absorbed, a situation must have previously emerged within which these concepts could be greeted as an aid for the expression of a problem already present.'[23] It is not the 'cultural conditioning' which is surprising but the ways in which the earliest Christians drew on and yet flew in the face of contemporary religious categories and in ways which ran the risk of ridicule in both a Jewish and in a Hellenistic environment. T. S. Eliot's dictum, 'Christianity is always adapting itself into something which can be believed', which is quoted in the Preface to *The Myth of God Incarnate*, is no more than a half-truth.

In this essay we have concentrated on two of the issues raised in *The Myth of God Incarnate*. Some aspects of the question of cultural conditioning have been explored briefly, but this is a major issue with wide implications. There can be no doubt that an incipient incarnational christology is found in a number of New Testament writings, but we have not attempted to discuss all the relevant passages. Instead we have sought to uncover the theological principles which lie behind one important strand of the evidence, passages which refer to the 'sending of the Son'.

Jesus as Son of God is sent into the world on God's initiative; this is God's supreme act of redemption. It is the 'sending' or 'giving up' of Jesus to the cross which is redemptive : the Son is no mere revealer who discloses heavenly secrets during a brief appearance on earth. The Son who is sent is unique, but his sending is not unrelated to the sending of the prophets to Israel; the parable of the vineyard makes this point particularly clearly, as does the epistle to the Hebrews (even though 'sending' is not mentioned explicitly). The 'sending' passages emphasize that the significance of Jesus is not to be seen in his achievements, his example of noble endeavour. God's salvation is not reward, it is gift and grace.

These theological principles must be retained in any attempt to restate the doctrine of the incarnation. They remind us that 'incarnation' must not be separated either from God's relationship with Israel or from the cross and the resurrection of Jesus. The incarnation must be central in Christian theology, but it must not be isolated (as it often has been) as the focal point.

The New Testament writings do rule out some estimates of Jesus which appeared in the first century and were to reappear again and again : Jesus was 'the prophet' *par excellence*, but he was more than this, however difficult it was to spell out the 'more than a prophet'. Jesus revealed God to men, but he was not a gnostic revealer of heavenly truths who appeared veiled in flesh. The New Testament writers spell out the significance of Jesus in a wide and amazingly rich variety of ways; they were unwilling to compromise either his uniqueness or his humanity. Should we not follow their lead?

NOTES

1. Cf. M. Wiles, 'Myth in Theology', *The Myth of God Incarnate*, ed., John Hick, SCM Press 1977, p. 164.

2. G. Ebeling, 'Time and Word', *The Future of our Religious Past: Essays in Honour of Rudolph Bultmann*, ed., J. M. Robinson, SCM Press 1971, p. 265.

3. Cf. M. Hengel, 'Christologie und Neutestamentliche Chronologie', *Neues Testament und Geschichte, Festschrift für O. Cullmann*, Mohr, Tübingen 1972, pp. 43–67. See also my note 'Samaritan Incarnational Christology?' in this volume.

4. Cr. E. Schweizer, 'Zum religionsgeschichtlichen Hintergrund der "Sendungsformel" Gal. 4,4f.; Rom. 8,3f.; Joh 3,16f.; 1 Joh 4,9' in his *Beiträge zur Theologie*

des Neuen Testaments, Zwingli, Zürich 1970, pp. 83–96; W. Kramer, *Christ, Lord, Son of God*, SCM Press 1966; J. Blank, *Paulus und Jesus*, Kösel, Munich 1968, pp. 250–303.

5. See W. G. Kümmel, 'Jesus und Paulus', *NTS* 10, 1963–4, p. 172.

6. I Thess.1.9f. is the only passage in Paul where the 'Son' is linked with the parousia, but even here the emphasis is on the divine initiative.

7. Paul's usual phrase is 'his Son' rather than 'the Son' or 'Son of God'. Exceptions are I Cor. 15.28; II Cor. 1.19; Eph. 4.13. Gal. 1.16 is imprecise. The sense could be similar to that found in Rom. 1.3b, or more probably, Gal. 4.4f.

8. R. P. Martin notes that the relation of the pre-existence of Jesus and his exaltation in Phil. 2.6–11 has rarely been discussed: *Carmen Christi*, Cambridge University Press 1967, pp. 247f. Martin summarizes J. Jervell's view that two diverse christologies are set cheek by jowl in the hymn.

9. R. Bultmann, *Theology of the New Testament*, I, SCM Press 1952, p. 293.

10. A. F. Segal, *Two Powers in Heaven : Early Rabbinic Reports about Christianity and Gnosticism*, Brill, Leiden 1977.

11. Ibid., p.8n.

12. Segal argues that whenever the second figure in heaven is seen as negative, we are dealing with a radically gnostic system; this happens in the later traditions.

13. Rom. 3.30; Gal. 3.20; I Cor. 8.4,6; Eph. 4.6; and cf. I Tim. 1.17 and 2.5.

14. F. Young, 'A Cloud of Witnesses', *The Myth of God Incarnate*, ed., J. Hick, SCM Press 1977, p. 27.

15. John 3.17 (cf. 3.16); I John 4.9.

16. E. Käsemann, 'The Structure and Purpose of the Prologue to John's Gospel' in *New Testament Questions of Today*, SCM Press 1969, p. 153f. See also E. Käsemann, *The Testament of Jesus*, SCM Press 1968.

17. Cf. G. Bornkamm, 'Zur Interpretation des Johannes-Evangeliums : Eine Auseinandersetzung mit Ernst Käsemanns Schrift "Jesu letzter Wille nach Johannes 17"', in *Geschichte und Glaube* I, Kaiser, Munich, 1968, pp. 104–21.

18. M. D. Hooker, 'The Johannine Prologue and the Messianic Secret', *NTS* 21, 1974–5, p. 44.

19. So R. T. Fortna, 'Christology in the Fourth Gospel' *NTS* 21, 1974–5, p. 502. Fortna argues that the Fourth Gospel is 'neither passion-narrative-with-introduction nor ; retalogy-with-sequel, but *one continuous passion narrative*, that is, a single account of Jesus' revelatory glorification via his death and resurrection.' Ibid., p. 504.

20. For a recent thorough discussion, see M. Hubaut, *La Parabole des Vignerons Homicides*, Gabalda, Paris 1976. Rather surprisingly, M. Hubaut does not refer to the Pauline and Johannine parallels we have discussed, nor does he consider the obvious link with the other Marcan 'Son' passages.

21. *Contra* R. Fuller, *The Foundations of New Testament Christology*, Lutterworth, 1965, p. 194. Cf. M. Hubaut's discussion, op. cit., p. 42.

22. It is impossible to discuss here the use and understanding of 'Son of God' found in Matthew and Luke. Recent scholarship has concentrated rather narrowly on the origin and development of the christological titles and has not given enough attention to the particular emphasis of the individual New Testament writers.

23. W. Pannenberg, *Jesus – God and Man*, SCM Press 1968, p. 153.

B (ii) Professor Stanton on Incarnational Language in the New Testament

Don Cupitt

Professor Stanton quotes Galatians 4.4: 'When the time had fully come, God sent forth his Son, born of a woman, born under the Law.' This and other similar texts he regards as incipiently incarnational in meaning, and he claims that Paul thought Jesus divine because 'the phrase "his Son" points to the "similarity", as it were, of God and Jesus rather than to their "difference"'. But there are some considerations which point the other way.

Since the doctrinal definitions of the fourth and fifth centuries Christians have become used to the idea that the Son of God is God of God, so that to say that the Son of God is incarnate is the same as to say that God is incarnate. However, the New Testament nowhere says that the Son of God is God of God. In pre-Nicene days the phrase 'Son of God' could be used to emphasize the *difference* of status between Jesus and God, as in the *Clementine Homilies* (16.15), where Peter tells Simon Magus:

> 'Our Lord neither asserted that there were Gods except the Creator of all, nor did he proclaim himself to be God, but he with reason pronounced him (*i.e.*, *Peter himself*) blessed who called him the Son of that God who has arranged the universe.' And Simon answered: 'Does it not seem to you, then, that he who comes from God is God?' And Peter said: 'Tell us how this is possible; for we cannot affirm this, because we did not hear it from him'.

A close discussion follows, in which Peter asserts that 'what is begotten cannot be compared with that which is unbegotten ... nor can it be asserted of him who has been begotten that he is of the same substance as he is who has begotten him.'[1] In the whole discussion the idea that 'Jesus is God' is treated as a heretical misunderstanding of the gospel. Harnack's analysis of the sense in which Christians of the second century thought of Jesus as divine still seems very accurate and judicious.[2] In a world in which Augustus had been called 'God of God' what is really impressive is how slow and cautious Christians were in edging towards the use of similar language.

There is in fact a considerable distance between these two propositions:

(*i*) Jesus is a pre-existent heavenly being close to God, whom God has sent into the world; and

(*ii*) Jesus is God incarnate.

Professor Stanton supplies evidence that (*i*) was believed by some from early times. But I suggest that he does not sufficiently emphasize the difference between (*i*) and (*ii*). I agree that the New Testament says (*i*), but (*ii*) is much less certain. The question is rather whether (*ii*) is the correct translation, or a possible translation, or a mistranslation into later language of what the New Testament says.

The nuances involved are very fine. John the Baptist is said to be 'a man sent from God', but is there a significant difference between the sense in which he is 'sent from God' and the sense in which Jesus is 'sent from God'? Does the statement that the Baptist is Elijah imply a belief in reincarnation? Professor Stanton adduces as evidence for Paul's belief in Jesus' divinity the fact that Paul calls Jesus 'his (i.e., God's) Son'. But how is one supposed to know that there is an *ontological* difference between the sense in which the Israelite King was God's Son and the sense in which Jesus is God's Son? Obviously the New Testament regards Jesus as God's Son in an ultimate or eschatological sense, but that observation by itself does not establish an ontological difference. On the contrary, you can just as well argue – indeed, I think you can more plausibly argue – that the whole drive of early Christian argument emphasizes the closeness and similarity of origin, status and destiny between Christ and Christians. In II Clement, for example, the church and Christ are given *the same* created, pre-existent and now eschatologically-manifested status. The whole discussion matches the two entities to each other.[3]

Another way of making the claim that the New Testament is 'incipiently incarnational' is to point to the way in which Jesus was from the mid-50s spoken of in idioms borrowed from the various intermediary beings that we hear about in the literature of the time – like the Wisdom of God, the Word of God, the Power of God, the divine Presence or Glory (Shekinah), the Torah and so on.

The status of these beings has been highly controversial for years, and is still not agreed. But one theory of them seems now ruled out. We ought *not* to think that God was at that time seen by the Jews as remote and inaccessible, so that reified intermediaries were needed to link God with men.[4] It therefore seems implausible to interpret the early Christians as claiming that because God himself is inaccessible, therefore the only way to God is through union with an incarnated intermediary that is Very God of Very God. Their contemporaries would have denied the premiss.

It seems more plausible to say that the intermediaries were manifold metaphorical ways of expressing God's gracious outreach towards the world and were *also* spoken of in ways that express the perfected creature's response to God, as when an intermediary is called God's image, a heavenly Man, a son or daughter of God, and a thing begotten or made by God that mirrors God.

Now early Christian language about Jesus is intensely eschatological. In him believers experienced both God's gracious outreach towards the world, and the beginning of the final perfecting of the world. So the idioms used in connection with the intermediaries were readily applied to him. But the language is for the most part not naturally incarnational in meaning. In the Pauline words (Col. 1.15ff.):

> [The Son] is the image of the invisible God, the
> first-born of all creation; for in him all things
> were created [including angels, etc.] – all things were created through
> him and for him. He is before
> all things and in him all things hold together.
> For in him all the fulness of God was pleased to dwell ...

Now it may be possible, with a good deal of squeezing, to interpret that passage along the lines of the later orthodoxy, and it may be possible to give it a platonic interpretation. But the natural sense of the passage, along with the rest of Paul's theology, is surely that Jesus is pre-eminent among all creatures (compare Rev. 3.14). As the bringer of final salvation in his own person he is God's perfect Man, the goal of all things, the last Adam, the first-born, the creature that mirrors God perfectly and therefore the one for whose sake and even through whom the world was made.

It is often said in the New Testament that a metaphorically pre-existent heavenly being of somewhat uncertain status has been sent into the world by God, but it is not said in so many words that God himself has become incarnate. It is said that Christ Jesus emptied (*ekenōsen*) himself, but not that God emptied himself. If we scrape and search for the incarnation in the New Testament we may miss its real message, that Jesus is the fulfilment of scripture, and the first and last in all creation because it is in him that final salvation has arrived in the world. He is the perfect Man, God's faithful Son, given to the world and now glorified as the one in whom God is all in all.

So far I have made merely historical observations, and it is notoriously difficult to make the transition from historical theology (what they believed) to systematic theology (what we believe). But I suggest that the Jewish-Christian exegesis of the New Testament is truer and a clearer guide to modern theology than the developed orthodoxy, because for us Jesus is not a superhuman figure whose life was a pageant of supernatural revelatory events. He was a first-century Jewish prophet of the Kingdom of God and teacher of salvation. I affirm that we can today experience and participate in the salvation he brought. It is still a world-ending and world-renewing experience. If we share it we can see why the New Testament writers spoke of Jesus as they did, and we can to some extent adopt their language. It is 'mythological' in character, but there is no harm in that provided we recognize that it is mythological, and do not try to turn it into dubious metaphysics. We have no reason today to postulate the existence of the odd population of heavenly beings in which people once believed, and to us it seems clear that a human being cannot intelligibly be spoken of as pre-existent. But if I have found salvation through Jesus' voice and person, I can quite intelligibly speak of him as the human ultimate and the crown of creation; the man who, by mirroring God, shows what the world is meant to be.

NOTES

1. Translation from the *Ante-Nicene Christian Library*, Vol. XVII (1870), pp. 252f.

2. Adolph Harnack, *History of Dogma*, New York: Dover 1961, Vol. I, pp. 186ff.

3. II Clem. 14, in J. B. Lightfoot, *The Apostolic Fathers* (1891), p. 91.

4. E. P. Sanders, *Paul and Palestinian Judaism*, SCM Press 1977 especially pp. 212ff. See also M. Hengel, *Judaism and Hellenism*, SCM Press 1974, Vol. I, pp. 153–175. On how modern theology should represent the relation of Jesus to God, we now have G. W. H. Lampe's *God as Spirit*, Cambridge University Press 1977.

B (iii)   Mr Cupitt on Incarnational Christology in the New Testament

Graham Stanton

I am grateful for Mr Cupitt's comments, for they do draw attention to some of the key issues in the current debate. Mr Cupitt wishes to drive a firm wedge between what he takes to be the 'real message' of the New Testament and the later doctrine of the incarnation. However, the 'real message' of the New Testament is far richer than he supposes, for he has selected one strand of the evidence which he finds congenial. Many strands of the New Testament evidence are not far in *intention* from the convictions which lie behind later incarnational doctrine. On the other hand, wherever later incarnational doctrine pays lip service to the humanity of Jesus or makes the incarnation *per se* the focal point of Christian theology, it fails to do justice to the rich variety of ways in which New Testament writers express the significance of Jesus.

While it is true that Paul does not seem to have reflected on the ontological status of Jesus, it is not quite accurate to claim, as Mr Cupitt does, the 'the New Testament nowhere says that the Son of God is God of God'. By and large such language was avoided, and I have said something about the reasons for this in my essay. The slowness and caution of Christians in referring to Jesus as God is, as Mr Cupitt notes, impressive : equally impressive is the fact that they edged towards such language and, on occasions, dared to use it. At least some of the following passages are taken by most scholars as examples: Rom. 9.5; Heb. 1.8; Titus 2.13; John 1.1 and 18, 20.28; I John 5.20. In a perceptive article B. A. Mastin has recently examined the Johannine usage carefully. He argues (plausibly in my view) that as a result of controversy between Jews and Christians the evangelist's three references to Jesus as God express not so much a functional christology but indicate *who he is*.[1]

Mr Cupitt presses the distinction between these two propositions:

(*i*) Jesus is a pre-existent heavenly being close to God, whom God has sent into the world; and

(*ii*) Jesus is God incarnate.

The New Testament does not speak explicitly of Jesus as *God* incarnate. Passages which seem to do this are qualified carefully in various ways; some examples from the Fourth Gospel were given in my essay. John 1.14 states that the *Logos*, not God, became flesh; the distinction is not unimportant. Some passages which do seem to affirm bodily that Jesus is God incarnate are notoriously difficult to interpret precisely. Colossians 2.9 may be rendered, as in the New English Bible, as 'For it is in Christ that the complete being of the Godhead dwells embodied ... ', but other interpretations are possible.

However, New Testament writers wish to say *more* than (*i*), or, rather, more than (*i*) as expounded by Mr Cupitt in terms of Jesus as 'the perfect Man', 'the creature that mirrors God perfectly'. In a wide variety of ways New Testament writers do speak of Jesus as 'divine'. This is not confined to the 'Sonship' theme or to pre-existence. It is not possible to rehearse the evidence here : it has recently been set out thoroughly and judiciously by Professor Moule in his *The Origin of Christology*. Few New Testament scholars would accept his judgment at every point, but it is hard to dissent from his general conclusion that for Paul, 'experience of contact with Christ takes very much the same "shape" as the "shape" of God in any theist's belief : he is emphatically personal, yet more than merely individual' (p. 97). A few pages later Professor Moule insists that 'even the most individualistic conceptions of the risen Christ, whether in Acts, in Hebrews, in I Peter, or in John, seem consistently to present him as something more and greater than what believers hoped that, by the grace of God, they themselves would become. In a word, they present him as *divine*' (p. 103).

Now whether the statement 'Jesus is God incarnate' is a *possible* 'translation' of the New Testament evidence will obviously depend on how one expounds 'Jesus is God incarnate'. There may be more appropriate ways of expressing the convictions of the New Testament writers. If there are, then they will certainly need to do justice to the constant insistence of the early Christians that Jesus was 'born of a woman' and that he transcended human categories.

Mr Cupitt claims that 'the whole drive of the early Christian argument emphasizes the closeness and similarity of origin, status and destiny between Christ and Christians'. There are certainly many passages in the New Testament which do stress that there are ways in which Christ and the Christian are similar, but the 'whole drive of the argument' runs in the *opposite* direction. Numerous passages insist that there is a *difference* between Christ and the rest of humanity.[2] At Galatians 4.4ff. Paul emphasizes that Christians are *adopted* as sons: God sent forth his Son ... to redeem ... so that we might receive adoption as sons ... God has sent the Spirit into our hearts, crying, "Abba! Father!"' In the Fourth Gospel there is a careful distinction between Jesus as the Son, who, unlike Christian believers, is never said to be born of God. Christian believers are children, *tekna*, but never sons, *huioi*, for Jesus alone is Son, *huios*. The epistle to the Hebrews refers to believers as 'sons' and to Jesus as 'the Son', but believers become sons only as the Son confesses them to be his brethren (2.10f.). Mr Cupitt refers to the splendid passage in II Clement to support his point that the early Christian argument emphasizes the closeness and similarity of origin, status and destiny between Christ and Christians. However, the opening verse confirms that even though II Clement is an unsophisticated treatise, the *difference* between Christ and the Christian was fully appreciated: 'Brethren, we ought to think of Jesus Christ, as of God, as of the Judge of the living and the dead ... for he had mercy on us, and in his compassion he saved us.'

There is both similarity and dissimilarity between Christ and the rest of humanity. The difference is as essential to the early Christian argument as the similarity.[3] For all their stress on the humanity of Jesus, both Paul and the writer to the Hebrews are unable, in the last resort, to ascribe to Jesus participation in our human sinfulness. As John Knox writes, 'They can think of him as sharing in our weakness, but hardly in our sickness.' Knox goes on to spell out the dilemma of early Christian thought about the humanity of Jesus: 'How could Christ have saved us if he were not a human being like ourselves? How could a human being like ourselves have saved us?'[4] So while Paul asserts that Jesus is 'the eldest among a large family of brothers' (Rom. 8.29b), or, to use Mr Cupitt's phrase, pre-eminent among all creatures, early Christian writers carefully mark out the *difference* between Christ and the rest of humanity. They insist both on the similarity and on the difference between Christ's humanity and ours and are prepared to let them stand side by side.

In his final sentence Mr Cupitt speaks of Jesus as 'the man who, by mirroring God, shows what the world is meant to be'. This seems to lead directly to a soteriology in which Jesus is our supreme example, to man's discovery of salvation rather than to God's initiative in sending his Son. The dispute between us is not just about christology, but also about soteriology, for, as Christian theology has always recognized, the two are linked inextricably.

NOTES

1. B. A. Mastin, 'A Neglected Feature of the Christology of the Fourth Gospel', *NTS* 22, 1975, pp. 32–51.

2. For a fuller discussion, see C. F. D. Moule, 'The Manhood of Christ in the New Testament', *Christ, Faith and History*, ed., S. W. Sykes and J. P. Clayton, Cambridge University Press 1972, pp. 95–110.

3. I am well aware that by calling attention to the *difference* between Christ and the rest of humanity, some would say that the *full* humanity of Jesus is being denied. On this see S. W. Sykes, 'The Theology of the humanity of Christ', *Christ, Faith and History*, pp. 53–72.

4. John Knox, *The Humanity and Divinity of Christ*, Cambridge University Press 1967, p. 52.

C The Finality of Christ
Frances Young

Most people would agree that Christianity has always tended to be exclusive. This persistent feature is widely assumed to be grounded in the doctrine of incarnation, understood as the final and complete revelation of God in Jesus Christ. What I wish to question is whether it *is* the incarnation which has produced this characteristic, or whether it is not really something quite different – in fact, whether the Christian insistence upon the finality of Christ does not have a certain independence of the belief that divine incarnation took place in him.

In my contribution to *The Myth of God Incarnate*, I suggested that in the New Testament Jesus 'was the embodiment of all God's promises brought to fruition', that 'such a characterization ... represents New Testament christology better than the idea of incarnation', and that 'it was in fact the germ of more and more christological ideas as the whole of the Old Testament was seen as fulfilled in Christ'. Now I would add that Christ's *finality*, in so far as the New Testament writers were convinced of it, was related to this fulfilment-theme, rather than to any coherently framed idea of his divine nature. In other words it is eschatology, not incarnation, which makes Christ final in the New Testament.

No one will find a treatise on the finality of Christ in the New Testament; the presence of the idea has to be discerned in material dealing with a wide range of issues. We may usefully begin by seeing what associations appear if we examine the actual use of words expressive of finality: (Some readers may like to continue on page 177.)

(i) *Telos* = end (We need hardly consider the one or two occasions where it means taxes.)

In Matthew's gospel, the word usually refers to the *End of the world*. Matt. 10.22: 'he that endures to the end, will be saved' is slightly ambiguous – it could in the context refer to the end of persecution and hatred; but there seems little reason to doubt that the eschatological interpretation is right, especially in view of the succeeding verse which speaks of the coming of the Son of Man. The three uses in ch. 24 (vv. 6, 13, 14) belong to an eschatological discourse concerned with the timing of the End. Only in 26.58 does the word occur in a more 'ordinary' sense: Peter went inside the high-priest's courtyard and sat with the guards 'to see the end', which presumably means the outcome of Jesus' trial.

In Mark's gospel, two out of three uses certainly refer to the *End of the world*: 13.7 and 13. In 3.26 we read: 'If Satan rises against himself and is divided, he cannot stand but has an end.' This is Jesus' reply to the accusation that he casts out demons by the power of Beelzebul, and the obvious meaning is simply concerned with the results of a hypothetical condition. This text is therefore *not* directly concerned with the end of Satan, though that might be described as one of the most important of eschatological events.

The use of the word in Luke-Acts is less consistent. It does not occur at all in Acts, and while it clearly means the *End of the world* in Luke 21.9, every other case is rather different:

1.33 'Of his kingdom there shall be no end': by negation, the word becomes a way of expressing eternity.

18.5 '... so that she will not wear me out with her continual (*lit.* to the end) coming': a phrase from the parable of the Unjust Judge and clearly an idiomatic usage.

22.37 is much more interesting: 'For I say to you that this scriptural word "And he was reckoned among the transgressors" must be fulfilled (*telesthēnai*) in me; for what is (written) concerning me has its end' (perhaps, 'outcome' or '*fulfilment*' would be a good translation). Here it is quite clear that the noun *telos* is connected with the verb *telesthēnai*, which frequently, as here, refers to fulfilment (see further below).

In John's gospel the word occurs once: 13.1 'he loved them to the end'. This could have a number of different meanings: it could mean 'to the end of his life', or to some other possible end, like the end of the world (unlikely in John's gospel) or the end of his mission (cf. 19.30 *tetelestai*); or it could simply be an idiomatic phrase for 'utterly' or 'for ever'.

In the gospels then we can establish four basic categories of usage, and a glance at the epistles shows that usages there fit into the same spectrum:

1. *Idiomatic and insignificant for our purposes*:
   To this category we may assign e.g. I Thess. 2.16 'at last' or 'completely'; II Cor. 1.13 'fully' or 'completely'; I Peter 3.8 'finally'.

2. *Non-eschatological reference to the end of something, e.g. life*:
   A few references in the epistles may be assigned to this category without comment e.g. II Cor. 3.13 'the end of the fading' (splendour of Moses' face); Heb. 7.3 'neither beginning of days nor end of life'.

We might also add I Tim. 1.5 'the end (i.e. aim) of our advice (precept) is love' and James 5.11 'you have seen the Lord's end ...', a reference to God's eventual mercy on Job after all his patient endurance.

But the vast majority that we might be tempted to place here in fact imply something like *ultimate outcome* and have overtones of judgment; i.e. they cannot be totally divorced from a possible *eschatological context*: e.g. Rom. 6.21–2 'What fruit did you get from the things of which you are now

ashamed? for their end is death. But now ... you have fruit producing sanctification, and its end is eternal life.';
or II Cor. 11.15 'their end will correspond with their deeds.';
or I Peter 1.9 'As the end (outcome) of your faith, you obtain salvation ...';
and cf. Phil. 3.19; Heb. 6.8; I Peter 4.17.

3. *Specific reference to the End of the world* (or associated uses):
 Most of the other references in the New Testament belong to this category:
e.g. I Cor. 1.8; 10.11; 15.24.
Heb. 3.6; 3.14; 6.11 (+ Rev. 2.26) – the phrase 'to the end' *could* have the meaning 'utterly' or 'for ever', but it most probably has an eschatological reference (*pace* Kittel) in these contexts.
I Peter 4.7.
Rev. 1.8; 21.6; 22.13 'the beginning and the end' – no doubt really referring to God's eternity, but in a strongly eschatological context.

4. *Fulfilment*:
 The noun does not occur again in quite the way Luke used it in 22.37, i.e. of the fulfilment of scripture, but there is one crucial text:
Rom. 10.4 'Christ is the end of the law'
which does not seem to mean simply its destruction but also its fulfilment, the expression of its purpose, cf. Rom. 3.31.

(*ii*) Words related to *telos*

(*a*) The verb *teleō* means 'I finish', and it is often used in that sense, e.g. Matt. 13.53 'when Jesus had finished these parables', or Rev. 20.5 'until the thousand years were finished'.
It appears in contexts like Luke 2.39, Rom. 2.27 and James 2.8 of 'fulfilling the law', i.e. performing its requirements.
It appears in a stronger sense of accomplishment or achievement in Luke 12.50 'I have a baptism to be baptized with, and how I am pressed until it is accomplished'. In both Luke and John, in fact, it is associated with the *fulfilment of scripture or of God's purposes*:
Luke 18.31 'Behold we are going up to Jerusalem, and everything written of the Son of Man by the prophets will be fulfilled.'
Luke 22.37: already discussed above.
John 19.28 'Jesus knowing that everything was already completed (or fulfilled – *tetelestai*) that scripture might be fulfilled (a related but slightly different verb *teleiōthē(i)*), said, "I thirst".'
Two verses later, Jesus cries, 'It is accomplished' (*tetelestai*).
 The same kind of usage is found in Revelation which speaks of 'the mystery of God as he announced to his servants the prophets' being fulfilled at the seventh trumpet (10.7); and of the 'words of God' being fulfilled when his purposes are carried out (17.17).

(*b*) The only frequent compounds of *teleō* are *synteleō* and *epiteleō*. Both are generally used in a straightforward sense of 'performing', 'finishing', 'completing'; but the first is significant in two places:

Mark 13.4 'what will be the sign ... when all these things shall be fulfilled? – enquiry about the date of the *End*; Heb. 8.8 'I will complete (i.e. establish) a new covenant....'

And the second (*epiteleō*) can also mean 'perfect': II Cor. 7.1 'making holiness perfect in the fear of the Lord'.

(*c*) The idea of *perfection* is more frequently expressed by the related verb *teleioō* or its associated words *teleios*, *teleiōsis*, etc.; but even this verb appears in some contexts in the sense of fulfilling or accomplishing, e.g. Luke 2.43, John 4.34, 5.36, 17.4, 19.28.

It is particularly important to note, however, that this verb is especially significant in the epistle to the Hebrews which contains nearly half the uses in the entire New Testament. In this epistle, the perfection of Christ's priesthood and sacrifice compared with those of the old covenant is an important theme (another characteristic word being *kreissōn* = better, superior), and Christ is actually called the 'perfecter (*teleiotēs*) of faith'. For Hebrews' author, *perfection* and *fulfilment* are ways of expressing Christ's finality.

In the Pauline epistles, perfection is seen in terms of the *eschatological goal*, e.g. the well-known I Cor. 13.10; Col. 1.28 etc.

(*iii*) *Eschatos* = last

It is perhaps important to remind ourselves that in spite of all the talk about 'the eschaton', such a word does not occur in the New Testament. However, the adjective *eschatos* = last is quite frequent and significant.

'The last day' is a Johannine expression occurring in John 6.39,40,44,54; 11.24 and 12.48.

'The last days' appears in Acts 2.17; II Tim. 3.1; James 5.3 and II Peter 3.3.

'The last time(s)' appears in I Peter 1.5,20; I John 2.18; Jude 18.

Paul speaks of the 'last enemy' being destroyed (I Cor. 15.26), of the 'last Adam' (I Cor. 15.45) and the 'last trump' (I Cor. 15.52).

Revelation uses 'the first and the last' as a title alongside 'the beginning and the end'.

The word is not only used in this strongly eschatological sense, of course; it is also used quite straightforwardly for 'last': e.g. Matt. 5.26 ' ... till you have paid the last farthing'. It occurs several times in the repeated synoptic saying, 'the last shall be first,' and so on.

Nevertheless, enough evidence has surely been produced to show that words expressing finality in the Greek Testament relate strongly to

(*i*) expectations of the End of the world

(*ii*) the fulfilment of prophecy.

To what extent, then is this sense of *finality* linked with Jesus Christ?

Clearly some of the passages already mentioned are important. Luke 22.37 *et al.* speak of *fulfilment 'in me'*. Romans 10.4 asserts

Christ is the *end of the law*. Luke and John speak of *Jesus accomplishing* the fore-ordained task. Paul calls *Christ* the last Adam, and he and the author of Hebrews associate perfection with the work of Christ. Revelation calls *Jesus* the *first and the last*.

But association of the End-time with the coming of Jesus Christ is much more basic to New Testament thinking than this short list of passages might suggest, and the disturbing and paradoxical character of this feature of New Testament thought has provoked continuing discussions of New Testament eschatology since the turn of the century. There is one thing that we seem to be able to say with certainty, namely that the early Christians identified *Jesus* with the expected Judge or Son of Man, to appear at the End, (rather than Enoch or Melchizedek, Old Testament characters who appear as candidates in other literature round about this time); and that they assumed that his return in this role was imminent. I Thessalonians 1.9–10 suggests that this was the distinctive content of the early Christian message: 'You turned from idols to serve a living and true God (so far, no difference from Judaism), and to await his Son from heaven, whom he raised from the dead, Jesus who delivers us from the wrath to come.' A second point which seems clear is that the eschatology of the early Christians was not just future. The 'kingdom' was already present in some sense in the activity of Jesus; the prophecies were already being fulfilled; the new covenant was already established in his blood; etc. So in the New Testament we find over and over again a tension between present reality and future hope, between prophecies fulfilled and prophecies not fulfilled. The 'balance' of this tension varies in different writings, the gospel of John, for example, stressing so much the present reality of judgment and the present gift of eternal life that his occasional descriptions of the future jar on the reader and have even been attributed to a later editor by many New Testament scholars. The important point for our purposes, however, is that this peculiar eschatological perspective whereby the End of the world, the fulfilment of God's saving purposes, is being experienced already, is entirely centred in Jesus Christ: 'If anyone is in Christ (he is, or perhaps, there is) a new creation; behold the old has passed away and the new has come into being' (II Cor. 5.17). 'As in Adam all die so in Christ shall all be made alive' (I Cor. 15.22); or through him: 'Behold I am coming soon bringing my recompense, to repay everyone for what he has done. I am alpha and omega, the first and the last, the beginning and the end' (Rev. 22. 12–13).

The related themes of fulfilment and eschatological finality, I suggest, are far more pervasive in the New Testament than notions of divine incarnation. In *The Myth of God Incarnate* I acknowledged that Paul's christology has incarnational elements – the development of notions of pre-existence alongside the eschatological expectations of Christ's return as Judge inevitably carried with it the corollary that in Jesus a supernatural agent of God was incarnate; but in Paul this figure is, in an important sense, a transcendent Man, created in God's image and appointed as God's representative (even in Phil. 2.5–11 behind which may well lie an Adam-typology). Christ is final for Paul, not as God incarnate, but as last Adam.[1]

A similar situation is found elsewhere in the New Testament. Broadly speaking we may say that there are plenty of indications that Jesus was treated as God's agent, whether human or supernatural; there are plenty of texts that imply that he carries to fruition God's fore-ordained purpose as revealed in the prophets; but there are precious few that explicitly and without qualification speak of Jesus as 'God' or 'divine'. The pre-existence or miraculous origin of the unique medium of God's eschatological action is occasionally assumed or stated (though not very frequently outside the Pauline and Johannine writings), and such texts have been taken to imply the Nicene doctrine; but it is by no means self-evident that the incarnational ideas of other New Testament writers, any more than those of Paul, implied anything like developed orthodoxy, and in any case it is clear that incarnational ideas are spasmodic in comparison with the constant recurrence of eschatological motifs. That Jesus inaugurated the End of history and will consummate its goal is basic to New Testament thinking and is intimately linked with the belief that he fulfilled all the predictions of the prophets. It was this rather than a doctrine of divine incarnation which constituted the basis of the New Testament claim to finality for Jesus Christ.

The chief apparent exception to this is the gospel of John. In the great christological debates of the centuries succeeding the New Testament period, it was the gospel of John to which the Fathers repeatedly appealed, so it is perhaps not surprising that it has also figured in discussion of *The Myth of God Incarnate*. In that volume I gave no attention to John's christology so let me make some attempt to rectify that omission here. Is it true that the basis of Christ's finality is to be found, for the author of John's gospel, in a doctrine of divine incarnation in Jesus Christ?

That the gospel is pointing in the direction taken by the patristic writers is quite plain. The essential thing about Jesus, for this author, the later apologists and many prominent Christian writers like Origen and Eusebius, is that he is the *true revelation of God*: 'No one has ever seen God; the only(-begotten) one (perhaps 'God' or 'Son', according to some manuscripts) who is in the bosom of the Father, has given an account of him' (John 1.18).[2] Whether or not the word 'God' belonged originally to this text, the implication seems clear; indeed, the culmination of the gospel comes when the risen Jesus is addressed by the words, 'My Lord and my God' in Thomas' confession of faith (John 20.28). On the face of it, Jesus is called God and appears as the divine Logos incarnate: 'The word was in God's presence and was God' (John 1.1); 'the word became flesh' (John 1.14). Quite apart from these explicit texts, there are three features of John's christology which lend themselves to a strongly incarnational interpretation, namely the Logos-doctrine, the Father-Son relationship, and the marked tendency to treat Jesus as more than merely human – a feature which led Käsemann[3] to the view that Johannine christology is a naive docetism. Let us examine each.

It is perfectly obvious that John's gospel gives us a portrait of Jesus which considerably heightens his supernatural character. The miraculous nature of his activity is sharpened by the insistence that the man was blind from birth and such a cure had never been known before (John 9.32), and that Lazarus was in the tomb four days before being raised (11.17). Jesus knows the minds of others (2.25) and is in control of his own destiny (7.6,30 etc.). The guards sent to arrest him recoil from him (18.6). He deliberately fulfils scripture on the cross (19.28). Not only so, but he openly acknowledges his Messiahship (unlike the synoptic accounts), and speaks of himself in such a way that accusations that he makes himself Son of God or equal with God have a certain plausibility. The key feature for Käsemann, however, is the presentation of the *glory* of Jesus: 'no other Gospel narrates as impressively as John the confrontation of the world and of the believers with the glory of Jesus, even in the passion-narrative.' He concludes that John presents a docetic picture of God's Son descending and ascending but identified with the glorified one throughout; there is no paradox of humiliation and exaltation – the cross is the hour of glorification simply because it is the way of return to the bosom of the Father. Such a picture has to be counterbalanced, I think, by taking note of the ambiguity, the irony even, implied in the narrative of John's gospel: Jesus' humanity is sufficiently real that only the believer can discern anything different about him. Jesus shares the grief of the mourner and the hunger and thirst of the traveller, and the story at least purports to be an account of a life full of incident and ending in a real death. Yet the Gnostics loved this gospel first; and it is to this gospel that we owe the docetic tendencies of the popular conception of Christianity. Jesus here appears as a supernatural figure incarnate, but does that mean he is God incarnate? Let us look at the other motifs which might suggest this.

The Logos-doctrine only appears explicitly in the prologue, though it is there by implication in much of the rest of the gospel, as for example when Jesus identifies himself as the Life, the Light, and the Truth. Placed at the opening of the gospel, this passage inevitably sets the tone of the whole, and demands from the reader that he see the significance of Jesus in cosmic terms. But does it say anything clearly about divine nature? The answer to that question depends upon the degree of personification intended in the passage, and its implications. It is quite possible to render the word 'Logos' as 'meaning' throughout, and understand 1.14 as simply stating that God's meaning was embodied in Jesus Christ (rather as we might speak of the Queen embodying British sovereignty) so that men had access to it through him.[4] I doubt whether that is quite all that is implied, largely because of the background. In the Old Testament the word of God and the wisdom of God are personified as agents acting out God's purpose on earth, and we find in contemporary literature the tendency to turn attributes of God into mediatorial figures, even angels, charged with doing God's will and performing his functions.[5] It is highly likely therefore that the author of John's gospel intended some kind of pre-existent 'being' who acted as God's agent and was in some sense derivative from God. Yet it is extremely difficult to ascertain how concretely this 'being' may have been conceived. The paradoxical statement 'The Logos was in God's presence and the Logos was God' is indicative of the uncertainty and lack of clarity about the situation. Since in rabbinic literature such language is undoubtedly mere 'periphrasis' corresponding to no reality, it is quite possible that the pre-existent Logos was an 'abstraction' rather than a 'personality' or some ill-defined combination of the two; and the same could be said of Truth, Light and Life. Of course, by identifying Jesus with this pre-existent attribute of God, the author of John's gospel was himself making it personal and concrete thereafter, and stimulating further development towards an incarnational doctrine. Whatever the situation, however, it is hardly God himself who was understood to be incarnate; it was an agent or instrument of God, and we may well ask how much this differs from the situation in the Pauline epistles.

So what about the Father-Son relationship? 'He who has seen me has seen the Father.' 'I and the Father are one.' 'No man comes to the Father but by me.' There is undoubtedly something exclusive and unique about this relationship as conceived by the author of John's gospel. That Jesus 'stands for' God in relation to man is certain, as indeed it is in many other parts of the New Testament. Yet the relationship implies not only unity but distinction; and the unity is most frequently portrayed in John's gospel in terms of agency, or of accomplishing God's purposes (See chapter 5, for example, discussing 'works', and passages referred to in the earlier discussion of *teleō*.) The Son is 'son of the Father' because he acts in accordance with the character and will of the Father; his opponents have the devil for father in the same sense (John 8.44). It is possible that when the author of John's gospel speaks of the only Son 'giving an account of' the Father (*exēgēsato* 1.18), he is thinking less of a gnostic or mystical revelation, and more of a telling out of God's purposes, i.e. the fulfilling of the course foreordained by God. Throughout John's gospel the submission of the Son to the will of the Father is a fundamentally important theme.

It is in the light of this discussion that the texts in which Jesus is explicitly called 'God' must be evaluated. In John 1.18, the one possibly called 'God' is 'in the bosom of the Father' and reveals an otherwise unknown God who is clearly other than himself; he is 'God' because he 'stands for' and reveals God. Similarly Jesus is God for Thomas because he has come to 'stand for' God; but he is not himself God, for a few verses earlier he himself said, 'I am ascending to my Father and your Father, and my God and your God' (John 20.17).

So whether the Fourth Gospel has advanced a great deal beyond the rest of the New Testament towards a fully conceived doctrine of the divine nature being incarnated in Jesus Christ is at least questionable. Fulfilment, the revelation and accomplishment of God's will and purposes, is more dominant than a first glance might have suggested. In Jesus is incarnated the *medium* through which God is seen, his purpose revealed and his fore-ordained will accomplished. As in the rest of the New Testament, the finality of Christ and his unique status are affirmed without any unambiguous doctrine of divine incarnation, and the most important basis of these claims is the assertion that in him all the prophecies or promises of God have been brought to fruition so that he becomes in a unique sense the agent of God's will and purpose.

In the space remaining to me, I wish to suggest that quite apart from the New Testament, which has been the chief concern of this paper, in the history of the Christian faith, the finality of Christ is a basic and persistent feature operating sometimes almost independently of the doctrine of incarnation. Once that doctrine was established of course it could always be appealed to, and thus it is difficult to argue a watertight case. But we may sink a couple of exploratory shafts·

1. The bas' ,upposition of the patristic period, from the apologists to t... cene period and beyond, was that Jesus provided *the* revel... he truth, the true way of life and the true religion. By con... no other claimants were worth considering (and there w... ty around). It is worth noting that even though some not... carnation came to be the basis of this claim, the fulfilme ... phecy remained its most powerful evidence:

> But in case anyone should meet us with the question, 'What should prevent it that he whom we call Christ, being a man born of men, performed what we call his mighty works by magic art, and in this way appeared to be Son of God?', we will now offer proof that we do not trust mere assertions, but are necessarily persuaded by those who *prophesied* of him before these things came to pass; for with our own eyes we behold things that have happened and are happening just as they were *predicted*; and this will, we think, appear even to you the strongest and truest evidence. (Justin Martyr, *I Apology* 30)

The background to such an argument lies in a culture in which even the government depended on books of Sibylline oracles and the technical expertise of astrologers or specialists in taking auguries. The argument retained its force for centuries and provided the framework for Eusebius' *Proof of the Gospel*. It was an argument which implied the finality of Christ, irrespective of claims to incarnation, since he alone was the fulfilment of the prophetic predictions. It is interesting to note that Athanasius argued *from* the claim to final revelation *to* the incarnation of a fully divine Logos. In other words, *a general acceptance among Christians that Christ was the final revelation, pre-dated the recognition of his full divinity*.

2. In the medieval and reformation periods, a theory of atonement came into prominence which has provided the language of gospel-preaching and hymns and prayers for generations of Christians, especially evangelicals. 'Christ died for our sins' has been understood to mean 'he received the punishment we deserved', and this has been justified by an appeal to the necessity of propitiating the wrath of God before forgiveness could be imparted; for

if God is a righteous God, the requirements of his justice must be met. In its essentials, this view of atonement hardly requires a *divine* Saviour. What is needed is a perfect man to pay the penalty mankind owed. A persistent theological criticism of this whole point of view has been that it divides the Trinity – Father and Son are set against each other in the atoning drama. In other words, this kind of doctrine of salvation through Christ is in certain respects inimical to the doctrine of incarnation.

It is of course true that it has always co-existed with the pre-supposition that the Christ who died was both God and man; it is also true that the best expositors and defenders of the theory have found it necessary to relate it to the classic Christian doctrine of incarnation, sometimes in order to justify the theory at all. Anselm in fact set up his conditions so as to require the incarnation: the debt owed by man is infinite, and only an infinite recompense can make satisfaction for it; therefore only a God-man could make the necessary offering. For R. W. Dale, who in the nineteenth century ably defended an objective theory of atonement against the critic-isms of liberal theologians, it was important that it was the Judge, the one identified with the moral law, who himself willingly under-took to meet the requirements of justice; only thus could he out-manoeuvre the moral objections to the theory advanced by his contemporaries. But the mere fact that such steps in the argument had to be consciously taken, surely goes to show that the theory itself largely operated, and certainly had its psychological force, independently of the doctrine of incarnation. The saving work of Christ in dying for our sins, and his revealing work as the incarnate Son of God, were two aspects of Christian understanding often not well-integrated with one another. More often than not the finality of Christ was primarily associated with the once-for-all atoning sacrifice which he offered.

In this paper I have suggested that it is not simply the doctrine of the incarnation which has produced or sustained the Christian claim to Christ's finality, but that other convictions have been involved. To subject the doctrine of the incarnation to critical scrutiny is not therefore bound to reduce the offence of Christian exclusiveness, nor is it necessarily to resolve the christological questions posed by the New Testament and Christian tradition. We still have to face the problem of the persistent claim charac-teristic of Christianity that Christ is in some sense 'final' or 'ulti-mate' for mankind.

This is not to say that any of the forms in which Christ's finality has been presented or understood in the past, is acceptable now. In spite of the current interest in eschatology stimulated by the theology of Pannenberg and Moltmann, it is doubtful whether the eschatological version of the claim to Christ's finality, linked as it is to the cultural conditions of the ancient world Jewish and Hellenistic, can now be revitalized outside rather specialist theological circles. The 'fulfilment of prophecy' cuts no ice as an argument in the current intellectual climate and present expectations of a cataclysmic End of the World are grounded not on hope in God's intervention but on secular pessimism. The 'penal substitution' theory of atonement continues to have evangelical appeal; but for many inside and outside the church it has proved increasingly unacceptable, if not positively offensive. If now the objections to incarnational belief prove valid, the classic grounds on which claims to Christ's finality have rested may all prove shaky. Yet in one form or another Christianity has clung to its conviction that Jesus Christ is in some sense final, that he has a unique and central role in theological understanding. The yardstick whereby so many heresies have been measured has been a loyalty to Jesus Christ which allowed no minimizing of his significance for the relationship between God and man. Christology remains at the centre of Christian theological exploration. Ultimately the question at issue is one of Christian identity – hence the emotive reaction to anything which suggests doubts or questions.

So the dilemma remains: If we affirm that God is Creator and then take seriously the fact that only a small minority of his creatures have had the opportunity to respond to him through Jesus Christ, it seems theologically offensive to continue to make exclusive claims to finality. On the other hand, in Christian faith and in Christian theology (whatever happens to the doctrine of incarnation), Jesus Christ has always been central and to dislodge him from that position would be to put Christian identity seriously at risk.

I think we have to face the fact that this dilemma is not easily resolved. Certainly an abandonment of identity in a vague syncretism, perhaps made respectable by the phrase 'religious ecumenism', would be a betrayal of the Christian heritage. I suspect that the only possibility of resolution lies in a positive acceptance of pluralism and an abandonment of the search for idealistic absolutes. What we make of Christ cannot be considered without reference to our total experience of God's world, a world in which everything is coloured by the specific particularities of individuals, cultures, historical circumstances and so on. (Have we not already discovered this in the ecumenical movement within Christianity? Uniformity is an impossible ideal, not merely in style of worship or ministry, but perhaps especially in theology.) No human individual, institution or movement can claim absolute or universal validity for its beliefs. Yet each human individual and group has a right to its own identity and dignity. So Christianity too may claim a right to its particular identity, and may foster the preservation of its tradition and its peculiar religious insights, even though claims to over-riding absoluteness have to be abandoned. In abandoning exclusive claims to a unique and final divine revelation in Jesus, and recognizing that all mankind has not and cannot be expected to see God in him, we should not be tempted to reduce the centrality of Jesus for Christian belief. Jesus Christ as the one through whom God has confronted us must surely continue to play a central role in Christian theology, for it is an essential element in Christian consciousness. We have to stick with the problem of christology, not abandon it or reduce it.

NOTES

1. See *The Myth of God Incarnate*, pp. 20–21 and notes.

2. There are a number of notorious difficulties with this text: (*i*) *monogenēs*, often interpreted as 'only-begotten' could simply mean 'unique'; certainly it can hardly have carried the technical associations of later trinitarian controversy. (*ii*) Whether or not this adjective was followed by a noun, and whether that noun was *hyios* or *theos*, is far from clear from the textual evidence. *Theos* is usually taken to be the more difficult reading and therefore more likely to be correct, and it also has strong ancient attestation; but it cannot be regarded as certain that it was part of the original text. See Sanders and Mastin, *The Gospel according to St John* (Black's New Testament Commentaries) p. 85 for arguments against the presence of either *hyios* or *theos* in the original text.

3. Käsemann, *The Testament of Jesus*, ET SCM Press 1968.

4. This is an attempt to convey to the modern reader the vague range of things which the word 'Logos' might have conveyed to a varied cross-section of the author's contemporaries: e.g. for the Stoics it could mean the divine rationality which was the basis of the universe (i.e. its 'meaning'), whereas to the Jew it could have meant the revelation of God's will and purpose (i.e. God's 'meaning' in a slightly different sense).

5. See *The Myth*, ch. 5, pp. 113–116.

6 · Christ and the Claims of Other Faiths

(i) The Uniqueness of the Incarnation
Brian Hebblethwaite

From time to time the suggestion was made, chiefly by John Hick, but also by Maurice Wiles and Don Cupitt, that there is no reason why, if incarnation is possible at all, it should only have taken place once rather than at many points in the history of religions. This opened up the whole question of the relation between Christianity and the other world faiths.

The suggestion that Jesus might have been one of many incarnations of God in human history betrays a complete failure to appreciate what the doctrine of the incarnation, in classical Christian faith, has been held to state. If God himself, in one of the modes of his being, has come into our world in person, to make himself personally known and to make himself vulnerable to the world's evil, in order to win our love and bind us to himself, we cannot suppose that he might have done so more than once. For only one man can actually *be* God to us, if God himself is one. We are to posit relation in God, yes, but not a split personality. Only one actual human person can be the vehicle and expression of the one God on earth. To think of many human beings as incarnations of God is to think of incarnation in a different sense – a derived metaphorical sense, namely, the embodiment of general characteristics. It is true that a whole number of loving, self-sacrificial men and women can manifest something of the loving kindness of God in their lives. But that doesn't make them God himself in person.

The scandal of particularity is only a scandal to those who have failed to appreciate what God has done. Indeed it is the particularity of God's action in 'setting his love in human neighbourhood' (Farrer) that makes God credible and lovable in an utterly personal way. The nub of the matter is what we mean by personal knowledge. I can know many facts about another at second hand from many sources. But when I meet that other face to face, I begin to know him personally – a totally different existential relation from what was the case before. Admittedly that is not a fair analogy for the relation between Christianity and other religions;

for God is present to all men in hidden ways, by his Spirit. He is not just the unknown transcendent God. He is immanent in the whole world, particularly in the worlds of religion and ethics. But here we have to spell out the difference between immanence and incarnation. Religious and moral experience can undoubtedly mediate God to us. We can enlarge on the opening verses of the epistle to the Hebrews: God has not only spoken to us of old by the prophets; he has also spoken to us through mystical experience, ethical concern and human love; but he has now spoken to us by a Son. And the Son, we discover, is very God of very God, God's human face, reflecting God's own glory, and bearing the stamp of his nature.

This unique incarnation, in which all knowledge of God is taken up and transformed into personal encounter, is not an isolated bolt from the blue. For Christian understanding, the whole of history pivots on the event of Christ's coming. The wider context of the history of religion and ethics, and the narrower context of the history of Israel, are to be regarded as providentially ordered, preparing the way for the incarnation. Moreover the whole future of man's relation to God, subsequent to the incarnation, is channelled through Christ, risen and ascended. His glorified humanity remains the focus of our knowledge of God both now and in the eschaton.

Admittedly we have to go on to speak of Christ in universal terms. He is no longer to be thought of as restricted to the particular slice of space-time that we read about in the gospels. Just as the men of the New Testament came very rapidly to think of him in cosmic terms as the one through whom the world was made and as the universal Logos of God, enlightening every man that comes into the world, so we look for his hidden, all-embracing presence in religion and ethics everywhere. But the specific, particular incarnation remains the key, the clue, and the criterion both of God's way with man, and for man's future in God. That clue is ironed out, that focus blurred, if we take the incarnation out of its total, world-historical context, and read it as one point among others of divine-human encounter. Christianity just is not like that. For better or for worse, the incarnation provides a total interpretative key by which all other knowledge of God is to be finally illuminated and transformed, just because it is God's own particular act in time and for eternity.

Consequently, I can make nothing of Wiles' objection (*The Myth* p. 11) that if incarnation is possible, it ought to be achieved in all men. The incarnation concerns God's dealings with us, now and for all time. He identifies himself with our lot in the closest possible way in order to draw us to him. I have argued that it makes no sense to suppose that he who made himself one of us might have been many of us. Still less sense (if that is possible) does it make to say that he might have been all of us. The purpose of the incarnation was to establish a new relation between ourselves and God. But the incarnation is not itself a *relation* between God and man. It includes that, admittedly, and Jesus' relation to the Father is the model for all divine-human relations. But the main point of the incarnation is not a matter of relation at all. It is a matter of identity. Jesus *is* God incarnate – for our sake and for our salvation. He draws near to us in Jesus. He is himself present and active precisely there. But he does not become you and me. To suggest that he might is not only a nonsense in itself. It makes nonsense of the purpose of the incarnation, namely, the restoration of *relationship* between God and ourselves.

(ii)   A Response to Hebblethwaite
John Hick

Brian Hebblethwaite is trying to prove that 'If God himself, in one of the modes of his being, has come into our world in person, to make himself personally known and to make himself vulnerable to the world's evil, in order to win our love and bind us to himself, we cannot suppose that he might have done so more than once' (p. 189). But I do not think that he succeeds in proving this. His argument (which appears above) boils down to this, that 'only one man can actually *be* God to us' (p. 189).

Much depends upon who is comprehended under the 'us'. It may be – though even this can be questioned – that only one man can actually *be* God to a given individual or to a particular group of individuals. But it does not follow – assuming for the sake of argument the viability of the notion of literal divine incarnation – that God, in one of the modes of his being, might not become a man (Jesus of Nazareth) within one particular stream of life, and also become a man (a different historical individual) within another separate stream of human life – say the Chinese civilization in the fourth or fifth century BC.

Many would accept that if there is intelligent spiritual life on other planets of other stars, a divine incarnation on such a planet would not have to be as the earth-man, Jesus of Nazareth, but rather as a member of the stream of life taking place on that other planet. If this is right, it implies that God could become incarnate more than once – and indeed, in principle, an indefinite number of times – for the sake of separate groups of people. And it could well be argued that the Chinese population in the fifth century BC was almost as separate from the population of Europe as are those of earth and another planet. Is it then really axiomatic that God could not have become incarnate separately within the great civilizations of the ancient world – China, India and the Mediterranean?

I am not, needless to say, suggesting that God *did* become incarnate (in Hebblethwaite's literal sense – see pp. 27f.) in ancient China and India. I am rather pointing to an inadequacy in the traditional Christian dogma – an inadequacy which was invisible to the early Christian thinkers, who knew virtually nothing of India and China, but which has become visible to us today.

Moving to the wider question of the relation between the Christian revelation and the other world religions, I think it can now be said that Christian thinkers and church leaders in this country have turned decisively away from the older view of those other religions as lying outside the sphere of God's saving activity. It is now widely accepted that God has been and is making his reality known to men and women, in both grace and demand, and is drawing them into his eternal life, not only within Christianity but also within the other historic streams of religious life and faith. And so the older assumption that all human beings must be converted to Jesus as their only Lord and Saviour, if they are to become acceptable to God, has given place to dialogue with people of other traditions on a basis of full mutual respect. For example, the British Council of Churches, with a view to the new cultural and religious pluralism of this country, declared in 1977 that 'We recognise that Britain is now a pluralist society of varied races, cultures and religions; we must respect those who practise different religions and adhere to different styles of life; a more varied society offers new opportunities to us all'.[1] And Bishop John V. Taylor, delivering in 1978 the first of a new series of Lambeth Interfaith Lectures, said that 'We believe now that the Ultimate Reality upon which the faith of all believers is focussed in every religion is the same. . .'.[2] And one could cite a number of other indications that this point of view is now becoming accepted orthodoxy within mainstream Christianity in this country.

But there is a reluctance to see that this new and more positive attitude to other religions has christological implications. The 'No salvation outside Christianity' attitude depended upon two main factors, one negative and the other positive – the negative factor being a lack of knowledge among most Western church members concerning the other great world faiths, and the positive factor being the conviction that Jesus Christ was uniquely divine, the one and only mediator between God and man.

The negative factor is now disappearing. A vast range of well presented information about the religions of the world is readily available to all who want it. What might, even a generation ago, have been excused as invincible ignorance is now culpable ignorance. It is no longer acceptable to say 'Of course I don't know anything about other religions . . .' and then go on to assume the salvific uniqueness of one's own religion. But the growing appreciation of spiritual truths and values within other religious traditions, and the developing recognition of them as authentic spheres of salvation, inevitably puts the Christian doctrine of the unique saviourhood of Christ under strain. If Christ was (literally rather than metaphorically) God incarnate, it would seem clear that the religion which he founded must be intended to supersede all other religions. Why should God wish anyone to follow a different religion from the one which he himself personally founded and in which he now lives by his Spirit? But having, in the light of reality, largely abandoned the project of the conversion of the world, whether in this or any other generation, do we not need to re-examine the assumptions which led to it?

A number of attempts have been and are being made in both Catholic and Protestant theology to reconcile the new spirit of interfaith dialogue with the old insistence that Jesus Christ was God incarnate and the Christian faith accordingly unique and superior. We have the suggestion that devout Muslims etc. may be 'anonymous Christians' (Karl Rahner); or that the world religions may constitute the 'ordinary' and the church the 'extraordinary' way of salvation (Hans Küng); or that non-Christians will encounter Christ, and have the possibility of salvation, in the life to come if not in this life; and other more tentative suggestions yet to be fully worked out. But these attempts suffer from a distinct air of artificiality, reminiscent of the epicycles added to the old Ptolemaic astronomy before the inevitable shift to a new model of the universe. I would urge fellow theologians to consider seriously the possibility of a more radical solution. Such a solution could begin by recognizing that the language of divine incarnation is a basic metaphor, and that the revelation of God's love in the human life of Jesus is one of many mutually supporting pointers to God, available to mankind in the great religious traditions of the world. (Since it is impossible to develop this idea more fully here, let me mention that I have tried to do so in *God and the Universe of Faiths.*[3])

NOTES

1. *Racism in Britain* – a Time for Decision: A Statement by the British Council of Churches, November 1977.

2. John V. Taylor, 'The Theological Basis of Interfaith Dialogue', *Crucible*, January-March, 1978, p 14.

3. John Hick, *God and the Universe of Faiths*, Macmillan/St Martin's Press 1973; Collins (paperback) 1977.

7 · Can *We* Believe in the Incarnation?

A (i)   The Centrality of Jesus for History
Lesslie Newbigin

All attempts to state the truth about what is the case have to make certain assumptions. Christian statements have traditionally been made on the basis of the assumption that (however difficult it might be to grasp) God himself was personally present in the man Jesus. The writers of *The Myth of God Incarnate* do not believe this. The statements of the grounds for disbelief rest, like all human statements, upon certain assumptions. These assumptions are not themselves questioned. For example, when it is said that 'in Jesus Christ I perceive something of God'[1] it is implied that we know enough about God apart from Jesus to be in a position to judge whether and to what extent we can recognize 'something of him' in Jesus. My purpose in this paper is to ask about these assumptions which underlie the argument. At the risk of over-simplifying the issues I suggest that the following three inter-related propositions are implied in the arguments of the book.

1. That there is a general religious experience of mankind in the light of which we have to understand Jesus.

2. That 'there is nothing intrinsically more secure in a know-ledge of God which claims to rest on "certain historical events" ... than in a knowledge of God which claims to rest upon more general historical experience (including that to which scripture bears witness) but which does not treat any particular events within that broad spectrum as essential'.[2]

3. That the facts about Jesus are inaccessible except in the broadest outline because what we have is not 'history' in a sci-entific sense but a series of interpretations of Jesus which come from first-century communities and reflect their experience within the accepted world views of their time.

It will be convenient to take these in the reverse order, since – if the facts about Jesus are inaccessible it is futile to talk about his finality for history.

The accessibility of the Jesus of history
All 'historical facts', it has been rightly said, are judgments of historical evidence. Even the most primary data of the historian (I

am not speaking of the archaeologist) are records which somebody made because they were judged to be worth recording. This is already a judgment of significance. And the selection of available material for study, the direction of research, the questions asked all depend upon the judgment of the historian as to what is significant. This judgment is in turn conditioned by the time and place in which the historian works, and the culture to which he belongs. It has often been remarked by writers on the art of the historian that the greatest historical writing tells us as much about the period of the writer as about the period which he studies. But this does not mean that their work cannot be trusted. On the contrary, they help us to understand the periods about which they write precisely because they themselves were trying to understand them in the only way in which anything can be understood – namely by seeking to grasp the data in the power of those concepts which they themselves had come to acknowledge as valid. If they did not do this they would not be great historians. We who in our time and place seek to understand the past are able to take their understanding as part of the material through which we ourselves come to understand. The fact that in doing so we recognize the convictions which shaped their understanding of the past does not mean that we regard the past of which they wrote as inaccessible to our understanding because their convictions stand between us and it.

When we turn to consider the story of Jesus, it is obvious that we do not have any 'bare facts', if this means uninterpreted facts. Our data are the testimonies of those who believed in him as Lord and Saviour. It is one of the often repeated statements of the text-books that, whereas up to a point about the end of the eighteenth century the story of Jesus was interpreted in accordance with the traditional faith of the church, at about that time 'the old dogmatic presuppositions were set aside and the modern scientific approach to the question of the history of Jesus began'. Obviously all historical study involves presuppositions; what happened was that one set of presuppositions was replaced by another. But what exactly was the change which took place at that point in the way the Western European tribes understood their history?

There seem to have been two stages. There was first the eighteenth-century concept of 'progress'. This was a typical product of the Age of Reason. It saw the new ways of knowledge developed in the seventeenth and eighteenth centuries as the key to unlimited future mastery over nature. It was not interested in the past; that was a period of darkness which had little to contribute to real knowledge. Interest was centred on the future when the last king would have been strangled with the guts of the last priest and all the irrational tyrannies of the past abolished. The second stage came with the Romantic Movement. Its characteristic product was the idea of development. In contrast to the idea of progress, this was interested in the past. It saw history as the unfolding of that which had been present from the beginning. Whereas the Age of Reason had seen the world in terms of time-less truths, valid equally for the Greek and Roman and for the Frenchman of today, the romantic age saw things as continually developing. It therefore became passionately interested in the past, and out of that interest the vast labours of the nineteenth-century historians were born. The fact that the ideas of progress and of development were later fused into a single general con-sciousness of movement towards an ever brighter future should not obscure the distinction between the two ideas in their beginnings.

How was the understanding of the story of Jesus changed by these movements? Two points must be made. First, the new pers-pective required that the story of Jesus be seen as part of a continu-ing story rather than as the once-for-all revelation of timeless truths which had no essential relation to an ongoing history. In the earlier view the story as enshrined in the text of scripture was itself the revelation, and no passage of time could change it. Although Augustine had made a decisive break with the classical concep-tions of history and had inspired the first attempt to write a true world-history based upon the biblical story, yet the succeeding generations had seen the encapsulation of this biblical history within the classical view of time as cyclical. Thus the writing of history up to the end of the eighteenth century was concerned with drawing out the rational and moral truths exemplified by the story rather than with the placing of events within a continuously developing process. Applied to the story of Jesus the new perspec-tive meant that text and history fell apart. Revelation was no longer a divinely guaranteed text; it was a series of events in his-tory of which the texts were the primary evidence, but which had to be studied as part of the whole history and with the same methods.

The second point is related but distinct. The presuppositions upon which the story was now to be understood were those of the nineteenth century concerning development. It was not just that the story of Jesus was seen as continuous with the entire secular history of the world; it was that this story was understood from a new centre. It was understood as the unfolding of forces imminent within history from the beginning, as a continuous and unbroken nexus of cause and effect every part of which is understood by relating it to what went before and after. From such a view the concept of a unique divine intervention from beyond history is excluded in principle.

The first of these two points is not in dispute in the present debate. The second is crucial. For this new perspective excludes the possibility of attributing 'finality' to Jesus in respect of the course of world history as a whole. It therefore leads necessarily to a disjunction between 'the Jesus of history' and 'the Christ of faith'. The judgment of the nineteenth-century historian about what is significant, about what is possible, and about what kind of evidence can be trusted, rested upon the assumptions of his culture; and when he applied his methods of research to the New Testament, he was necessarily searching for an interpretation of the data which could be fitted into these assumptions. The records as he found them had all been written on the basis of a different understanding. The nineteenth-century historian could therefore only see them as coming between him and the 'real' Jesus. There followed the long effort to get behind the 'Christ of faith' to the 'Jesus of history' – or rather to speak more accurately, to replace the interpretaton of Jesus which was based upon one understanding of history with one based on another. It is not surprising that the result was a series of questionable fragments.

The issue here is not between 'history' and 'faith'; it is conflict between two different faiths. All understanding of history rests upon some provisional belief about the meaning of the whole. The Christian faith is a particular way of understanding history as a whole which finds in the story about Jesus its decisive clue. The real nature of the conflict has been misunderstood because the church has failed to grasp the implications of the new understanding of history and its bearing on the nature of revelation. Instead of meeting the challenge of a rival world-view with a fresh attempt to relate the gospel to world history (such as Augustine made), the Western churches have (in general) accepted the relegation of the gospel to the 'private sector' where it takes its place as one of the ways of personal salvation and abandons its claim to be the clue to the understanding of the whole public life of mankind. The attempt to define a 'sacred history' apart from the whole history which all peoples share may be seen as part of this withdrawal movement. It was natural that when this attempt failed, the question of the relation of Christianity to the other religions should become the burning issue for Western Christians (in contrast to

Christians of – for instance – Latin America where the burning issues are related to Christian faith and Marxism). Here in the West the church seems to have tacitly reversed the refusal of the early church to accept the protected position of a *cultus privatus* and to be regarded as one of the forms of private *gnosis*.

The significance of historicity for faith

I have argued that all understanding of history rests on some kind of faith. But does faith have to rest upon history? Does it matter whether 'it really happened'? J. H. Oldham, writing in the heat of the conflict with the Nazi movement, wrote: 'The Christian faith ... implies that events took place which changed fundamentally the relations between God and man and instituted a new era in human life. History now possesses a centre. From this centre it derives its ultimate meaning.'[3] Maurice Wiles, writing in the present year, says: 'The exact historical status of the events traditionally associated with the Christian faith has to be assessed by historical means, and the outcome of that investigation will frequently turn out to be "not proven".'[4] What is at issue between these two positions?

Wiles identifies two forms of the counter-position which he describes as 'strong' and 'weak'. The former, ascribed to Barth, says that to separate Christian faith from historic events makes the faith false; the latter, ascribed to John Baker, says that the separation reduces the certainty with which the faith can be held. Wiles deals with Barth by accusing him of begging the question, but when we are dealing with different ultimate faith commitments this argument cuts equally both ways. In defence of Barth one may suggest an analogy. While much information about a person may be obtained by collecting and organizing the reports about him from all sources, this is not equivalent to the knowledge of him which is given through the words and gestures and acts which he directs to me personally. If a person does in fact address me in this way (as Christian faith asserts that God has done), and if I decide that nevertheless I should prefer to get my information about him from generally accessible sources, it would surely be fair to say that the knowledge I would gain would be different in kind from what I would have obtained by listening to him. Professor Wiles has kindly drawn my attention to a statement of Barth when he was challenged on this point: the theologian, says Barth, 'must answer directly and without qualification, without being ashamed of his naivety, that Jesus Christ is the one and entire truth through which he is shown how to think and speak'.[5] Wiles remarks that he finds this a very unsatisfactory answer, but why should it be thought so? On what grounds can it be shown that the understanding of how things are that is obtained from this child-like attention to Jesus as the clue to it all is inferior to that which can be obtained by the attempt to develop one's clues for grasping the vast complexity of experience? Indeed is not the former stance more appropriate for a creature before its creator, and for a forgiven sinner before its saviour?

In answer to the 'weaker' form of the contrary view Wiles writes that 'there is nothing intrinsically more secure in a knowledge of God which claims to rest upon "certain historical events" whose historicity is regarded as essential, than in a knowledge of God which claims to rest upon a more general historical experience (including that to which scripture bears witness) but which does not treat any particular events ... as essential.'[6] Now it is obvious that 'general historical experience' is a very large, complex and ambiguous entity. It would be a bold man who could claim that general historical experience proves, or even faintly suggests, that the one in charge of the universe is like Jesus. In fact we do not grasp general historical experience at all except by means of models and concepts which we take as provisional clues. The question at issue is: where do we find these clues? What is popularly conceived to be the 'religious' approach to experience is that one finds the clues in certain mental and spiritual experiences which are widely shared among human beings – described in such phrases as 'a sense of the transcendent', a 'feeling of absolute dependence', an awareness of 'absolute demand and final succour', or the mystical experience of the oneness of the Self with the All, or in other ways. Judaism, Christianity and Islam – on the other hand – claim to find the clues in particular events, events which they are under obligation to make widely known. The distinction can be seen most sharply by comparing the doctrines of man to be found in the Upanishads with those of the Old Testament. In the former the ultimate truth about man is sought in his interiority, in the deepest recesses of his being where all relations with the sensible world and with other human beings have been left behind. In the Old Testament, by contrast, the truth about man is seen in his relatedness to his neighbour and in his responsibility to God for both his neighbour and for the world in which God has placed him. I think that the Indian tradition has been more powerful in shaping Western ideas than the biblical. Consequently there is a reluctance to tie the revelation of ultimate truth to concrete historic events. Wiles (see above page 10) asks that we separate the 'categorical religious demand' from being 'tied to the historical person of Jesus in a strictly metaphysical way' (as in the traditional doctrine) and insists that it is 'the categorical element that belongs properly to religious faith' which must be preserved.

Does this tying up to history matter? To the devout Hindu it does not matter whether the facts about the Battle of the Kurukshettra were as stated in the Gita; what matters is that he has in his hands the sublime teaching of the Lord to Arjuna. Why should not I, as a Christian, be equally content with the New Testament? The past is past and cannot be anything else, but I have in my hand the record of it and on this I feed my soul? What more do I need? Why, as a Hindu friend once asked me, should I be so foolish as to risk the salvation of my soul on questionable events in history? What is at stake?

I answer that what is at stake is the full humanity of man. More precisely, it is the question whether man is to be understood ultimately in terms of his inward, private spiritual life alone, or whether he is to be understood in terms which include both this and also the public life which he shares with the whole of the rest of mankind and with the world of nature in a single cosmic history; whether 'salvation' is only of 'the soul' or of the whole human being – a participant in the whole history of man and of nature. Let me spell this out in the following affirmations.

1. The present which I now live and experience will become the past for future believers. My way of understanding the past must be valid also for their way of understanding my present. If with regard to the past I hold that the 'happenedness' of alleged events does not matter because it is the truths, values, experiences to which they bear witness that matter, then the same must apply to the life I now live. In that case the things I actually do, the part I play in the shared life of my time, do not matter; what matters is the truths, values etc. (the 'categorical religious demand') to which I bear witness. But if, on the other hand, what I do really matters; if it really matters whether my insights are translated into action on the stage of public events and not simply treasured in the inner room of my soul, then the same must apply to the events of the past.

2. It is always possible to believe that history is a kind of shadow play, that nothing really happens. Much religion has assumed this and advised the prudent to forsake the shadows and seek the real beyond. I keep a daily diary but, like others, I have to admit that there are many days when there is nothing significant to record. Perhaps it is my blindness which prevents me from seeing what is

significant. There have been long stretches of time when it seemed to a whole people that there was nothing to record. Indian history before the time of the Muslim invasions has had to be almost entirely recreated by Western scholars, for in the Hindu view history was not a bearer of significance. The question which cannot be avoided is: are there significant happenings, events which by their actual 'happenedness' make a difference to the whole human story, or is it true, as Collingwood seems to have taught, that history exists only in the mind? I here confess my belief that there are happenings which are significant in the sense that they change the course of the story and not just the way men think.

3. But one must ask: significant for what? In telling the story of a small society or institution it is usually not difficult to identify the events which were specially significant for that story. But no society exists apart from the wider society of nation and world, and the final judgment of what is significant even for a small society will depend upon a judgment of what is significant for the whole story. But the story is not yet finished; how then can we know what is significant? It is always possible that there may be a surprising end and therefore no firm conclusions can be drawn by induction from the evidence so far available. It follows that there can be no escape from the necessity of a prior decision, which can only be an act of faith, as to the clue which will be accepted as the starting-point for understanding.

4. This clue could be something in the public sphere of observable events or it could be something in the inner experiences which we all share and which are not necessarily bound up with particular events – even though one may be able to point to a time and place when attention was first drawn to this common experience. In the latter case the events of history will be seen as illustrations of the spiritual realities which are common to all human beings. The insights shared in common among many religious traditions will be prized as essential clues, and the exact historical status of the circumstances alleged to have surrounded the enunciation of these insights will be unimportant. The future will be seen in terms of the perfecting of the individual human soul and there will be no interest in an eschatology which looks to a shared future for the human family.

5. If the former alternative is chosen then – as Oldham insisted – everything will depend upon the faith that history has a centre from which it takes its meaning. The public history of mankind will be seen as a coherent reality which has a real centre and a real end. The centre (in the Christian understanding) is the life and death

and resurrection of Jesus. The end is not, of course, the end-product of historical development as conceived in the eighteenth-century doctrine of progress; to think that would be to deny the judgment upon history which is embodied in the cross. The end is the new creation of which the resurrection of Jesus is the first-fruit. But this new creation is the true consummation of the shared history of mankind and of nature. It is symbolized not in the idea of disembodied survival for the individual, but in the vision of a city which is at the same time the gift of God and the true goal of the story of civilization. The meaning of the story as a whole will have been grasped in the only way which is possible, not by induction from the generality of experience but by a revelation in the form of happenings which are grasped by faith as the self-communication of the one whose purpose the story embodies. The 'happenedness' of these events which form the clue to the whole will be essential to the faith. And the faith will be expressed in a life of discipleship in the shared life of humanity, seen not just as illustrations of the faith or as exercises in personal spiritual growth, but as participation in the story whose centre has been discerned in the events.

6. I suggest, therefore, that the issues in the discussion between Maurice Wiles and John Baker have to be re-stated. It is not (as Wiles says) a matter of greater or less certitude about the same beliefs; it is rather a conflict between two ultimate beliefs. At the beginning it is a question of where we are to find the clues for understanding the human situation. In the end it is the question whether the shared public life of mankind has a place in the ultimate purpose of God, whether 'salvation' refers to the destiny of a soul conceived as an entity apart from the total human person, or to the destiny of the human person considered realistically as part of history and nature. It is, I think, the question which the primitive church decided in principle when it declined to accept the status of a *cultus privatus*, or to allow the Christian faith to be assimilated to the private *gnosis* characteristic of the spirituality of the period.

7. If I am right, the issue to which the discussion leads us is whether the church accepts or challenges the view of our contemporary Western culture which relegates Christian faith to the private sector and adopts other models for its interpretation of world history and therefore of current public affairs. Here we come back to the matter discussed in the first section of the paper. There is a reciprocal relation between the question of the accessibility of the facts about Jesus and the question of the necessity or otherwise of

a belief in the 'happenedness' of these facts, just as there is a reciprocal relation between the models by means of which one seeks to grasp the facts and the facts themselves. One's judgment about the reliability of the apostolic testimony to Jesus will depend upon whether or not one shares their belief in the unique and decisive character of his person and work, or whether one seeks to interpret Jesus by means of models drawn from other experience. In the first case the New Testament witness to Jesus will be taken as a trustworthy clue to be followed in seeking to understand experience and to share in the public life of one's time and place. This does not mean laying aside the critical tools fashioned during the last 200 years of scholarship, but it means that these tools will be used from within the commitment to Jesus as Lord and not from within some other commitment. Alternatively, if other clues are taken as decisive, then the testimony of the apostles will have to be understood in terms of these clues – as in the many re-interpretations of the *religionsgeschichtliche* scholars. In both cases one is arguing in a circle, but that is characteristic of all systems of fundamental belief.

8. I have spoken of Christian faith as a judgment of historical evidence. It is essential to add that this is not a judgment made once for all and therefore petrified in a fixed tradition. It is a living and developing thing because the believer is constantly called upon to meet new situations and other fundamental commitments, and is again and again called upon to re-test and re-think his faith. Here is the Christian form of the circularity of which I have spoken. The whole enterprise of Christian discipleship is both a continuous exegesis of and a continuous revision of the original commitment to Jesus. It is therefore a proper and necessary duty of theologians to attempt, as the authors of *The Myth* have done, to re-interpret the story about Jesus in terms intelligible to our culture. The formulae developed in the first five centuries naturally used the language of their time and much of it is unusable today. I think that, in contrast to the traditional language about 'nature' and 'substance' it is proper in our situation to take the new under-standing of history as the most important element in our culture for the understanding of Jesus. The life, death and resurrection of Jesus are – I believe – the decisive events in God's history with his creation. Some at least of the authors of *The Myth* believe this, but they are inhibited from giving adequate expression to it by tradi-tional ideas of God drawn from other sources. If Jesus is decisive for history, then his presence is God's presence – unless God has abdicated. Why do these writers not believe this? Because of a

prior conception of God which makes it inconceivable that God should be involved in history. But we must ask for the credentials of this 'God'. Is he not, in fact, a typical 'no-god', one of the 'vanities' of which the Bible speaks, a product of human devising? For myself I cannot look to this 'god' for my salvation. But I can look to Jesus Christ, and I can follow the goodly company of Christian thinkers who have learned to follow him as the Son through whom we come to the Father in the power of the Spirit and thus come to know the living God through his own saving action.

Jesus in the context of the religious experience of mankind

This brings me to the first of the three assumptions which I have to criticize, 'that there is a general religious experience of mankind in the light of which we should formulate our statements about Jesus'. The word 'God', as I have just stated, when used in contemporary English speech, is usually understood to refer to a Being (conceived in unitarian terms) about whom some knowledge is generally available; it is assumed that this knowledge is what religion is about: and that Christianity is one form of this general class which we call 'religion'. In this climate of opinion it is natural to assume that the claims about Jesus should be judged in the context of this wider (and prior) reality. In so far as 'God' is known apart from Jesus we obviously have a standpoint from which we can assess claims made about the relation of Jesus to God. Thus Wiles rejects the view that 'Jesus is to be identified with God' in favour of the view that 'he symbolizes and expresses God's action towards the world' (see above page 7). In the Christian tradition Jesus is spoken of as the 'Word' of God. A word (which from one point of view is a series of vibrations in the air or marks on paper) symbolizes and expresses the intention of its author. Words can have differing degrees of authenticity in respect of the degree to which they constitute a true self-communication of the speaker. The letter to the Hebrews says that God, who spoke in many and various ways by the prophets 'has in these last days spoken to us by a Son ... who bears the very stamp of his nature and upholds the universe by his word of power'. The synoptic tradition similarly speaks of a continuity and contrast between the prophets and Jesus. What is here affirmed is that Jesus does 'symbolize and express God's action towards the world' but in such a way that – in contrast to the prophets – he *is* God's active presence in the world.

Wiles' rejection of this rests, I think, on a doctrine of God drawn from other sources than the Bible. That is a separate question. The point here is that of the relation between the word which is Jesus and the other words. I have insisted that the other words must be evaluated in the light of Jesus and not vice versa. Wiles, if I understand him, rejects this as a false or unnecessary dichotomy and maintains that we can and must understand Jesus in the context of the wider religious experience of mankind – however deeply Jesus may transform our understanding of that experience. Is this not reasonable? Should we not place Jesus among, rather than over against the other witnesses to God?

In reply to this question I can only point to that which is the centre of the preaching of the gospel – to the cross. There was indeed a knowledge of God among the people whose life was rooted and nurtured in the faith of Israel; but in the name of that faith Israel solemnly and deliberately rejected Jesus as the enemy of God, as one under the curse of God. This is the crux of any discussion about the continuity of Christian faith with the wider religious experience of mankind. Of course the discontinuity is not total; total discontinuity is inconceivable. If something was totally discontinuous with my present experience I could not be aware of its existence. But it is necessary and proper to speak of a radical discontinuity between that perspective in which Jesus is perceived as enemy of God and that in which he is perceived as Lord. This is – I submit – a case in which there can only be 'either-or' and not 'both-and'. One does not, to put it another way, reach a true view of how things are by viewing both of these as variations of the common religious experience of mankind. I do not deny that such a view is possible. It is in fact widely held. My claim is that it is not true.

It can be argued against this that the gospels indicate a certain continuity in the experience of the disciples: even before the resurrection they are described as believers, disciples, followers. Presumably they had some real knowledge of God then? Indeed, yet all the four gospels insist with almost wearisome reiteration that before the resurrection the disciples did not and could not understand, and that in the end they all deserted, denied or betrayed him.

Certainly there is a continuity, but it is a continuity perceived from the new perspective and not otherwise. Saul of Tarsus could see Jesus only as the enemy of the law; it is only after the experience of life in Christ that he can understand that Jesus is the fulfiller of the law. There are, I believe, relevant analogies in the field of natural science. There is continuity between Newtonian physics and that of Einstein, but it can be seen only from the standpoint of the latter. There is no logical process by which Newtonian physics can accommodate the theories of Einstein. There is a leap, a conversion, a 'paradigm shift' (T. Kuhn). One can usefully interpret Newton from the point of view of Einstein, but not *vice versa*. In an analogous way one can speak meaningfully from within the perspective of the Christian faith of a real self-communication of God in the wider experience of mankind (not merely, be it noted, religious experience). From a perspective outside the Christian faith, on the other hand, the gospel is and remains incomprehensible. It is impossible that a man should be 'God's presence and his very self'. The same Paul who knows (as a Christian) that Christ is the fulfiller of the law, knows also that the gospel can only appear a scandal to the Jew and nonsense to the Greek. I do not believe that this element of scandal can be eliminated from the faithful communication of the gospel. This is not a love of irrationality for its own sake. It is not to echo Tertullian's *'Credo quia absurdum est'*. It is to recognize that a wider rationality which can justify the ways of God to man is not obtainable except on the other side of that radical change of perspective which has traditionally been called conversion. The precise character of that shift will vary with circumstances. The shift involved for a Hindu is not the same as that involved for a Jew or a Marxist. The presuppositions will be different, and will by no means necessarily be religious. Those in our day, for example, who are being converted from Marxism to Christianity certainly do not have to graduate by way of theism. What is common to all is that there is a radical shift of perspective. The word attributed to Jesus in his conversation with Nicodemus succinctly describes the situation: unless one is born anew he cannot see the kingdom of God. That the crucifixion of a Jew is the final and decisive manifestation of the rule of God in the universe – this is something which is strictly incomprehensible from a point of view other than that of the one who has been converted to total discipleship. But from that point of view this becomes the clue with which one begins a fresh understanding of the whole of experience, including those experiences which have been associated with the word 'God'. But then, obviously, one does not begin by asking how the story about Jesus can be related to the previous understanding of God; one asks rather what way of understanding the word 'God' can begin to do justice to the new situation. And it is out of this questioning that the doctrine of the Trinity has been developed.

The attempt to view the Christian story from the perspective of the general religious experience of mankind is attractive. It eliminates the scandal of which Paul speaks. It enables one to see Jesus, as the Hindu does today, as an example of the god-filled life. But there is a price to be paid. The general religious experience of mankind, if no event in history is allowed decisive place, does not and cannot furnish clues as to the meaning of history as a whole. Indian religion has taken this way, and it follows that Indian religion is dominated by the quest for a way of escape from the endless and meaningless cycle of existence. Contemporary English Christianity, sharing the general loss of faith in a significant future which has followed our loss of a sense of a national role in world affairs, is strongly tempted to go this way – as Christopher Dawson prophesied many years ago. It is helpful to turn at this moment to Augustine, who lived through the disintegration of the old pagan view of history to which we are now tempted to return, and who explored with all his intellectual powers the world of religious experience apart from Jesus. For Augustine discovered that a totally different quest is possible, that it is possible by the grace of God to be converted and to find in the gospel the starting point from which the whole of human experience can be seen in a new light. And while conversion cannot be brought about by any arguments from general religious experience, a Christian believer can and must ask whether there is anything in the history of religion comparable with that to which the gospel bears witness, and whether there is any other place than the cross of Jesus where the real issues of human existence are dealt with at so profound a level. I believe that the task of a Christian theologian is not to seek to place the story of Jesus within the general religious experience of mankind, but to place the myths of our contemporary culture in the light which streams from him when he is acknowledged as Lord.

NOTES

1. See Frances Young, *The Myth*, p. 13.
2. Maurice Wiles, 'In what sense is Christianity a "historical religion"?', *Theology*, LXXXI, January 1978, p. 12; reprinted in *Explorations in Theology 4*, SCM Press 1979, pp. 53–65.
3. J. H. Oldham, *The Church and its Function in Society*, Allen & Unwin 1937, pp. 103f.
4. Wiles, loc. cit.
5. E. Busch, *Karl Barth*, SCM Press 1976, p. 435.
6. Wiles, loc. cit.

A (ii) Comment on Lesslie Newbigin's Essay
Maurice Wiles

I welcome Lesslie Newbigin's concentration on some of the fundamental assumptions that underlie our discussions, especially as I dealt somewhat cursorily with that aspect of the debate in the first section of my own survey paper. But even papers about fundamental assumptions have fundamental assumptions of their own, and in this comment I want to draw out some of the basic assumptions that I found in his paper and would want to call in question.

1. At the very outset of his paper, Newbigin criticizes the statement 'In Jesus Christ I perceive something of God' on the ground that it implies a sufficient knowledge of God apart from Jesus to judge whether and to what extent we can recognize 'something of God' in Jesus. If the remark to which he takes exception had implied, yet still maintains his objection. For later on (p. 208) he changed by what we see in Jesus, Newbigin would have good ground to complain. But he acknowledges that this is not what is implied, yet still maintains his objection. For later on (p. 000) he protests against an understanding of Jesus in the context of the wider religious experience of mankind, even with the proviso that such an understanding of Jesus may profoundly transform our understanding of that wider experience. I regard such an extreme and exclusive insistence on Jesus as the source of any true knowledge of God as a narrowing and distorting perspective – and on that point I believe myself to have the main stream of Catholic tradition on my side.

The kind of difficulty that his position gets him into is well illustrated by his turning for support to the claim that it was in the name of the faith of Israel, with its knowledge of God, that Jesus was rejected as one under the curse of God (p. 208). If this is evidence for the strong case that he is trying to make out, it makes it very difficult, if not impossible, for him to do justice to the continuity between Jesus and the faith of Israel, which he explicitly acknowledges, as every Christian must. And what would be the implications of the gross crimes and acts of apostasy that are to be found on occasion in the history of the Christian community?

2. Newbigin rightly points out the difficulty of finding clues from within general historical experience that point towards a coherent meaning in history as a whole. Much of it seems to us to lack significance (p. 204); much militates against any conviction that the one in charge of the universe is like Jesus (p. 202). None of that do I wish to dispute. The difficulties are enormous. But he then goes on to claim that no answer to those difficulties is possible unless decisive place is allowed to a particular event (p. 210) and that that event is seen as 'the self-communication of the one whose purpose the story embodies' (p. 205). No one would want to deny that if a meaning is to be found in history, it will be because some events are seen as of outstanding significance, and for the Christian the event of Christ will be the most significant of all. But I do not see that he has made out his case that there would have to be *one* event of a different order of decisiveness, or that that one event would have to take the form of a divine self-communication as distinctive and direct as he postulates. To use his own analogy, we frequently grasp the meaning of a story not just from one key incident in which the author lets us into his secret, but from a series of more or less ambiguous clues at different points in the story.

3. Newbigin has some very interesting and perceptive things to say about the rise of critical historical study. He also goes on to stress that there is no such thing as a purely objective history, but that every historian sees things and writes from a particular perspective. With all that I am in substantial agreement. But I think he seriously overplays his perspectival card. He speaks as if the various perspectival views were fixed and incorrigible. Purely objective history may be an impossiblity, but it is nonetheless true that critical historical study may reveal factual evidence of a kind that forces us to modify the perspective from which we had initially approached our historical study. In the past the perspective from which many Christians approached the study of biblical history led them to see the biblical records as factually accurate throughout; but in course of time the evidence revealed by critical study forced most of them to modify that view. So when Newbigin writes that 'one's judgment about the reliability of the apostolic testimony to Jesus will depend upon whether or not one shares their belief in the unique and decisive character of his person and work' (p. 206), I want at the very least to enter a strong note of caution. Such a belief may properly affect the prior expectation with which one approaches the historical study involved. But it cannot by itself determine the outcome of one's judgment. The evidence may lead one to modify the degree of confidence with which one can assert

the 'happenedness' of particular events of which that testimony speaks. And if that requires some corresponding modification of the belief with which one had first come to the study, then such modification is both possible and necessary.

4. It was this last point that I was particularly trying to make in my *Theology* article which Newbigin refers to at various points in his paper. But as I said in the paper itself, I did not (and still do not) see it as committing me to 'advocating a total divorce between Christianity and history'.[1] Yet that is how Newbigin, working with a very sharp dichotomy between inner experience and public history, understands it. It is certainly true that there are religious traditions which give primary, or even exclusive, importance to withdrawal from concern with public affairs and which see man's communion with God as solely a matter of private, inner experience. But I do not think he has made out a case for claiming that my approach to incarnation, or that of the other authors of *The Myth of God Incarnate*, involves any such exclusive valuation of private, inner experience. One way in which he expresses the different implications of his approach and mine is that only his will be interested in 'an eschatology which looks to a shared future for the human family' (p. 204) and able to maintain that 'the shared public life of mankind has a place in the ultimate purpose of God' (p. 205). I think there are great difficulties in making satisfactory sense of those concepts, but they are difficulties which I am as anxious to grapple with as he is. Nor do I think they are any easier of solution for him with his way of understanding God's action in Jesus Christ than they are for me with mine.

NOTE

1 'In what sense is Christianity a "historical religion"?', *Theology*, January 1978, p. 13; *Explorations in Theology 4*. SCM Press 1979. p. 64.

B Relativism in Science and Theology
John Rodwell

In my earlier contribution I attempted to show how some of the ideas of Karl Popper might be relevant to rescuing theology from the dilemma created by the Logical Positivists, a dilemma which I see perpetuated in various ways by the authors of *The Myth of God Incarnate*. There is a further issue which I touched on but briefly there, one on which the Popperian view has itself been criticized: it is the question of relativism. Briefly the issue, as it concerns us here, may be stated as follows. Even if we concede that religious propositions are in some way connected with reality, and not meaningless in the sense of the Logical Positivists, it may be that such propositions are so closely related to the cultural contexts in which they arose that they are inaccessible to other cultures and generations and may indeed tell us more about the contexts than about the reality they were intended to relate to. Under such circumstances, what purchase can the others have or expect on even the strongest propositions of the original culture, and what hold do or can any of us have on what really is? Such questions are a powerful undertow throughout *The Myth of God Incarnate* and I wish now to examine, first, how seriously the authors have taken the issue and, second, what developments in the philosophy of science might be of help to us in considering the problems it raises.

The book offers a variety of programmes to account for the growth of the traditional incarnation doctrine. Frances Young considers the New Testament and Patristic contexts;[1] Michael Goulder examines the contemporary Samaritan background;[2] John Hick offers us a comparison of the process of divinization of Jesus and Gautama.[3] I am not qualified to comment on the detailed evidence adduced in each case but there is a general observation I wish to make. Although I fully acknowledge the care with which these reconstructions have been undertaken and the sincerity with which they are presented, I detect a certain ease and security in the subsequent dismissal of the traditional doctrinal alternative.

We have already seen that, for some of the authors. the elucida-

developed is tantamount to a mechanism for rejecting that proposition[4] and this seems to be common to most of the contributors. This assumes a certain neutrality of vision which can appear condescending. It is as if the authors have found a place from which they may, with equal levels of freedom, survey the entire sweep of human history. John Hick tells us that it was 'natural and intelligible' that the divinization of Jesus should have occurred given the conditions of the cultural milieu (p. 176) with the inevitable implication that such a milieu was encumbered with preconceptions from which each of us (or at least the author) has freed himself. Likewise, Leslie Houlden speaks of rescuing Paul from his own inability to make what to us (or at least to the author) is a virtually self-evident contemporary distinction.[5]

Beneath the condescension lie two assumptions. The first concerns the relationship between an observer and the thing observed in each particular culture. Leslie Houlden says:

> When I am told what 'son of God' meant in the first century, the matter remains abstract until I hear to whom it meant it. So we set out to identify the picture of Jesus each writer saw, and we describe the christologies by reference to the titles in which the writers express them. We give an account of the christology of Paul by telling how he uses terms like Christ, Son of God, Lord, and wisdom with reference to Jesus (p. 126).

In the discussions at which these papers were originally presented, another of the authors expressed this point starkly by saying that he could not see the difference between 'what someone saw as happening' and 'what happened'.

The second assumption concerns the inaccessibility of different cultures and ages. As well as the gap between what happened and what was seen to happen, there is a gulf between what was seen to happen and how we see what was seen. Leslie Houlden puts it thus:

> ... if I get as far as being aware of the gap between my picture of (Paul's) thought and his own, as far as being baffled and tantalized by it, can I either profit from these emotions or do anything to bridge the gap? The profit in the emotions lies in the feeling of them. All I can do towards bridging the gap is to perceive it (p. 127).

Maurice Wiles echoes a similar sentiment when in the opening chapter of *The Myth* he talks of it being 'more reasonable' for us to see the traditional incarnation doctrine as an interpretation 'appropriate' to the age in which it arose (p. 4).

In turning, however, to their own cultural context, I am not convinced that the authors, despite their disavowals, are aware of the extent to which they are themselves culturally conditioned. For example, Frances Young warns us against relying on a crude mechanistic analysis of our own age and then goes on to offer a description of it which, to many intelligent people, would be just that; she then uses it as a basis for concluding that 'heavenly powers have given way to earthly forces' (p. 31). Or again, consider the various titles or descriptive names proposed for Jesus as an alternative to 'God incarnate': the 'as-if-God' (p. 39), 'the unique focus of (men's) perception of and response to God' (p. 42), '*the* man of universal destiny' (p. 57), the exemplar of a faith based on 'homopraxis' (p. 62), the proclaimer of the 'principles of Spirit' (p. 209), 'God-acting-towards-mankind' and 'God-in-relation-to-man) (p. 181). Each of these carries with it certain implications about contemporary ways of looking at the world which are neither fully acknowledged nor unfolded. To take one of the most attractive, '*the* man of universal destiny', I know many Christians who would, while rejecting traditional incarnation doctrine, be very wary of defining Jesus along an axis that included Joan of Arc or Sir Winston Churchill, however far down the line. The authors thus feel free to analyse previous cultures while standing rather uncritically within their own.

But there is a greater inconsistency when it comes to the gap between ourselves and different ages and cultures. Alongside the recognition of the inaccessibility of other milieux there is a clear acknowledgment of the possibility of links. For example, Michael Goulder, though proposing a rather tight relationship between the traditional incarnation doctrine and what he sees as its context, admits the power of the myth to capture the imagination of men in cultures to some extent different (p. 84). Frances Young speaks of a 'common ground' between each individual's faith and that of Jesus' immediate followers (p. 39) and believes that 'Jesus Christ can be all things to all men because each individual or society, in one cultural environment after another, sees him as the embodiment of their salvation' (p. 42). Or again, Don Cupitt asserts that 'in history, a man proclaimed the possibility of transcending history; and we, in history also, can verify his claim in practice' (p. 205). And finally, all the contributors clearly resent the implication that they are not speaking with a legitimate Christian voice within the community which can be traced back to Jesus.

It would be quite wrong to cobble together, on behalf of the authors, a single coherent view on this matter. (Anyway their own inconsistencies make this impossible but I return to this below.) However, I think we may fairly say that they all give a good deal of weight to the importance of the context in which theological propositions originally arose and that this must count heavily against our being able either to recover the original truth of the matter or to accept the original interpretation of it.

The continuing presence of God lends a grandeur and a comfort to the relativized scene. I do wish, though, that the acknowledgment of the effects of this sort of relativism had been made in the light of similar developments in other disciplines – most notably in sociology, social anthropology, the studies of language and literature and in science.[6] This might have helped the authors free themselves from the delusion that they labour, as theologians, under particular difficulties, might have allowed us all to detect a common philosophical base for the discussion and could have enabled us perhaps to benefit from the experience of others in handling the problems that the relativist approach raises. Lesslie Newbigin and Nicholas Lash in neighbouring essays bring to bear their own insights on the deficiencies of the authors on this matter. I wish myself to see how developments in the philosophy of science affect the discussion.

I take it that, for some of the authors at least, the recognition of relativism weighs heavily against the sort of views I expressed in my first contribution about the irrelevance of the original context of a proposition for its serious consideration as a working hypothesis. We recall that for Popper there is no logic of the creation of hypotheses and that any process is acceptable for their genesis (apart from induction). This view has been substantially criticized, most notably by Thomas S. Kuhn.[7] Basically, Kuhn doubts whether scientists can be as innovating as Popper suggests. In 'normal science', to use Kuhn's term, scientists work within 'paradigms' which provide the indispensable equipment with which to view the world. Though a somewhat diffuse concept, a paradigm can be seen to include sociological components such as recognized scientific achievements and sets of political institutions, metaphysical components such as clusters of received beliefs, a general epistemological viewpoint or an organizing principle and artefacts such as textbooks, instrumentation and grammars.[8] Together these provide model problems and solutions for a particular community of practitioners at a particular time. A person learns science by being socialized into their shared paradigm and thereafter he cannot look at the world except through the framework to which he has committed himself.

All this strikes me as an approach which the authors of *The Myth of God Incarnate* would find very congenial, though it would not work entirely to the advantage of their position. First, the concept of the paradigm, though rather woolly, might enable us to avoid the sharp distinction in credibility implied, for some, in the terms 'myth' and 'hypothesis'. Second, it might allow us to acknowledge a greater subtlety than Popper at first sight permits in the relationship between a proposition and the context in which it arose. Thus could we give some value to the communal life of, say, the early church and its members and the wider social and political constraints they experienced. We could, for example, acknowledge that there is more to a creed than its written existence after a council: there is the historical background to the council's convening, the sociology of its deliberations and the methods and artefacts of promulgation resulting from it.

The important question here is: 'How much weight would we give to such factors?' The distinction between Popper and Kuhn on this particular point has been sharpened up in the alternative: 'Logic of Discovery and Psychology of Research?'[9] Though both admit that they are closer than this antithesis implies, there is a point where they part company. Popper admits that we are prisoners . . .

> . . . caught in the framework of our theories; our expectations; our past experiences; our language. But we are prisoners in a Pickwickian sense: if we try, we can break out of our framework at any time. Admittedly, we shall find ourselves again in a framework, but it will be a better and roomier one; and we can at any moment break out of it again.[10]

Kuhn considers that to assert that paradigm frameworks are 'simultaneously essential and freely dispensable is very nearly a contradiction in terms'.[11] I cannot see this myself or, at least, I would follow Popper in striving for the balance and thus avoiding indoctrination by the spirit of the age.[12] This latter is always a possibility but it should be avoided. Further, I do not doubt that it *was* avoided by some of our Christian forbears. I do not think it quite fair to assume, as the authors do, that we ourselves are Popper's Pickwickian prisoners while our ancestors in the faith were Kuhnian captives. This was the first of the inconsistencies I detected in their approach.

The second is more difficult to deal with. Let us return for a moment to Kuhn and consider how individuals or groups might move from one paradigm to another. Kuhn says that this occurs through a 'paradigm-shift', that is, a relatively sudden and unstructured event like a gestalt-switch, a sort of conversion experience in which something previously obscure becomes illuminated. After such a revolutionary change of allegiance, the individual or group would not simply see objects as something different, but would actually see different objects. They would be responding to a different world, would regard different things as constituting valid evidence, and so on. The upshot of this is that succeeding paradigms would be 'incommensurable'.[13]

This clearly finds echoes in *The Myth of God Incarnate*, in, for example, Leslie Houlden's inability to do more than 'perceive the gap', but we should be fully aware, in a way in which I think the authors are not, of the far-reaching implications of this sort of statement. In general, Kuhn considers that there is no neutral language whereby we might judge the claims of succeeding or competing paradigms or translate the elements of one into those of another. Yet he is not totally consistent: he can speak for example, of our being able to see that a new proposal might be 'on the right track' (even though we are still in our old paradigm)[14] and he admits that 'accuracy, scope, simplicity, fruitfulness, and the like' might be good reasons for making a choice between paradigms (even though we are fully bound up with only one of them).[15] This is exactly the same sort of oscillation to which the authors succumb in their haziness about the nature and extent of our connection with the Christian past.

The oscillation is possible for the authors because they have, as Dennis Nineham detects in his somewhat mischievous epilogue, left for themselves an escape road down the slippery slope of relativism. It is the acknowledgment, across the gap, of some sort of uniqueness for Jesus based on the reliability of the historical record. Dennis Nineham considers that his companions are altogether too glib in being able to assume this sort of connection with the past.[16] Joining with them in rejecting the traditional attempt at picturing Jesus, he also wishes to close off this particular route.[17] And, of course, he is right, if one is concerned to pursue their logic to its conclusion. Thus, his question follows naturally:

> In a situation of galloping cultural change, which has brought the doctrine of the literal divinity of Jesus into question, is it any longer worthwhile to attempt to trace the Christian's ever-changing understanding of his relationship with God directly back to some identifiable element in the life, character and activity of Jesus of Nazareth?[18]

Let us take the logic to the end and see how it affects the idea of truth. Popper considers that Kuhn exaggerates the difficulty of the translation of paradigms into an impossibility and that, in science, critical comparison of competing theories and frameworks is always possible.[19] He does believe in 'absolute' or 'objective' truth[20] and considers that this can be reached out for. Kuhn, on the other hand, considers that truth may, like proof, be a term with only intra-theoretic applications. He sets himself apart from those who wish . . .

> . . . to compare theories as representations of nature, as statements about 'what is really out there'. Granting that neither theory of a historical pair is true, they nonetheless seek a sense in which the later is a better approximation to the truth. I believe nothing of that sort can be found.[21]

Yet he also maintains that 'one scientific theory is not as good as another for doing what scientists normally do',[22] manages to talk about scientific 'progress'[23] and about 'knowledge' and 'evolution-toward-what-we-wish-to-know'.[24] Clearly he likes to have it both ways and he does say that in one sense he is a relativist and in another not.[25] One sees why but not quite how.

How far does Dennis Nineham's position reflect this ambivalence? In his analysis, he makes use of a distinction employed by Norman Perrin between historical (*historisch*), historic (*geschichtlich*) and faith-knowledge.[26] Historical knowledge, Dennis Nineham has himself ruled out and, because ultimately historic knowledge depends on it, this too falls. The hope lies with faith-knowledge, with (quoting Perrin) 'knowledge of Jesus of Nazareth which is significant only in the context of specifically Christian faith, i.e. knowledge of him of a kind dependent upon acknowledgment of him as Lord and Christ'.[27] Obviously, we are here in the realm of Kuhn's intra-theoretic truth and Perrin himself states that the tests exclusively valid for this kind of knowledge would be of quite a different kind from those applicable to historical knowledge: 'the understanding of ultimate reality it mediates, the kind of religious experience it inspires, the quality of personal and communal life it makes possible, and so on.'[28] Seeing preaching as one way in which people are confronted by faith-knowledge, Dennis Nineham goes on to say:

> Their experience is that if this Christ is truly preached and they truly listen to, and hear, the preaching, he does something to them, he faces them with an inescapable choice.[29]

What does 'truly' mean here? In one sense the word seems to imply a circular, self-corroborative type of assurance to be tested within the closed world of the listening congregation. Yet, elsewhere, Dennis Nineham talks of the need of men for an imaginative account of how God relates to the world which will ensure a 'meshing in with the rest of their sensibility'.[30]

In so far as he has a final resting place, Dennis Nineham seems to opt for Maurice Wiles' proposal for 'some sort' of link between Jesus and contemporary Christianity, albeit in the weaker form, perhaps by asking that there should be no signal contradiction between the preached Christ and the historical Jesus 'in so far as we can recover him'.[31] But this then seems to lead us back to the very difficulty we started with.

This vacillation is, then, common to all the authors – and indeed to most relativists. In admitting the possibility of relativism, they straightway take on, to varying degrees, the principle of incommensurability and thus forfeit the opportunity to effectively criticize the noble struggles of earlier ages to interpret their understanding of Jesus. They also lose the chance of a dialogue with the Popperian position on the question of the exact role of context and culture in the framing of propositions. Their persistent desire to break the circle of the relativist position, to seek out and maintain the historical connection and to attempt a link with 'what is really out there' is, though not consistently expressed, a hopeful sign, not the flaw in the argument, but the sign that the argument is mistaken. It now needs to be rigorously pursued, perhaps initially by facing the wider consequences of their present position. For example, what would happen to prayer and mission, and indeed to any Christian activity which claims a connection with the wider world, if religion were to be seen as a 'form of life' or 'language-game'?[32] What would separate our kind of religious belief from obsession and what could count against it, if we were to have no rational basis for choice between one belief system and another?[33] What would prevent the framework of belief being manipulated for gain if the community of the faithful (or the bishops or theologians) decided the rules of the game or if the culture called the tune?[34] These questions are not new and, indeed, certain of the authors have addressed themselves to them on other occasions, but they are still open and it would be profitable now to return to them. Most important of all, perhaps, we should ask ourselves what we can say about a God whose creation and whose connections with it are interpreted in relativistic terms. I do not doubt the very considerable faith of the authors in God but it would be a mistake to imagine that the strength of faith depends on the slimness of the visible connection between ourselves and him or that the demand for a vigorous link is a sign of immaturity in this apparently grown-up world. For the moment, I do not find my earlier anxieties allayed, nor my critical and pastoral impulses offered the chance of fulfilment by their approach.

NOTES

1. Frances Young, 'A Cloud of Witnesses', *The Myth of God Incarnate*, ed., John Hick, SCM Press 1977, pp. 14–30 and 'Two Roots or a Tangled Mass?', pp. 87–121.

2. Michael Goulder, 'The Two Roots of the Christian Myth', *The Myth*, pp. 64–86.

3. John Hick, 'Jesus and the World Religions', *The Myth*, pp. 168–170.

4. See above p. 68.

5. Leslie Houlden, 'The Creed of Experience', *The Myth*, p. 129.

6. Roger Trigg has gathered together some developments in a variety of fields in his *Reason and Commitment*, Cambridge University Press 1973.

7. Thomas S. Kuhn, *The Structure of Scientific Revolutions*, The University of Chicago Press 1970. Kuhn's style might be termed poetic and I have paraphrased his ideas on paradigms but for the original proposals see pp. 23–51.

8. Margaret Masterman has provided a valuable analysis of the paradigm concept in her 'The Nature of a Paradigm', *Criticism and the Growth of Knowledge*, ed. Imre Lakatos and Alan Musgrave, Cambridge University Press 1970, pp. 61–66.

9. The title of Kuhn's first contribution to ed. Lakatos and Musgrave, op. cit., much of which is given over to the Popper/Kuhn debate.

10. Karl Popper, 'Normal Science and its Dangers', ed. Lakatos and Musgrave, op. cit., p. 56.

11. Kuhn, 'Reflections on my Critics', ed. Lakatos and Musgrave, op. cit., p. 242.

12. Popper, op. cit., pp. 52–53.

13. Kuhn, *The Structure of Scientific Revolutions*, op. cit., pp. 66ff.

14. Ibid., p. 157.

15. Kuhn, 'Reflections on my Critics', ed. Lakatos and Musgrave, op. cit., p. 261.

16. Dennis Nineham, 'Epilogue', *The Myth*, pp. 186–7.

17. Ibid., p. 201.

18. Ibid., p. 202.

19. Popper, op. cit., p. 57. It has not escaped my notice that, in this reference, Popper specifically contrasts science with theology. Some readers may consider that this vitiates much of what I have said in both my contributions. Clearly, I do not but it would be good to pursue this point with Popper, and especially to know how much it was a specific reply to Kuhn who, in certain respects, sounds 'theological' and 'religious' in his treatment of science.

20. Ibid., p. 56.

21. Kuhn, 'Reflections on my Critics', ed. Lakatos and Musgrave, op. cit., p. 265.

22. Ibid., p. 264.

23. Kuhn, 'Logic of Discovery or Psychology of Research?', ed. Lakatos and Musgrave, op. cit., p. 20.

24. Kuhn, *The Structure of Scientific Revolutions*, op. cit., p. 171.

25. Kuhn, 'Reflections on my Critics', ed. Lakatos and Musgrave, op. cit., p. 264.

26. Norman Perrin, *Rediscovering the Teaching of Jesus*, SCM Press 1967, pp. 234–5.

27. Ibid., p. 234.

28. Ibid., p. 241.

29. Nineham, *The Myth*, p. 200.

30. Ibid., pp. 201–2.

31. Ibid., p. 200.

32. To see what happens to prayer see, for example, D. Z. Phillips, *The Concept of Prayer*, Routledge & Kegan Paul 1965.

33. This, of course, takes us back to the 'University Debate' in ed. A. Flew and A. McIntyre, *New Essays in Philosophical Theology*, SCM Press 1955. For a more recent discussion of the question of religion and truth see Patrick Sherry, *Religion, Truth and Language-Games*, Macmillan 1978.

34. The questions of elitism and power within relativism are discussed by D. L. Phillips, *Wittgenstein and Scientific Knowledge*, Macmillan, New York, 1977.

C Christology and the Future of Truth
Nicholas Lash

My previous contribution may have seemed excessively abstract and unhelpfully negative. I now propose, therefore, briefly to illustrate my suggestion that the contribution of the systematic theologian to christological debate may consist in an attempt to reflect on those aspects of our contemporary human experience which might find appropriate expression in christological categories. I shall do this by offering what we might call a 'christological meditation' on the principal themes of Professor George Steiner's 1978 Bronowski Lecture, *Has Truth a Future*?[1]

An exercise such as this can, of course, only 'work' to the extent that, for the reader, theological (and, *a fortiori*, christological) questions are, or are allowed to become, *also* (but not 'merely') anthropological questions: questions concerning the meaning of human existence. To put it very crudely: it seems to me that much of the recent debate about 'incarnation' has proceeded (on all sides) on the assumption that christological questions can be appropriately handled in isolation from both theological and anthropological ones; that christological questions are not, whatever else they are, inevitably questions both about the meaning of 'God' and about the meaning of 'me'. Because I do not share this assumption, my purpose, in this paper, is impressionistically to indicate that there are (and have long been, in the history of theology) quite other ways of perceiving the problem. One of the reasons why I am unable to align myself either with the 'mythographers' or with some of their more confident and strident critics is that I am convinced that it is the problematic that has provided the framework for much of the debate that is mistaken. Before the question as to whether or not Jesus is God incarnate can be appropriately answered, either positively or negatively, we need, as I said earlier, to reflect on *what sort of question* that might be supposed to be. It goes without saying, I hope, that my concern in this essay is not with 'proof' or 'demonstration', but with understanding. Apologetics has its place, but it is no substitute for, and is frequently the enemy of, serious theological reflection.

The fruits of a 'meditation' such as this cannot, of course, stand substitute for the work of the critical historian. Thus, for example, questions concerning the extent to which christological issues were already, for the authors of the New Testament and the Fathers of the church, at the same time both theological and anthropological issues, are questions of historical fact. They are, however, questions of fact that cannot be resolved by positivistic appeals to the 'data'. There is a hermeneutical problem, whether we like it or not. And one of the tasks of the systematic theologian, as I see it, is to help his colleagues the historians to reconsider, from time to time, the range of questions to which they suppose New Testament, patristic, medieval and modern theological texts to have provided, in their often very different time and context, elements of a response.

The greater part of Professor Steiner's lecture reads (at least superficially) like a celebration of and an *apologia* for that 'eros of the mind' which Bernard Lonergan has called the pure, detached, disinterested, unrestricted desire to know. Lonergan's massive study of human understanding begins with a story: 'the story of Archimedes rushing naked from the baths of Syracuse with the cryptic cry, "Eureka!"'.[2] Steiner also begins with Archimedes, but with his death: 'Bent over a problem in the geometry of conic sections, Archimedes did not hear his killers coming. He perished, as it were, in a fit of abstraction' (p. 3).

As Lonergan speaks, paradoxically, of a 'detached desire', so Steiner speaks, paradoxically, of a 'hunger' (p. 4), a 'lust' (p. 4), whose defining feature is its disinterestedness (cf. p. 5). In all times and in all places, human beings – whether farmers or hunters, builders or mathematicians, lawyers or administrators – have sought practically applicable knowledge and understanding. But in Greece (for which Archimedes stands symbol) there arose, in addition, a concern for 'the abstract, the inapplicable, the sovereignly useless. Application, when it comes at all, comes *after*. It is the bonus, the impurity of condescension that may come of truth' (p. 3). Moreover (and here, on the first page, Steiner foreshadows the dark dilemma of his conclusion) this concern, this quest, this pursuit, this disinterested passion, is a quest for truth 'for its own sake. Not ... or not in the first place, for the sake of justice on earth, of a better life for the common man, of wealth or political power' (p. 3).

There is, in the story of this quest's historical emergence, a 'scandal of particularity'. Whatever the reasons, sociologically or biologically, it is undoubtedly the case, says Steiner, that 'the concept of abstract truth and of the pursuit of abstract truth, be it at the cost of good sense, of social utility, of economic benefit, of life itself, springs up in one place and one place only, and at one specific and singular time in our history' (p. 4).

Steiner insists that this peculiar obsession, so particular in its origin and history, so universal in the range of its ambition, is 'predatory. It is a hunt, a conquest' (p. 5). At least until the concluding section of his lecture, the image of the 'hunter' dominates his description.

Underlying this pursuit of truth for its own sake, enabling it, providing it with its dynamism and determining its morality, is one unquestioned axiom, one founding article of faith: the conviction 'that human dignity, excellence, prosperity and happiness can only benefit from the hunt after truth' (p. 6). And he describes this foundational conviction as 'the implicit theology of liberalism' (p. 6). It is the conviction that 'the truth shall make you free' (p. 6).

This commitment to the quest of truth for its own sake 'has not gone unchallenged' (p. 6). Professor Steiner sketches four lines of attack upon it – lines that are ancient, recurrent and, today, are powerfully conjoined to call in question its legitimacy and possibility.

There is, firstly, what he calls the 'mystic' or 'irrationalist' attack (p. 6), the insistence that 'the criteria of authentic discovery are not experimental control and refutability, but an immediate and visionary light that seizes upon the soul' (p. 6). Such intuitionism 'entails a posture which is contemplative, which sees action, notably of the questing mind, as impatient and predatory' (p. 7).

The second line of attack comes from what theologians sometimes call 'revelational positivism'. Appealing to 'systematic religious and supernatural revelation', it sees the rational, scientific quest for truth as exposing 'to chance and seemingly violent renovation those very concepts of truth and of proof to which a revealed religion must attribute everlastingness and perfect internal coherence' (pp. 7–8).

Thirdly, there is what Steiner calls 'the romantic existential polemic' (p. 8), the spirit of Wordsworth and Kierkegaard, 'attempting to recall men and women to the mystery of their incompletion' (p. 8), reasserting 'the scandal and wonder of human freedom as against the dictates of mathematical postulates and the prohibitions of logic' (p. 8).

Finally, there is the 'relativist or dialectical' attack, springing from an awareness that all talk of 'truth' is socially constructed, culturally specific and historically conditioned. It insists, not that truth is not to be sought, but that the object of the quest and the modes of pursuit are complex variables depending on the social context (cf. p. 9).

I have said that, according to Steiner, all four lines of attack are ancient and recurrent. What gives their conjunction a new power, a new persuasiveness, in our day, is that, as he puts it: 'For the first time, one can conceive of a fundamental incongruence, of a fundamental coming out of phase, between the pursuit of truth and equally demanding ideals of social justice, or, even more centrally, between truth and survival' (p. 10). Developments in nuclear physics, in anthropology and in genetic engineering, for example (and they are but examples) confront us, immediately, practically and starkly, with an absolutely fundamental dilemma. For the first time in human history, it seems, we are challenged to choose *either* for the future of truth *or* for the future of man. 'There are', says Steiner, 'doors immediately in front of current research which are marked "too dangerous to open", [and] which would, if we were to force them, open on chaos and inhumanity' (p. 15).

No 'return to innocence' (p. 16) is possible. 'The obsession with objective and abstract truth is imprinted on the western mind . . . We shall continue to ask wherever the question may lead, however dangerous the answer might prove to be' (p. 16). Perhaps, after all, 'the rage for insight, the hunter's cry . . . is leading us into ambush' (p. 17). Bronowski, Steiner supposes, would have distinguished 'between suppressing truth and pursuing new truths at any human cost' and would have said that 'if man's endurance as a more or less decent creature depends on leaving certain doors closed, then so be it' (p. 18).

'But the other answer', says Steiner, 'is also possible. We hear it, unquenchable, from the dark of Thales' well, and from the blood-stained garden in Syracuse. It says to us that truth matters more than man. That it is more interesting than he, even when, perhaps especially when, it puts in question his own survival. I believe that truth has a future. Whether we do is less certain. But man alone can suppose this. And it is this supposition, first put forward in the Mediterranean world some three thousand years ago, which is the mark of his glory' (p. 18).

Not the least important thing to notice about this 'other answer' is that it is personal, confessional in form: 'I believe that truth has a future'. If someone were to object that, because Steiner's answer is 'personal', is expressive of a commitment, it is thereby deprived of 'objectivity', they would, I suggest, betray their subscription to a discredited account of human rationality.

To justify that sweeping and polemical assertion would demand at least a book on developments in European philosophy and interpretation theory from Schleiermacher and Marx to Heidegger, Gadamer and Habermas. So let me put it another way. Towards the end of 'Interpretation and Imagination' (above p. 25) I remarked that a measure of critical self-understanding is a necessary condition of an accurate 'reading' of the past. The exercise on which I am engaged in this essay can only succeed in the measure that Steiner's answer, and the 'christological rereading' of it which I shall offer shortly, are 'heard', not as merely theoretical statements (somebody else's reply to somebody else's question) but as possible forms of our personal, practical response to the perceived questionableness of our self-understanding, identity, responsibility and fragile sanity.

I would now like briefly to backtrack, and put one or two questions to Steiner's account. My first question concerns the appropriateness of the image of the 'hunter', the 'predator', as a generalized characterization of man's quest of truth for its own sake. That this quest has often been thus construed, I admit. And, in so far as it has, the quest has been marked by an arrogance, a hubris, a concealed lust for power. It was, after all, Bacon who both promulgated the maxim *'scientia propter potentiam'* and who saw the scientist as nature's 'torturer'.

Steiner does entertain the possibility that there has been, in Western man's pursuit of truth, 'an imperialism analogous to that of his colonial conquests and economic exploitations' (p. 16). The issue is an historical one. There have indeed been periods in which the pursuit of truth for its own sake appears to have been dominantly 'imperialistic' in conception and strategy, but there have also been periods in which, without loss of passion or singlemindedness, the quest has been more modest, more attentive, more contemplative. And perhaps in our own day the perceived logic of scientific discovery is tending to become less predatory, to recover that mood, not of exploitation but of wonder, of attentiveness, which characterized the birth of the quest in ancient Greece. Perhaps a better model than that of the hunter would be of man as the 'shepherd' of truth.[3] (Nor is that suggestion merely a verbal concession to the ecologists.)

Thus to qualify the appropriateness of the 'predatory' image is also to call in question the crusading, buccaneering tones in which Steiner contrasts the quest of truth for its own sake with its four antagonists. He presents us with a hero, a noble and possibly tragic hero, challenged and beleaguered by four forms of plausible unreason. How else to interpret his rhetorical comment, apropos the contemporary confluence of the four lines of attack, 'All about us are the drop-outs of reason' (p. 10)?

It is, I suggest, inadmissible sleight-of-hand to identify scientific rationality with the pure quest for truth, and to imply that other modes of man's cognitional activity stand suspected of irrationalism and self-interest. The nearest he comes to recognizing this is in his admission that the struggle 'between dogmatic christianity ... and Galilean or Darwinian science ... is not one between unreason and rationality ... [but] between rival claims to logic and to proof' (p. 7).

I am not suggesting that it is possible easily to reconcile, either in practice or in theory, the 'internal variety of the forms of reason and truth'.[4] I am not even suggesting that we should necessarily suppose such reconciliation to be, even in principle, achievable. I am only suggesting that the fundamental contrast on which he invites us to reflect – the contrast between the pursuit of truth for its own sake, wherever it leads and whatever the cost, and the abandonment of that quest in favour of the security of socially acceptable goals of justice, humanity, common decency and a common life – cuts right across the distinction between scientific rationality and other dimensions of man's quest for and perception of truth.

The fundamental contrast is, I believe, as stark, as troubling, as he suggests. Only insensitivity or ignorance can shelter us from experiencing that contrast, at least from time to time, as presenting us with an option at once unavoidable and intellectually and morally intolerable: an option *either* for the future of truth *or* for the future of man. As experienced, such an option fundamentally calls in question all our intellectual and moral values. It extinguishes our self-assurance in a darkness from which there is no 'sensible', 'common-sense', 'liberal' or 'moderate' escape. In our situation, these good words too easily become the slogans of evasion, of *mauvaise foi*.

Professor Steiner, as we have seen, suggests that another answer is possible. Let us follow him through it again, in exploration of my hypothesis that the paradoxes of classical christology were attempts at a similarly non-evasive response to the question of human existence.

Steiner suggests that the disinterestedness of the pure quest for truth 'could be our singular dignity' (p. 16). Suppose we construe that 'dignity' as 'vocation', as responsibility conferred? The first Christians perceived, in the manner of Jesus' living and dying, an unswerving fidelity to vocation, an unaltering obedience to truth perceived, not in the clarity of propositions, but as the mystery fathering his existence, conferring his dignity, his responsibility. Jesus' pursuit of truth for its own sake, his obedience to the Father, put in question his survival. It was not sensible to go to Jerusalem.

Jesus' pursuit of his vocation, his obedience to truth, entirely lacked the character of the predatory. In the line of Ezekiel, his disinterestedness, his integrity, was rather that of the shepherd of truth.

Moreover, the gospel accounts of Gethsemane and of the cry on the cross do not suggest any reassuring intellectual resolution of the perceived incompatibility of the future of truth and the future of man. In so far as compatibility was asserted, it was asserted in darkness, in the manner of his dying. There was not, and could not have been, prediction of the outcome.

For those who would see in Jesus, and in his fate, the definitive revelation of God, there are, from the standpoint of the existential dilemma with which we are concerned, two ways of reading subsequent Christian interpretations of his significance. One way is to turn his tragedy into comedy, to see him as providing us with a 'happy ending', a slackening of the paradox, a resolution of the dilemma. That is the route taken by the docetic currents in christology, domesticating divinity into a miraculous commodity placed at our disposal. Christianity as a machine for dispensing painkillers: *deus ex machina*.

The other way is to read the confession of Jesus' divinity, of his 'consubstantiality' with the Father, as the expression of a recognition, in Jesus and in the manner of his living and dying, of the identity of the future of man and of the future of truth, and of the radical dependence of the future of man on the future of truth.[5] Thus to declare the significance of this man is to risk saying that, *if* man has a future in truth, then the way to that future is only open in the measure that truth is taken, in practice and in theory, to matter more than man. The imitation of Christ cannot have a structure different from that of his pursuit of his vocation, his achievement of his dignity. Unless a grain of wheat fall into the ground . . .

And if there is, in the discourse of Christian confession, thus conceived, an unstatable joy, it arises from the conviction (the grammar of whose expression is closer to a request than to a claim, to prayer than to assertion) that man is not constitutive of truth, but that truth, which *has* a future, is constitutive of man, is the ground of his dignity and the promise of his glory.

However, the assertion that 'truth matters more than man' needs to be handled with considerable care. Only too often, some such claim has been employed to justify the most appalling inhumanity. No individual, no group, no generation is entitled to declare any other individual, group or generation dispensable in the name of truth. It may well be – and it is this, in part, for which I am arguing – that the practical recognition that 'truth matters more than man' is a necessary condition of displacing the stubborn, anxious egocentricity of individual, tribe, clan or nation, and so of entering into deeper truth, but for one individual or group to use such recognition as a justification for suppressing or sitting light to the dignity of other individuals or groups is to dress the pride of Lucifer in the mask of *metanoia*. It may be expedient for one man to die for the people, but it is not for those who wield political power to say so or to act upon the conviction. Perhaps we should amend Professor Steiner's text to read: truth matters more than *us*.

In my earlier contribution to this collection, I suggested that the way in which several of the contributors to *The Myth of God Incarnate* distinguished between 'literal' and 'metaphorical' or imaginative discourse seemed to embody some highly questionable presuppositions concerning rationality, objectivity and imagination. I took as my slogan a definition of 'imagination' as the intellect in quest of appropriate precision. With the aid of this definition, I argued that many of their assessments of classical christological models and metaphors were flawed by a twofold failure of the imagination: on the one hand, a failure to hear the *questions* to which the christological languages of the past were forms of response and, on the other hand, an insufficiently self-critical 'hearing' of the way in which those same questions confront us and challenge us today. And I suggested that it was in attempting to meet the second of these requirements that the systematic theologian could be of service to the critical historian, assisting him to meet the first.

I have therefore tried, in this second essay, to enlist Professor Steiner's aid in helping me impressionistically to formulate that question to which christological confession would be, at the level of language, the characteristically Christian form of response. The question concerns the future of truth and the future of man. Christian responses to it have been risked or undertaken in a rich variety of conceptual schemes and metaphorical constructs, many of which may today be unintelligible or unusable. (Even an extremely 'high' doctrine of the authority of tradition would not, for example, commit its adherents to the continued use of the conceptual furni-

ture of Nicea or Chalcedon.) But one of the permanent respon-
sibilities of Christian theology is to attempt to hear, yesterday and
today, the questions in response to which Christian confessions
were formulated in the past and are to be reformulated in the
present. Only when we have done this are we in a position to
decide what models, metaphors and analogies might least inade-
quately, today, clothe such confession.

By way of conclusion, therefore, let me offer an adapted version
of Professor Steiner's final paragraph. We may decide that the
quest for truth is to be abandoned, that aspects of truth are to be
suppressed or, at least, not sought for. But the other answer is also
possible. We hear it, unquenchable, from the darkness on Gol-
gotha, and from the blood-stained garden in Gethsemane. It says
to us that truth matters more than we do. That it is more interesting than us, even when, perhaps especially when, it puts in question our own survival. I believe that truth has a future. Whether we
do is not comparably certain. But man alone can declare this. And
it is this declaration, enacted in the Mediterranean world some two
thousand years ago, which is the mark of his present and future
glory.

NOTES

1. Unless otherwise indicated, the page-references in the text are to the published version of this lecture (BBC Publications 1978). I am grateful to Professor
Steiner for his encouraging comments on a draft of this paper.

2. Bernard J. F. Lonergan, *Insight*, Longmans 1957 reissued Darton, Longman
& Todd 1978, p. 3.

3. Cf. Ralph Harper's discussion of 'Heidegger, the shepherd of being', *The
Sleeping Beauty*, Harvill Press 1955, p. 51.

4. Renford Bambrough, *Reason, Truth and God*, Methuen 1969, p. 129.

5. May I remind the reader for whom that reference to 'consubstantiality' seems
suspiciously abrupt that I am not asserting that the significance of Jesus may only be
thus interpreted. I am simply offering a suggestion, in the context of our contemporary human experience, as to what it was that those who first thus articulated
their Christian faith sought to affirm. Central to the thrust of my 'meditation' is the
assumption that, for the Christian theist, commitment to truth *is* commitment to the
concrete mystery of God; that the 'order of words' and the 'order of things' con-
verge to identity. in God. To put it another way: I am supposing the Christian's
commitment to God to be commitment to truth substantially conceived. On what it
is to conceive of truth, and of God, in the order of 'substance', cf. G. C. Stead,
Divine Substance, Clarendon Press 1977.

A Summing-up of the Colloquy:
Myth of God Debate
Basil Mitchell

I have done my best to be an impartial chairman, but I shall not attempt an entirely neutral summing up. Instead I shall give my own response to the discussion and, in so doing, betray the fact that my background is philosophical rather than theological.

As it happens, a surprising amount of our discussion has been concerned with problems of a broadly philosophical character. Here are some of them:

1. By what process of reasoning can we hope to decide such a question as whether to retain the 'traditional' doctrine of the incarnation?

2. To what extent, in endeavouring to answer such questions, are we inevitably subject to cultural conditioning, or – if this is different – influenced by underlying presuppositions? Is there any way in which presuppositions can be tested, so that we can decide whether or to what extent to continue to be guided by them?

3. Does it follow from the answers to 1 and 2 (or is it independently true) that we can only with difficulty understand, and rarely, if at all, make our own the thought of previous ages?

These are questions, it is important to notice, of a quite general kind which can be raised about any body of knowledge or system of ideas having a continuous history. They have been the subject of vigorous controversy among philosophers of history and even among philosophers of science. They are far from being peculiar to theology, although theologians often talk as if they were.

About the first question there was more agreement than at first sight appears. The 'mythographers' argue that the doctrine of the incarnation, as traditionally understood, is unintelligible or, at any rate, highly paradoxical; that its spiritual and moral value can be given as good or even better expression by viewing it as myth rather than literal truth; and that it is not to be found in the New Testament. The 'traditionalists' reply that, although paradoxical, the doctrine has not been shown, and cannot be shown, to be logically incoherent; that to regard it as 'mythological' in the sort of sense intended is to weaken its spiritual and moral significance; and that the New Testament contains much that implies or antici- pates it. It is apparent that the mythographers' case is a cumulative one, and so is that of their opponents. And there is, for the most part, a welcome absence of the sort of mutual incomprehension which so often bedevils philosophical and theological debates. Both parties recognize the force and relevance of the arguments that the other adduces. There are two features of the debate which add to its difficulty. We are operating for much of the time with expressions that are used in extended or analogical senses, so that it is hard to decide precisely what their implications are; and we are dealing, characteristically, with very varied considerations which cannot be ranged on any simple scale of probability. This only serves to show that theology as an intellectual discipline is closer to the humanities than to the sciences. I have the impression that it is rather characteristic of theologians to look for stronger proofs than the nature of the subject allows, so that they often fall an easy prey to scepticism.

About presuppositions, I think no one in the debate denies that we inevitably have them. As emerged from John Rodwell's paper, if we are to make sense of our experience at all we need some interpretative framework, and this will normally be something that, in the first instance, we take over uncritically from others. It does not, however, follow in the least that we can only proceed on lines laid down for us from the start. We can learn to criticize our presuppositions; and, although we cannot criticize all of them at once, we can criticize them piece-meal and, perhaps, so radically that we end by revising them completely.

In our discussions the question of presuppositions was raised especially by Lesslie Newbigin. He stressed that we inevitably approach the study of history with presuppositions, and suggested that the mythographers, like many modern theologians, take for granted an 'evolutionary world view' (not his expression, but Maurice Wiles's) which runs counter to the fundamental Christian claim that certain events in history provide a crucial clue to the meaning of the entire process, and to the character of the God who alone gives it meaning.

This is a question of central importance in the debate. The mythographers hold that we know much of what we do know of God independently of Christ; Lesslie Newbigin maintains that, without the incarnation, we lack a decisive clue as to the nature and the purposes of God. There was among the participants much diversity of view about our knowledge of God, both as to how we know him and what we can know of him, and this cut right across our other disagreements. Nicholas Lash and Don Cupitt, for example, appear to share a considerable degree of agnosticism. I was myself surprised by how little mention was made, even by Lesslie Newbigin himself, of revelation. For if a clue is looked for as to the meaning of history, and history can have a meaning at all only if God gives it one, it would seem to follow that we can come to know of this meaning only in so far as God himself chooses to disclose it; and the incarnation, as proclaimed in the first chapter of Hebrews, would be the supreme instance of such disclosure. As always, human analogies are inescapable; we can get some way towards understanding another person's character and purposes by relying upon close observation of his behaviour and our own spontaneous responses to him (our 'experience' of him), but such clues on their own are likely to remain somewhat ambiguous. What we chiefly need is for him to *tell* us what he thinks and feels and intends. Despite the difficulties in applying this analogy to divine revelation, I doubt if Christian theology can afford to dispense with it altogether.

It is quite possible that the reluctance of many contemporary theologians to employ the concept of revelation *is* associated with their acceptance of an 'evolutionary world view' which is thought to rule out anything that might be described as divine 'intervention' in the historical process. If so, this presupposition would operate even more strongly against a doctrine of incarnation, and I think it does. Whether such an evolutionary world view is at all entailed by the methods or the discoveries of science is highly disputable. But it is often thought to be, and not only by Christian theologians. Here, perhaps, we have an example of a widely pervasive assumption, which forms part of the prevailing secular culture, and is open to an intellectual critique which Christians and others are free to direct against it. Whether that critique is sustainable is, of course, one of the questions about which we differ; but its possibility is sufficient to dispose of the idea that we are so culturally conditioned as to have no choice in the matter.

The third question, that of relativism, I pass over, without wishing in any way to minimize its importance. It is too big a question to comment on in passing, and it calls in question the objectivity of science as well as that of theology. The only point I would make is that we need to distinguish between an entirely general cultural relativism which would, for example, make Aristotle every bit as opaque to us as St Paul, and a more modest relativism which would adduce particular reasons why the culture of a given time and place (e.g. first-century Palestine) is peculiarly resistant to our understanding.

A further question naturally falls into place at this stage, which has also figured in our discussions. Is there a recognizable body of Christian doctrine which we can distinguish and discuss: or are the various expressions and formulations of Christian belief throughout the centuries so diverse that almost all we can say about them is that they proceeded from people who called themselves Christians? Is there, indeed, a 'doctrine of the incarnation'? Traditionalists are bound to hold that there is. Mythographers need not and some of them do not.

It has, I think, to be conceded to Maurice Wiles, Frances Young and Don Cupitt that it is hard to discern a simple continuous identity of doctrine from the earliest days of the church till now. There are enormous difficulties about characterizing, let alone defining, the beliefs in which Christians are, and have been, agreed. But I have to confess, as a layman, that when I turn from the hymns of Fortunatus to those of Luther, Wesley and Newman, I do not feel myself confronted by sheer discontinuity. The 'family resemblance' is strong and deep and this becomes even more evident if I compare them with characteristic expressions of Hindu or Buddhist piety. The word 'motifs' was introduced into our discussion and can be of use here. There are a number of motifs of which recognizable versions have been present in Christian thought at different times and places, though not all of them at all times and all places, and not always with the same emphasis. Hence a Christian 'shape' is discernible, and it is for this reason that I am unwilling to share John Hick's contention that, if Christianity had moved East and not West, it would have assumed an entirely different form.

Many, if not all, of the mythographers would be prepared to accept this, with the rider that what has survived through the centuries and received expression in hymns and prayers and other devotional works is the *myth* of the incarnation rather than any statable doctrine. And the myth, they would say, is not to be taken as literal truth, for any attempt so to interpret it involves us in palpable contradiction. On this question of the nature and role of myth I believe we have made real progress. It was one of John Rodwell's main contentions that there is no clear line of demarcation between science and myth. As W. V. O. Quine, the American logician remarked, 'the myths of Homer's Gods and the myth of physical objects differ in degree, not in kind'. If this is true, it is not, in all contexts, useful to distinguish between myth or metaphor on the one hand, and literal, i.e., scientific, fact on the other. It depends upon the sort of myth one has in mind. There are some myths which conform to John Hick's definition, whose function it is to provide what T. S. Eliot called an 'objective correlative' to an attitude or emotion. Clearly there are myths which express or symbolize eternal truths. But myths may also perform a genuinely explanatory role, and, if they do this anywhere, they may be expected to do it in theology, where we are confronted by a reality which it must strain our intellectual powers to grasp at all. So we ought to ask not just, 'Is the incarnation a myth?' but what sort of myth it is. If it is agreed to be of the genuinely explanatory kind, then we may endeavour to give it more precise philosophical expression. We are unlikely wholly to succeed, because it is characteristic of myths to have a certain inexhaustibility about them; or, to vary the metaphor, a continuing resonance. It would seem to follow that the theological enterprise involves a constant attempt to approximate to a truth which cannot in the nature of the case be captured in any final formulation.

But if the myth is to be of any relevance to human life, we must be able to draw some inferences from it; hence the issue of logical coherence cannot be dodged. About this a great deal more work requires to be done. We were, I think, largely agreed that to say of anyone that he is both God and man is not a clear case of a logical contradiction, as it is to say of something that it is both round and square. As Nicholas Lash pointed out, we do not have any clear and accepted account of human nature, let alone of divine nature, in terms of which it could be shown that a single being could not partake of both. Nor is it clear that there is any one class of which both God and man are members. Nevertheless it was also agreed that the doctrine is highly paradoxical, for the attributes we ascribe to God are not, for the most part, such as we can intelligibly ascribe to a man. Nor is it altogether easy to understand how God can divest himself of these attributes by 'voluntary self-limitation' (C. F. D. Moule).

But, as Michael Goulder notices, modern physics contains some notable paradoxes and it is thought preferable to retain them unresolved rather than sacrifice the greater simplicity, elegance and comprehensiveness which is achieved by their acceptance. Michael Goulder himself is not prepared to retain the paradox of incarnation, but this is because he does not believe that it secures any comparable gains for the understanding of religious truth. At this point, then, in the debate the cumulative character of the arguments becomes especially evident. For, if myths can be explanatory and explanations can embrace paradox if sufficient reason is given, it becomes necessary to ask whether the doctrine of the incarnation in something like its traditional form is needed to give Christianity its full coherence and significance.

We discussed this issue under the heading 'The Moral and Religious Value of the Incarnation' and someone may well ask what relevance this has to its truth. Why should an interpretation of Christian doctrine which enhances its moral and religious value be any more likely to be true than one which does not? The answer must lie in our doctrine of God. If, as Christians believe, it was through the life and death of Jesus that God chose to redeem mankind and bring men into communion with him, we are bound to prefer that interpretation of the whole event which is the more congruent with what we know of his character and purposes.

Thus John Hick refers to the death of Jesus as the supreme instance of creative suffering through which God's love is revealed to the world, and Frances Young and Maurice Wiles both contend that God was indeed involved in the sufferings of Jesus, in a way that symbolizes his presence in every human tragedy. But they also insist that to regard God as having been involved in the sufferings of Jesus in some unique way would detract from the moral and religious value of the myth. For it makes God's presence in the suffering of all men less intimate and less complete than it might be.

To this the traditionalists reply, with Brian Hebblethwaite, that in Christ God is involved in a new and special way, as he could not be with all men, but that 'in Christ' all can share in a new pattern of communion with God, and that Jesus *shows* God's love and his involvement in human suffering in a stronger sense than the mythographers allow.

With this discussion we reached the heart of the debate, and it was perhaps inevitable that we should venture only a little way into so difficult and profound a topic. But the earlier patient attempts to achieve some degree of clarity about the underlying philosophical differences seem to have opened the way to a direct and unconstrained expression of our convictions and our perplexities. There could be, at this point, no doubt that the participants shared in a Christian faith that they were all seeking with equal seriousness to understand and articulate. The disagreement about the sense in which the life and death of Jesus shows God's love is related to the earlier one about the need for a 'clue' to the nature and purposes of God. Brian Hebblethwaite, like Lesslie Newbigin, believes that if, and only if, God has himself on the cross borne our sorrows, can we have warrant for finding the love of God revealed in the death of Jesus. We should then have a clue to the character and purposes of God of a different order from any inference we might try to draw from the course of human history or the nature of our own religious experience. And the same could be true of our assurance of the promises and the forgiveness of God. The mythographers, for a variety of reasons, deny that such a clue is either necessary or possible.

The dispute about the nature of God's involvement in suffering up to a point follows the same lines, and turns on the question how we can know that God is involved in suffering. Maurice Wiles suggests that the doctrine of the incarnation has, perhaps, done its work too well, so that it is no longer conceivable to us that God should not fully share in the tribulations of his creatures. If this is now a fundamental axiom for Christian thinking, it is not surprising that we should not feel the need of any special warrant for it. And yet the questions still remain: how we know that God shares our sufferings, and in what way he is able to share them.

The religious demand underlying the debate was movingly presented by Frances Young. If God wills to help us in our distress, as we must believe he does, it is not enough that (to speak anthropomorphically) he shows sympathy; he must, in some fuller sense, be present with us in our pain and grief. We are not alone in our suffering, but God has in Christ endured temptation and pain, and persecution and death, and continues to be with us when we endure them. None of us wished to repudiate this claim. The dispute was about what it means. The mythographers deny that the moral and spiritual value of the claim depends upon God's having been identified with Jesus in some way other than he is identified with all men. Indeed they argue that the claim is weakened by any such distinction. How could there be any initial limitation upon God's capacity to know human suffering of a sort that could be remedied only by his actually becoming a man at a particular point in history? Moreover for this belief to have present power to comfort us, we need to know that Jesus was a man just like us and that God is present with us, and with all who suffer, in the very same way that he was with Jesus. Brian Hebblethwaite and others like him, reply that what Frances Young asks for is what the traditional doctrine has always given, an assurance that God is with us through the indwelling of Christ, but this reply is felt by the mythographers to be unsatisfying because it seems to them to introduce an intermediary where none is needed, and to bring the divine Son close to us at the cost of removing the divine Father further from us.

No one who reads the papers that were presented on this topic, or who heard the discussion, could believe that theological reflection is remote from the realities of human existence. It is tempting here simply to acknowledge mysteries and reject all further attempts to penetrate them as futile and even trivial. Yet in this case I feel bound to ask whether enough account has been taken in the mythographers' approach of what is implied by divine transcendence. As Frances Young points out, what we chiefly look for in people who could help us is the kind of sympathy which comes from their having suffered too. But can God, the transcendent creator, suffer as we do? How could he, not simply know and understand, but actually experience the kind of distress which is totally obsessive and disabling? No doubt the main tradition of Christian theology has been unduly influenced by presuppositions derived from Greek philosophy in insisting on divine 'impassibility', but for any adequate theism it must be true that in God joy is more fundamental than sorrow, life than death. And, following through Frances Young's human analogy, so far as it can take us, we find that the people who can help us are not those who continue to be overwhelmed by suffering, but those who have in some way overcome it. Thus if we are to know that God has shared our lot, we need to know that he has been subject to the limitations of human nature which are the necessary conditions of pain being for him what it is for us. If this is true, there is a logic of condolence to which the traditional doctrine, if it is intelligible, conforms.

'If it is intelligible.' If one thing emerged from our discussions it is that the problems which confront contemporary Christian theologians are of enormous difficulty and complexity. In this respect they resemble those that exercise the practitioners of every serious academic discipline today. There is not one of them that does not, if it has any vitality at all, face questions of a daunting kind about its methods, presuppositions and fundamental concepts. It would not support the claims of theology to be an exacting intellectual discipline concerned with matters of ultimate importance if it alone were to be exempt from such problems. Theology is not to be identified with Christian faith, and the relation between the two has always been somewhat uneasy; but the church has never for long been content with an unexamined faith. It will be apparent from the general tenor of my remarks that on most of the issues I incline towards the traditionalists, but even from that standpoint the kind of debate in which we are engaged is a necessary part of the process by which the church at any time endeavours to approximate to the fullness of truth.

Appendix

(i) Samaritan Incarnational Christology?
Graham Stanton

The most strikingly original essay in *The Myth of God Incarnate* is Michael Goulder's 'The Two Roots of the Christian Myth'. Dr Goulder argues that Paul appropriated the idea of Jesus' incarnation in the course of dialectic with the Samaritan (Christian) missionaries in Corinth and Ephesus between AD 50 and 55. This novel hypothesis deserves more scrutiny than it has received in recent discussion of *The Myth of God Incarnate*. A full discussion is not possible here, as Dr Goulder's hypothesis raises a large number of very complex historical issues. However, I do not think that there is any evidence to support the speculation that Paul's 'incarnational' christology has been influenced by Samaritan views. Other currents within first-century Judaism provide a much more likely background.

Our knowledge of Samaritan views in the first century is very sketchy. Dr Goulder reconstructs five features of Samaritan theology before outlining what he takes to be distinctive emphases of a Samaritan christology.[1] But part of his evidence for Samaritan theology in the first century is drawn from Samaritan traditions. In most cases the Samaritan sources have yet to be studied with historical critical methods, and the editions and translations of Samaritan traditions which are available are often inadequate.[2] Although Samaritan studies are still in their infancy, from the traditions as they have survived there appear to be wide divergencies within Samaritanism; these may be accounted for by change and development over the centuries.

The Samaritans should be seen as one of the strands in a very diverse first-century Judaism.[3] On nearly every issue they seem to have taken a conservative stance. So on *prima facie* grounds binitarian or 'incarnational' views which compromised monotheism would seem to be extremely unlikely. Where, then, is there any evidence which would suggest that Samaritan views influenced the development of incarnational christology?

Dr Goulder refers to two traditions which are the lynch pins of his case: a passage in the Samaritan document Memar Marqah VI. 3 and Luke's report in Acts 8.9f. that Simon Magus claimed to be 'somebody great', 'that power of God which is called Great'.[4]

I would accept that Marqah VI. 3 may well be as early as the first century for the reason which Dr Goulder gives : it does use what could be interpreted as dualist or binitarian language, whereas other (later) evidence suggests that the Samaritans were staunch monotheists. It is probable that following the rise of Christianity the Samaritans, along with Judaism generally, became more reluctant to use dualist language and more cautious in their references to hypostases of God and to intermediaries. But I am not convinced that Marqah VI.3 is any more 'binitarian' or 'incarnational' than other passages from first-century Jewish traditions. Philo, for example, is often extremely bold and refers to the Logos as a 'second God', but without conceding that monotheism was thereby compromised.[5] In short, the Marqah passage is not unlike Hellenistic Jewish traditions about the Logos and Wisdom of God which have often been taken as part of the background of some aspects of New Testament christology.

Dr Goulder claims that Acts 8.9f. provides evidence that Simon Magus took himself to be an incarnation of one person of a Samaritan binity.[6] Luke takes pains to emphasize that Simon was a magician, but Simon's claim, which Luke reports, has teased scholars for a very long time and is certainly puzzling. What is implied by Simon's claim to be 'somebody great', and his followers' claim, 'This man is that power of God which is called Great'? If Samaritan views in the first century (in so far as we can reconstruct them) were monotheistic, how could Simon have claimed to be an incarnate deity if he was a Samaritan?

Was Simon a Samaritan? Luke does *not* say so explicitly! Most readers of Acts assume that he was, simply because he is linked by Luke with Samaria. But many Gentiles lived in Samaria; not all inhabitants of Samaria were members of the Samaritan 'sect'! So Luke may well have used a tradition about Simon Magus which originally stems from a Hellenistic environment. Simon's claim and that of his followers then becomes very much more intelligible. We may compare the response of the crowds at Lystra to Paul and Barnabas: 'The gods have come down to us in the likeness of men' (Acts 14.11). As an inscription in Greek from Lydia is strikingly similar to the words used by Simon's followers in Acts 8.10,[7] we do not need to assume a Jewish or Samaritan background.

Dr Goulder's own interpretation of Acts 8.9f. is along very different lines. He assumes that Simon was a member of the Samaritan sect.[8] The evidence for the latter comes from the references to Simon in various second-century (and later) Christian traditions.

With the possible exception of Justin, the later Christian traditions must be read in the light of the bitter struggles in the second century against Gnosticism and the belief that Simon was the arch-heretic and arch-Gnostic.[9] They are much later than Luke's account and much more clearly part of Christian propaganda. I do not see why they should be preferred to Acts 8 as sources of historical information.

Dr Goulder believes that Samaritan Christians were a powerful section of the first-century church. His case is based on several lines of evidence, at least three of which are, in my view, very flimsy. The references in Hegesippus and various church Fathers to Christian, Jewish-Christian, Gnostic and Samaritan sects are notoriously difficult to sort out and assess as evidence for *second-century* Christianity; they cannot easily be used in our efforts to reconstruct first-century Christianity.

The correlation between details in the Samaritan Torah and Targum against both the Massoretic text and the Septuagint in the early chapters of Acts does not necessarily suggest that Samaritan influence was at work in mainstream Christianity. Both Hebrew and Greek text forms were fluid in the first century, so we cannot attach too much weight to readings which Samaritan and New Testament traditions seem to share.[10]

On the basis of the use of *Hebraioi* in II Corinthians 11.22, Dr Goulder speculates that Paul's opponents referred to in II Corinthians were Samaritan Christians. But as he himself notes, Jews called themselves *Hebraioi*. Dr Goulder does not mention that Paul refers to himself as a 'Hebrew of the Hebrews' at Philippians 3.5. Are we to conclude that Paul was a Samaritan? Are the *Hebraioi* of Acts 6 Samaritans? No doubt individual Samaritans did become Christians, but they are enveloped by a mist which is at the moment almost impenetrable.

I do not dispute the importance of Samaritan studies for students of early Christianity and of the rise of Gnosticism. But rigorous historical criticism must be used in study of Samaritan sources, as well as of Jewish and Christian traditions about the Samaritans. Samaritan views in the first century are unlikely to have been more 'binitarian' or 'incarnational' than other currents within Judaism. A link between Simon and the Samaritan religious sect is not made explicitly in our earliest source, Acts, and the claims of Simon and his followers in Acts 8.9 do not necessarily have to be interpreted against a Samaritan or Jewish background. So even if Paul did come into contact with Samaritan Christians, it is extremely unlikely that his christology was influenced by Samaritan views.

NOTES

1 *The Myth of God Incarnate*, pp. 69–75.

2. See R. Pummer, 'The Present State of Samaritan Studies : I', *Journal of Semitic Studies* 21, 1976, pp. 55ff.

3. See especially R. J. Coggins, *Samaritans and Jews*, Blackwell 1975. I am grateful to Mr Coggins for his assistance and advice on Samaritan questions.

4. Goulder, *The Myth*, pp. 70ff.

5. See A. F. Segal, *Two Powers in Heaven : Early Rabbinic Reports about Christianity and Gnosticism*, Brill, Leiden 1977, pp. 159ff.

6. Goulder, *The Myth*, p. 72.

7. See W. Baur's lexicon, *sub* 'dunamis', 6; also F. F. Bruce, *The Acts of the Apostles* (commentary on the Greek Text) Tyndale Press, 1951, pp. 184f.

8. This *may* have been Luke's own view, even though he does not say so explicitly. If Luke has used a tradition about Simon's activities in the geographical area of Samaria which originally had a Hellenistic setting, he has probably placed it in Acts 8 on the assumption that the Samaritans were 'half-Jews'; the *Gentiles'* 'Pentecost' does not come until Acts 10.

9. See K. Beyschlag, 'Zur Simon-Magus-Frage', *ZThK*, 68, 1971, pp. 325–426, and also his important book, *Simon Magus und die christliche Gnosis*, Tübingen 1974. Beyschlag argues that there is no historical foundation for the assumption of a pre-Christian Samaritan *Frühgnosis*. See also R. Bergmeier, 'Zur Frühdatierung samaritanischer Theologumena' *Journal for the Study of Judaism*, 5, 1974, pp. 121–53, especially pp. 146f.

10. R. Pummer, 'The Samaritan Pentateuch and the New Testament' *NTS*, 22, 1976, pp. 441ff.

(ii) The Samaritan Hypothesis
Michael Goulder

I am grateful to Graham Stanton for his appreciation of my
Samaritan proposal as being original; and hope that I can counter
his criticisms. 1. 'Our knowledge of Samaritan views in the first century is very
sketchy': so theories based on them are bricks without straw.
Samaritans were conservative; 'so on *prima facie* grounds
binitarian ... views ... would seem extremely unlikely'. So far
Professor Stanton has produced two arguments against my
hypothesis. He then withdraws them: 'I would accept that Marqah
VI.3 may well be as early as the first century.' So although our
knowledge is sketchy, it is allowed that we 'may well' have vital
evidence for first-century Samaritanism; and since the passage in
question is straightforwardly binitarian (being a conversation between 'the original God' and 'the Glory'), it goes flat against our
prima facie expectations. Thus the two first arguments are acknowledged to prove nothing. They are then tacitly resurrected in the
very next paragraph: 'If Samaritan views in the first century (in so
far as we can reconstruct them) were monotheistic ...' – i.e. not
binitarian! It really is too easy to argue from our ignorance and
from our *prima facie* expectations, to concede the validity of evidence that we do know something to the contrary, and then to
ignore it. For an even closer implied contradiction, compare the
'wide divergencies within Samaritanism' due to 'change and
development', followed two sentences later by 'On nearly every
issue they seem to have taken a conservative stance'. But conversation is resistance to change and development, is it not?
   2. There seems to be a plain implication in Acts 8.9f. that
Simon Magus thought he was an incarnation of God.[1] Professor
Stanton seeks to escape from this by following R. P. Casey's[2] suggestion that Simon was not a Samaritan, because Luke does not
say so explicitly. But we do not always expect explicitness: Luke
does not say explicitly that Peter was a Jew either. The implicit
understanding seems obvious. Acts tells of the church's mission in
Jerusalem, Judaea, Samaria and to the uttermost parts of the

earth: the crisis over the admission of Gentiles took place over the conversion of Cornelius in Acts 10, and it is this which permits the Gentile mission (Acts 15.7ff.). So it is assumed that all converts before Cornelius are circumcised, Jews, Samaritans or proselytes, including the Ethiopian eunuch and Simon in Acts 8. Further, Justin (who for some reason is allowed as a 'possible exception' to the unreliability of second-century evidence), himself from Samaria, says that Simon was a Samaritan, and even tells us his home village, Gitto; adding that in his day almost all the Samaritans in Rome worshipped him (I Apol. 26).

3. The evidence I cited for a substantial Samaritan section of the early church is not three- but sixfold: (*i*) Luke's ambivalence to the Samaritan mission, (*ii*) Hegesippus' list of the first heresiarchs, three of whom (out of five) have Samaritan connections, (*iii*) textual links between the New Testament and Samaritan Torah and Targum, (*iv*) three passages in John's gospel (1.42–51; 4.1–42 and 8.48) which suggest Samaritan membership in his church, (*v*) Samaritan links with the epistle to the Hebrews, (*vi*) the united testimony of the Fathers that Gnosticism had its roots in the teaching of the Samaritan Christians, Simon and Menander. All of these points need exposition, and I would agree that too much can be made of (*iii*). But it is no way to argue down a thesis simply to omit from consideration points (*iv*) and (*vi*), which are, I should have thought, ungainsayable evidence for my hypothesis (though not of course proof of it). Nor shall we progress by relaxing on the 'notorious difficulty' of sorting out the patristic evidence and refusing to use it for understanding the first-century situation. Apostolic Christianity grew into patristic and sectarian Christianity somehow, and our task is to find hypotheses which will satisfy the not inconsiderable evidence we have.

One such hypothesis is that the *Hebraioi* of II Corinthians 11.22 were Samaritans. This would enable us to see Paul's opponents in the two Corinthian epistles as the same people (since those in I Corinthians deny the resurrection of the dead, as Samaritans did), instead of two completely different groups of gnostical and Jewish preachers playing Box and Cox, as they do in so many commentaries.[3] Both Jews and Samaritans called themselves Hebrews on occasion, but Paul uses the word *Ioudaioi* 26 times, and *Hebraioi* in two passages, both in the context of 'confidence in the flesh other men think to have' (II Cor.11.22; Phil. 3.5). It seems reasonable to think that he used the word of himself then because his opponents called themselves Hebrews ('Are they "Hebrews"? So am I'), but that his natural word was 'Jew'; and his opponents' self-designation as *Hebraioi* would suit Samaritans, who could not all themselves *Ioudaioi* because they were not. I should explain Acts 6 by Luke's ignorance, a hypothesis required in general by all commentators on the chapter. Samaritan Christians were not, as Professor Stanton suggests, a few individuals: Justin says that Gentile Christians in his day outnumbered those from among the Jews *and Samaritans* (I Apol. 53), and see Epiphanius' description of the Samaritan-type Ebionites he knew (Pan. 30. 15–18).

A further instance of unhelpful argument is the point about Philo. Dualism could, it is conceded, be Samaritan; but it could also derive from Philo; so that Samaritan possibility can be forgotten. But the direct influence of Philo has been canvassed for more than a century, and is (to my knowledge) almost universally rejected. Neither in John nor in Hebrews do we find a way of thought remotely like Philo's; whereas I have adduced passages from Samaritan sources which do correspond to the stress in Genesis 1 and Exodus 34 which comes out in the Johannine Prologue and II Corinthians 3.1–4.6. My living Samaritan dog is better than Professor Stanton's dead Philonic lion.

4. Professor Stanton refers to my proposal as 'speculation', and the same word is used, more harshly, by Professor Moule (p. 148 above). It is interesting to contrast his rather pejorative use of the word with the attitude of the doctrinal critics of *The Myth* in this volume. 'It is imagination ... that is the decisive function of the scholar' (Gadamer, cited by Dr Lash). The whole of Dr Rodwell's commendation of Popper is in the same direction: 'What we should be aiming for are statements with a low probability and a proportionately high information content ... We should not crave to be right but take risks in our theorizing.' I cannot but enjoy his ironic commendation of my 'baroque' hypothesis. F. M. Cornford wrote, 'Many literary critics seem to think that an hypothesis about obscure and remote questions of history can be refuted by a simple demand for the production of more evidence than in fact exists. – But the true test of an hypothesis, if it cannot be shewn to be in conflict with known truths, is the number of facts that it correlates, and explains.'[4] The Samaritan theory is a bold and plausible explanation of a great many features of the early church, including the rise of Gnosticism and of incarnational christology, neither of which has been adequately explained, and it deserves an attempt at refutation, not a reproach for 'speculating' on the basis of such 'flimsy' evidence as we do possess.

NOTES

1. Cf. E. Haenchen's commentary on Acts. ET Blackwell 1971.
2. R. P. Casey, 'Sinion Magus', in *The Beginnings of Christianity*, ed. F. J. Foakes-Jackson and K. Lake, V, pp. 151–163.
3. Cf. C. K. Barrett, *The Second Epistle to the Corinthians*, A. & C. Black 1973, p. 6.
4. Cited by J. L. Weston, *From Ritual to Romance*, Cambridge University Press 1920, flysheet.

Indexes

Index of Subjects

Index of Names